Murders Galore
© Stuart Bonnington 2021
First published 2021

ISBN 978-0-6453587-0-4

Printed by IngramSpark, Melbourne, Victoria

Cover illustration PBPublishing

DEDICATION

To Jay
This book would not be possible without her.
Her tireless support and suggestions made my job so
much easier.

Thanks also to friends who have provided support to
help me maintain a sense of proportion and to retain
a sense of humour.

case 1

melting pot murder

CONTENTS

	Prologue	1
1	South Africa: Linda	5
2	South Africa – Before	9
3	Apartheid – Moving to Australia: Linda	16
4	Australia – A Tough Country: Cliff	21
5	Australia – Lucky for Glen	29
6	Australia – Benefits from Aunty Polly: Glen	34
7	New Zealand – Growing Up: George	38
8	Australia – The Melting Pot	52
9	Tough Being a Police Officer: Linda	57
10	A Trip Home: Linda	62
11	Ballarat shop – Commerce: Glen	66
12	The Mysterious Aunt Polly Gamble	69
13	Business Prospects: George	73
14	Possibilities: Glen	77
15	Investigations – After the Fire	82
16	More Police Probing	94
17	First One-on-One: Cliff	102
18	Personal Development: Linda	105
19	Police Work: Dig Dig Dig	108
20	Number 1 Suspect	111
21	In the Clear?	116
22	Who Employs Lombardi and Khoury?	119
23	Brought in Again: Glen	124
24	Deep Enquiries: Tony Lombardi	126
25	Police Review	129
26	Explanations: Glen	132
27	Reluctance: John Khoury	136
28	Reinterview: Tony Lombardi	141
29	Result!	148

case 2

double jeopardy

CONTENTS

Prologue   153

1   The Moretti Family   155

2   Carry-On Courier Company   160

3   DS Linda Alexander   164

4   Incident No 1   167

5   Incident No 2   170

6   Co-ordination   173

7   Incident No 3   177

8   Police Work   182

9   Family Summit   184

10   Back to Basics   187

11   Continuing Grind   192

12   Burning Leaves   198

13   Incident Room Summary   200

14   Forging Friendship   204

15   Progress   207

16   The Big Shed   211

17   Back to Moretti's   224

18   Adelaide   232

19   Wiltshire   234

20   Back to Gisborne   247

21   Search Warrants   265

22   Chasing the Big Guys   270

23   Gisborne Police Station: Incident Room   275

case 1

melting pot murder

Prologue

It was mid-winter, about 3pm on a cold clear Saturday in Ballarat, regional Victoria, Australia.

Boom! Boom!..... boom! Explosions rang out around an inner-city address on the corner of Don Place and Pleasant Street. It was an old weatherboard home/shop that appeared to be having a clean-up sale. There quickly followed another smaller explosion that sent a huge plume of dust and smoke up through the rusting corrugated iron roof.

"What was that?" exclaimed a kid out on the street with his head buried in the boot of his old Ford. Other neighbours were out on the street looking in wonderment at what was now a fire, the building burning like a packet of matches.

"For God's sake, someone call the Fire Brigade," screamed a bystander. Someone rushed off to do that, knowing that Ballarat City Fire Brigade (within the Country Fire Authority or CFA) was not far away in East Street. Famous for its castellated parapet building.

"Anyone got hoses?" yelled another, now in panic. "Was anyone inside?" asked someone else, as people milled around. The old weatherboard shop was now fully engulfed in flames.

Some time went by before the sound of a siren could be heard and there were anxious enquiries among spectators wondering if anyone had been inside? Close neighbours knew there was some sort of clearance sale underway but they did not know anything about the owners.

By the time the Fire Brigade arrived, the shop was fully ablaze and extreme heat and pungent fumes made a close approach dangerous. The Brigade Captain quickly took charge and instructed his team to keep the public back and to do an 'around the premises' search, to decide if any rescue plan could be initiated. The heat emanating was incredible, so containment rather than extinction of the fire was enacted.

One of the firefighters reported back to his captain that around the back, huddled in a van, there was a mildly burnt and terrified "hippie looking" young man. The firefighter thought he looked a bit weird; skinny jeans, back to front cap, body-hugging T-shirt bearing rude signs, and with pierced nose, ears and eyebrows, and a funny haircut with a purple streak in it.

"He's a bit hysterical," he reported to the Captain, "but seems not seriously damaged. We think he is a kid called Tony." His Sandman van was also undamaged.

To make sure, an ambulance was called, and a check also made to confirm police were on the way. Fifteen minutes later, a very young constable arrived in his police car and conversed with the Fire Brigade captain for a summary. The captain had found two people who claimed to have been inside when the explosion took place. They also claimed they were associated with the business and were looking at stock to buy or sell. They were Cliff Richardson and Barbara McKenzie. Barbara's friend Melanie Ortega, a Frank Camorra and a young man called Tony Lombardi possibly related to Frank Camorra—had maybe also been on the premises?

Initially, not much attention was given to survivors but after a second Fire Brigade truck arrived, and then Senior Police Detective Sergeant Fred Thomas (the most senior officer in Ballarat), and as the remnants of the building slowly sank down to eye level and the smoke and fumes continued, the serious questions were posed.

The site was cordoned off and 'Wait and See' behaviour instigated by the police. It was beginning to get dark so a constable was posted to secure the site. Names, addresses and telephone numbers of Cliff and Barbara and also young Tony were taken by the police, as were details from the other possible witnesses.

Cliff, Barbara and Tony were invited to the Police Station to give further information. While they were still there, DS Thomas got an urgent call from his constable and the CFA men on site, saying that it appeared there were the remains of two people amongst the debris. It also appeared that one person could have suspicious extensive head injuries.

DS Thomas exclaimed, "Bloody hell, that's all I need on a Saturday afternoon." And to himself, 'Jesus Christ, and Patrick's just gone off on holiday for a fortnight!' Ruing the timing of his second in command Patrick, he instructed the constable to securely block off all access to the site, and both the CFA and his police officers must prevent all and any trespassing. He instinctively knew this was going to be a big deal which would require delicate handling and an ability to deal with the Press. DS Thomas immediately swung into 'formal protocol' mode and contacted his immediate superior to check on next best steps. How quickly could a forensic pathologist's report be obtained?

A real scramble began to gather together all the personnel needed for a major inquiry. Help was requisitioned from the bigger Footscray Police Station, who agreed to send two officers from their Criminal Investigation Department to Ballarat.

So, from Footscray, Detective Sergeant Fred Wilson, who had the air of a conscientious and incorruptible officer, and young Detective Constable Linda Alexander (a 'two-striper') arrived together on Sunday morning. DS Wilson was known and liked by DS Thomas. However, Wilson indicated that he could only spend a day in Ballarat, but he was assigning DC Alexander to them for as long as necessary. He accompanied that statement with a complimentary summary of her detective 'nous'. She could stay as long as needed as part of her ongoing training.

"There is a case to be solved here, with two deceased and badly burnt bodies—and an indication of foul play with one showing extensive head injuries. There is much work to be done to uncover what is a possible murder," he summarised.

"Good experience for her."

1

South Africa: Linda

1980. This is Linda Alexander at eighteen. She had always had the certainty of unconditional support from family, friends, and country. The result was confidence and some smugness from a superior lifestyle. Linda had innocence resulting from a selectively narrow childhood because of where she was born. The isolation from the real world had given privileges and protection from some of the more unpleasant realities of life. She was a virgin by her own choice and had never been in a rush to alter that status. Her single-sex education made her well aware of the theories and excitement and potential thrills of intercourse, and she was well aware of the consequences, physically and socially.

Linda had a regular boyfriend who she had known for years as their families were neighbours. More importantly, their parents were friends and approved of the friendship. Harry Hockfeld was also eighteen and was a handsome, six-foot-tall, well-proportioned, tanned athlete and a successful scholar. Linda was in many ways similarly blessed. Their relationship was warm and friendly and they enjoyed each other's company. Their manners and behaviour charmed everyone. They attended functions together and were observed regularly holding hands and having warm embraces. They were discreet in where and when they had more passionate cuddles and kisses and body exploring sessions.

With absolute trust the relationship had blossomed into more passion and explorations of body and sensitivities. Both were attending University and were increasingly aware of the effects of world opinion on their country's welfare and their futures. Linda's family future was being quietly researched and was daily falling more into place in such a way as to make best use of her parents' skills and experience. Young people were less depressed by the likely future until it sank in as a compulsion! Apart from regular meetings Linda and Harry exchanged short notes of love and commentary over a range of local and international happenings. Sport, but not much politics!

Johannesburg is a city blessed with enviable weather. For the major part of the year there is clear blue sky, windless conditions, and ideal days for swimming pools and barbecues. Such a day was being enjoyed by Harry and Linda at the Hockfelds' luxurious home on a day that the gods must have combined to achieve—or was it just karma! No university lectures and Harry's parents away for two nights, plus it was the domestic helper's day off. A light poolside lunch, a stolen glass of Stellenbosch wine from Dad's collection, swimming, fun diving and chasing, and enjoyment as good as any two, young people can have in one another's company.

Laughing, giggling, and with extravagant movements as their temperatures rose, touching and whispering became more positive. Generous-sized towels aided the drying off in the sun and rubbing all parts of the scantily clad bodies. For a long time, the two had believed they had mild ESP that gave them quick mental 'tune-ins'. Rubbing one another's backs with warm and fluffy towels sent shivers and shock waves through their bodies. They were still a little shy around their bodies but potential nudity caused no problems since they had been to plenty of parties where dispensing of garments was common. They had genuine respect for each other and no violations were likely. They began to look deeply into one another's eyes, non-blinking, trying to get inside the mind and soul. Holding the fixation as they touched and caressed. They murmured to each other "How can I reach inside you to keep you for ever!" "Can we be soulmates through thick and thin?" and "To hell with apartheid and the consequences." And Linda popped into the conversation, "You know I take the pill!" She did not add that like her contemporaries she was just as curious about sex but had never felt the need, urgency, or pressure to 'go all the way'. Harry was undoubtedly her number one passionate friend with whom she was totally in sync.

They continued to embrace and chatter words of love and endearment. The happy removal of remaining clothes was almost ritual as they stroked and massaged all parts of their bodies. The warmth and thrill rushed to all extremities. Exploration with tongue in the mouth, around the eyes and ears and down the neck gave rising ecstasy as excitement and temperatures rose. Warm and enthusiastic responses flowed as fingers delved into hair, down backs and advanced over boobs and above knee height. Linda kept moaning, "I love it whatever you are doing please don't stop!" Bodies rubbing together became more and more energetic until with grunts and moans and total mutual agreement Harry entered Linda's hot and receptive body. Loud exclamations of happiness and joy as they mutually pressed forward to achieve her first ever orgasm. Linda was full of delight and Harry equally thought he had done well. They both thanked one another for the enjoyment and fun and recovered quickly to do it again. Body and mind in fulfillment.

As the afternoon progressed, talk about the future rose to the fore as did that of their aspirations and the inevitable handicaps created by the isolation that South Africa was experiencing. Amongst the sentiments of love and closeness Linda said, "Life has dealt up a shithouse future." Harry was not quite so emphatic but recited his parents' motto: "We aren't going anywhere."

Although not wanting to inflame the atmosphere, Linda reluctantly admitted she had a burning resentment that unilateral family decisions had been made without due consultation with her. Harry equally was angry about being deprived of the love of his life with no obvious ability to respond. Young love is not always accommodating. They rambled over ways to keep in touch from Australia, and the vital need to remain friends. Linda's Dad was to blame, and they both felt better after berating his decision making. Linda shouted, "Dad's way is 'his way or the highway'."

After tears, grief, crying, and accusations of how selfish her father was, an element of calm entered the discussion. Linda emphasised her wish to stay in South Africa but realised it was probably a forlorn hope. She vowed, "I'll never love another the way I love you. I want to drown in your love. Flood me with your touch." It seemed like forever for both of them, before the bounce of youth and the new "world adventure" slowly sneaked in.

2

South Africa: Before

Growing up as a young girl in Johannesburg in the South Africa of the 1960s had not been a hardship. Particularly if you were protected from apartheid, which was then the ruling political regime. With well-educated, successful parents providing a solid home basis there were not many problems. Linda Alexander had attended a quality English-speaking private girls' college. Her older brother, Brendan, had attended a similar boys' college. Both children had been delivered and picked up by car on a daily basis. They were privileged and isolated from the hardships of life faced by the black majority.

Linda's parents, both second or third-generation South Africans, held well-paid professional positions in Johannesburg. Father John, a medical practitioner, had graduated from the University of Cape Town and done additional training in London. Mother Prue, (nee Pretorius) had an Afrikaans background, and had graduated from Stellenbosch University with a B.Com and was employed by mining giant Gencor Ltd. They had met as students of the two universities, socialising between groups that usually regarded one another as from different factions i.e., English-speaking vs Afrikaners.

They married in 1958 and settled in Johannesburg, and formed a strongly united family accommodating their historical differences. The family home in Sandton, north of Johannesburg CBD, was almost across the road from the notorious and disgraceful slums of

Alexandra, and was a typical property for a high-income family, able to insulate themselves from the obvious inequalities. Half an acre of well-maintained grounds, a tennis court, a swimming pool, three-car garage, all protected by two-metre-high fences and lockable gates, supported by obvious guard dogs. A fortress of a kind!

Complementing the attractive lifestyle, there were two live-in black helpers who had barely adequate accommodation, furnished with the most minimal of comforts. Duties included cooking, cleaning, gardening and all levels of maintenance. Security was paramount. It was understood that home helpers were like "extended family" and they received their full board and keep. They were trusted, and how wonderful it all seemed. It was common for small children of some of the home helpers to play on the property with Linda and her brother while work was being done. No discrimination amongst kids.

Into this melting pot of wealth, vibrant capitalism, ambition and energy, mix the ambitions and envy of intelligent plotters from all over (internal and external); the so-called 'Coloureds' from Cape Town, the Portuguese from Mozambique and Angola, Zimbabweans, second and third-generation British and European immigrants and many more; all with ambitions to make their fortunes while they could; the local black majority playing the 'waiting game' to utilise the huge bounty emanating from the expertise and energy provided by generations of people seeking the opportunities associated with the wealth from local gold, diamonds, copper, nickel, and other metals.

Apartheid made the melting pot even more explosive. The most notable of all anti-apartheid protesters, Nelson Mandela, was in jail on and off (mostly on) between 1962 and 1990. The arrogance of superiority in apartheid was at its height with the use of an Afrikaans-language Bible.

Home safety and security became bigger issues for parents as they worried about the effect that fear (by osmosis) was having on all. 'White' parents were taking more and more steps to cottonwool their children from all and sundry. Houses were locked up each night and sleeping sections were created with locked-off secured bedrooms and piercingly audible burglar alarms. They had not really realised they were prisoners in their own homes. The children did not know anything else. Hand guns were abundant. Door locks on cars were extra strong and automatically locked into action as soon as the car moved off. Many drivers had hand guns on them or in the glove box.

Tourists were not necessarily exposed to the local underlying fear, and they loved and appreciated the diversity of the country and the national game parks. The outside world was gradually marshalling its opinion about basic human rights in South Africa. How had this unique situation evolved?

The family psyche for most white South Africans had developed through their history, over several generations, with all the built-in prejudices that this involved. To reverse their attitudes, deep changes were needed.

The past 200 or so years had burnt into southern African white and other ethnic groups huge amounts of historical and psychological feelings and attitudes. Backgrounds were even more complicated when dissecting European influences without considering the wonders of the Bantu people: their tribes and many languages, their sophisticated making and use of iron tools to aid cropping and the herding of goats, sheep and cattle. Add to that the influence of Persian and Arab travellers and traders and the remarkable mix gets more complex and diverse.

Colonisation of various forms was retained in personal historical family records, influences and resentments for generations. Battles, wars and fights of varying sizes and outcomes became events to celebrate or bemoan through the ages.

For the whites (locally called Europeans) the major historical and combat events took place around the turn of the century (c1900) and influenced relationships in Southern Africa from then onwards. The British had established themselves in what was called the Cape Colony and this ultimately resulted in what became known as the two Boer Wars. The second war, the most famous—or infamous, depending on parentage—lasted from 1899 to 1902 and was primarily about Britain's status and control of Southern Africa. An important background to these events was that the original Dutch settlers, known as the Afrikaners (or Boers; farmers) considered they had been robbed in 1806 by the British taking possession of what was known as the Dutch Cape Colony. Ultimately, this led to the Boers beginning the great exodus (or Trek) from the Cape to go north and inland. This occurred from 1830 onwards. These Boers became known as the 'Voortrekkers'—famous pioneers, pathfinders and absolute legends to all future Afrikaners.

The Voortrekkers were comparatively uneducated, low-status farmers, with an obstinate determination to better their lives and prospects. They were Dutch-speaking settlers, travelling mainly by wagon trains from the Cape into the interior to escape British Colonial control. They were very religious, with a background from Protestant Calvinist Holland, and were Members of the Dutch Reformed Church, which became a crucial part of Afrikaner nationalism in South Africa. The Boers felt that the British governors did not help them fairly in disputes with neighbouring tribesmen and their biggest complaint was the emancipation of their 'slaves'. Prior to the great Trek, most farmers totally relied on their 'Blacks' for cheap labour, and the compensation they were to be given was not enough for them to remain solvent. The Boers' resentment towards successive British administrators continued to grow.

In time, they founded and established two Boer republics: the Orange Free State (Free State) and the South African Republic (Transvaal).

The discovery of diamonds and gold in 1867 in the Witwatersrand in Transvaal had prospectors of all ages, types and creeds, nationalities and skills, flocking to the area. Boer resentment of the British administration continued, as did that of the Black population overall, and anti-white-superiority attitudes grew.

Imperialism vs republicanism festered away. Roman Dutch law vs British law was another big difference. The names of Cecil John Rhodes and Paul Kruger became rallying cries. New arrivals, called 'Uitlanders' (who were not only from Britain) could become naturalised and vote under different qualifications of time and residence at very short notice. It all added to the resentments bubbling away in the melting pot.

It had been realised that trying to bring together South Africa under a single British Confederation uniting the Boer republics, independent Black states and British colonies could not work until the strong Zulu kingdom had been defeated.

Then the famous Boer Wars one and two occurred. Even Winston Churchill was a participant, at the time a young soldier in the British military. The second Boer War occurred from 1899 to 1902, lasting almost three years. This war greatly influenced thinking and attitudes of all modern South Africans. It was a war about British status and control of South Africa. A war between well-equipped and trained British soldiers versus 'commando style' fanatical warriors (the Boers) on horseback. No doubt leadership played a part. Although it was 'White v White', and British versus Afrikaner, both sides welcomed into their forces other 'soldiers' from all over the world.

The Boers declared war on the British on October 1899 on behalf of the two Boer Nations. The Boers were free thinkers; they 'fought and ran away' to fight another day. They did it with great skill and resourcefulness. Battles were bloody and killing often indiscriminate. The British captured cities and towns but the Boers controlled much of the countryside. The prizes were the Orange Free State and South African Republic (Transvaal).

At the peak of the war, the British had nearly 500,000 soldiers in South Africa—the Boers no more than 80,000 soldiers. Momentum flowed back and forth over the years but large British reinforcements made ultimate defeat for the British unlikely. Bloemfontein, the capital of the Orange Free State, was captured and even though Paul

Kruger (the leader) escaped to Europe, he was unable to win support against the British.

The skilful Boers created chaos with their brilliant 'hit and run' guerrilla-style tactics. The British retaliation of scorched earth and the first of harsh, segregated prisoner of war camps, which involved the inhumane treatment of women and children, caused international rage and condemnation. The Boers retaliated with raids deep into the Cape Colony, where General Jan Smuts became famous. A Boer peace offer in 1901 was rejected as the British insisted on the annexation of the two republics. Finally, the Boers lost their independence in May 1902, with the Peace of Vereeniging Treaty being signed and accepted. It was widely seen as an alliance of British and Boer against black Africans.

In summary, 100,000 lives were lost. 20,000 British troops, 14,000 Boer troops, and more than 20,000 non-soldiers died—and many Boer women and children from sickness, starvation and ill health. Strained relationships between all participants remain today and will probably last forever.

In spite of British hints to black Africans that in return for their support, or at least neutrality, black Africans could have rights after this war, the Treaty specifically excluded political Black rights in a reorganised South Africa. The British and the Boers co-operated towards the now common goal of white rule.

More recent ugly Southern African conflict is displayed in events such as the the Kenyan Mau Mau Uprising (rebellion), between 1952 and 1960; the Sharpeville Massacre in 1960—in which the white South African Police fired on black people in the Sharpeville Township near Vereeniging, south of Johannesburg, in response to a non-violent demonstration against apartheid. Sharpeville was a major turning point in South African history because of the police use of live ammunition (as opposed to the usual batons) and the use of British Saracen armoured vehicles. It was a flashpoint and the beginning of what would become a mass exodus of people over the next decades. Detailed plans were hatched to exit, taking maximum assets out of South Africa.

Other horrifying events affected life in South Africa and further contributed to the carefully planned exodus, among which was the Soweto Uprising of 1976. This spread quickly from Soweto ('South West Black Township', south-west of Johannesburg) and changed the South African socio-political landscape for ever.

In 1974, the language of Afrikaans had been made compulsory alongside English as a medium of instruction in all Black schools. Young black students began mobilising themselves. This uprising spread countrywide with deep cultural change and repercussions. Within various groups, e.g. the Black Consciousness Movement (BCM) and SASO (South African Students Organisation), detailed planning against the hated 1953 Bantu Education Act (anti-apartheid) gathered support.

The uprisings continued into the following year and images of SA Police firing on peaceful demonstrators led to international revulsion and condemnation. It was probably accurate to say that the 'English-speaking' were more sympathetic to integration and independence than were the Afrikaners. The cumulative effect of all the disputes and battles, (not to mention the rising situation in neighbouring Zimbabwe, or Southern Rhodesia), was deeply etched into the psyche of Southern Africans of all backgrounds. Even the most loyal and nationalistic South Africans realised that they had to leave for a decent future.

When the Alexander family experienced a serious home break-in, it was the last straw for them, coming after John had been pressured to join the 'Broederbond' organisation, and mother Prue had made it clear that she did not want to have to carry a gun.

3

Apartheid – Moving to Australia: Linda

For the Alexander family, the volatile melting pot history of South Africa culminated in the family decision to emigrate to Australia. Apartheid was no longer acceptable or comfortable, and fear of what the future held made the painful decision unanimous. Easy, but more emotional for the parents as they were well aware of world opinion.

Careful planning, even plotting, was necessary. Monumental decisions and actions for friends and family members were initiated with extreme confidentiality. Rules about how much money could be taken out of South Africa were strict: How to swing into action to 'get out and get in' and to maximise assets at both ends was a huge challenge.

Qualifications were invaluable because of the recognition internationally of the quality of education in South Africa. Confidential inquiries confirmed high-level positions were available in Australia. Linda's brother Brendan had recently obtained employment with a giant Anglo-American company, in the London Office.

A very small but significant event in the eyes of most South African men took place in New Zealand in 1981 when traditional Rugby Union rivals the Springboks and the All Blacks were scheduled to play the final and deciding match of a Rugby series. The controversial tour had been disrupted by protests about apartheid throughout New Zealand at every match. The culmination occurred in Auckland in September 1981, at what became known as the "Flour Bomb Test". The match was disrupted by a small aeroplane pulling a large anti-apartheid slogan dropping flour bombs onto the crowd. The All Blacks won 25 to 22 by a penalty kick in the last minutes. But no further Rugby Tests were played for many years and it constituted one more step towards the end of the apartheid era.

Linda was at Wits Uni in Johannesburg doing B. Com and BA degrees. Her heart was not really in it as she was well aware of the family's plans to leave and the undoubted repercussions. Linda was studious and serious and well aware of history. She wore her long blond hair firmly pulled back into a bun style and had dark-framed glasses that she wore most of the time. She had a no-nonsense exterior. Added to that, she had martial arts training and was very athletic, although still prim and proper, and more and more aware of the need for personal security.

The average home in Johannesburg was a fortress. It had not really occurred to Linda how strange that was. She could be naïve, to the point of sometimes commenting, "Why is there so much attention about how black people are treated when we provide them with so much!"

So how best to 'smuggle' valuables through the export/import systems of the two countries? Innovative individuals stood at both ends, legally and illegally, and included in the equation was the question as to whether or not, "you have the balls to risk it?" A parent's problem, not the children's!

Furniture and motor vehicles were clearly a target. Anything that had or could be modified to add small hidden tubes or hidden storage areas—pipes, false walls, or covers over existing frames; even in walking sticks, hats, clothes, and using miscellaneous human 'mules' to assist.

The South African bureaucracy was mainly controlled by Afrikaners, and bribery and corruption were endemic. Further down, the black population was always prepared to undermine the disciplines (for a price) just to be negative and undermine White authority. To maximise what could be taken with the Alexanders, and then to assist in re-establishment in Australia, a great deal of planning and manipulation needed to take place. A small contribution in possibilities and knowledge came from Brendan and his associates in the UK. The greatest value and practical action was the direct route, using every subterfuge on offer.

The official banking system in all and any way was utilised. The family fortune took a haircut with the move, but the sacrifice of assets, cash and some personal mementos was considered part of the price of the decisions made. After what seemed a never-ending saga of time, frustrations and petty restrictions, the family of three (John, Prue and Linda) finally arrived in Perth. They were not immediately aware of the tensions of their history quietly slipping away. The deeply etched prejudices between Afrikaners and the English-speaking South Africans had always been just below the surface. Prue Pretorious had married John Anderson in 1956, and as a child Linda was always aware of some of the family antagonisms over their marriage.

The good news was that as a result of applications submitted prior to their departure, John was immediately appointed to a senior hospital position in Perth. There were constraints attached to how quickly he could seek other employment. It took a little longer for Prue to secure a position but mining company BHP offered her employment in their Perth administration office. Her previous Gencor experience was a real plus.

Linda enrolled at the University of Western Australia campus in Nedlands in Perth to complete a law degree, which included having to become familiar with Australian (British) law. The family was fortunate to rent a suitable four-bedroom house in Claremont, an upmarket Perth suburb. The location was ideal for their new life. There was a high percentage of 'new' Aussies living, working and studying in these areas, and although their accents were an immediate giveaway of where they were from, the family quickly formed new social cliques. They were new Aussies with an inbuilt attitude of isolation, but Linda was aware of where she wanted to go and that she looked good and fitted in well.

Linda now wore white-framed glasses with her long blond hair pulled back. She maintained a serious demeanour, and although a conscientious student, mixed easily with fellow students. They enjoyed pop music and danced to the Rolling Stones, Bon Jovi, Prince and Whitney Houston. She began to enjoy 'Aussie' humour and quickly became good at giving back—with interest—as much as she got! Her sporting prowess helped her integration. Although the inane humour was sometimes just too much, as this example from a uni friend: "The great Aussie Game Hunter was stalking in the jungles of Africa looking for lions and tigers to shoot, when he stumbled across a beautiful woman lying naked in a clearing; 'Wow,' he said. 'Are you game?' She gave him a seductive smile and said, 'Why, yes I am!' So, he shot her!" Linda was expected to think this hilarious. Sigh.

Probably because of the quality of her education in South Africa, Linda's Uni results were excellent and she progressed easily through each level of her law degree studies and graduated. While doing her Articles of Practical Legal Training and Articles of Clerkship in a large central-Perth legal practice, she became attracted to the idea of joining the police force. "Why on earth would you do that?" everyone asked.

Linda replied, "My parents grew up in a society full of bias and bigotry, and I am bored with the lack of responsibility of my contemporaries—and I want some legitimate, lawful excitement. Mum and Dad have their careers marked out."

When she tried to be totally honest with herself, she admitted she enjoyed her own company, was an isolationist, confident in handling her own emotions. As a young woman she had become adept at her own counselling—able to look in on herself. 'I can handle that and arrive at my own opinion given the chance to consider what I know,' she felt. Very mature, reflecting some of her background. In the process of answering the many questions in the formal police application, she found herself comfortable about aptitude and psychological attitudes, plus the medical and fitness requirements for police service. Her life in South Africa, the law-and-order issues and the everyday use of guns had given her a wider experience of life than the general run of Australian police applicant.

Her brother Brendan was still in London and, intrigued by the possibility of having a policewoman sister, wrote her an encouraging letter, also revealing that he was formulating plans to join the family in Australia. Everyone seemed more thrilled about the latter idea than having Linda join the Australian police force!

The police application steps were comparatively easy to complete once education and Australian citizenship points were clarified and established. Linda was accepted. Although quite confident, she had not yet acknowledged to herself that she was a 'pretty straight two shoes!' (i.e. very serious). On the social side of Australian life, she was schoolgirl innocent. This was illustrated when she asked one of her new girl friends, "What exactly is chlamydia and herpes that I hear you talking about?"

4

Australia – A tough country: Cliff

For Clifford (Cliff) Richardson, growing up in Creswick, central Victoria in Australia, in the 1970s was not a lot of fun!

A small, west-central town eighteen kilometres from Ballarat and 122 kilometres from Melbourne, Creswick was similar to the close-by towns of Clunes, Maryborough, Talbot and Buninyong. They all had a rich history associated with the Australian Gold Rush of the 1850s to 1880s, and to a lesser degree with reforestation and sheep farming. With the exception of nearby Daylesford, most of these central Victorian regional towns in the 1970s were socially and economically 'challenged'. They could be described as dirt-poor, although they all had some attractive buildings that had resulted from the era of gold wealth, e.g., mechanic's institutes, hotels, heritage council buildings and libraries. Regular farmers markets were an opportunity to trade home-grown products as well as the local gossip.

A normal daily diet when Cliff was growing up started with porridge made with water, and the evening meal usually consisted of meat of some type and three boiled vegetables. Their own garden would produce some vegetables, and apple pie was a regular dessert. Bread from the local bakery was always on the table. Chicken was considered a luxury, and after the first meal was used to the nth-degree for soup. The saying 'waste not, want not' was clearly part of the family motto. Another: 'make, bake, grow and sew', was used by many families and diligently practised. Lean living was an absolute reality for many.

The fragile economy for most regional towns was extensively supported by employment by the local council, the traditional general store, the hardware and plumbing store, the railways, the hotels, and the mines. In Creswick, it was also the Woollen Mills. Times were lean and marginal families had attitudes that had been influenced and hardened by history and harsh memories of the Great Depression of the 1930s. It was tough, hard country, with high unemployment levels and a climate that was unforgiving of failure or poverty. There was an underlying non-compromising attitude in hardship.

Clifford Montgomery Richardson was born in 1955. The name was chosen by his father Ray, who only ever called him Cliff. The grand name was chosen because his father thought it may give him increased status in the adult world.

Ray was an average second-generation Australian with forebears from the UK. Home was a rundown twenty-acre sheep farm on the town fringe. Family income came from Ray's labouring for a local builder, some extra mowing, and was supplemented with wool and meat sales from 'the farm'. Cliff's mother, Mavis, worked as a domestic house cleaner when she could.

'Cliffie' as he grew up, could best be described as 'lumbering'. He was a large-boned teenager, big for his age, with little or no obvious talent scholastically or athletically. He was quite well liked by his peers, as he really did not have a mean bone in his body. He had big strong arms and legs that had real power when applied to a given task. Not a great conversationalist, but when pleased he had a magical wide smile. However, the very short-cut black hair and his plain, blunt, pockmarked features did not help first impressions.

Cliff was judged by many to perhaps be a bully because of his looks and demeanour. He had been teased from the time he was a small boy about his posh name, "Clifford Montgomery!" Regular razzing along the lines of "Who do you bloody well think you are, you big ox?"

Provocation strained his fuses. Mavis tried to help with her input of, "Sticks and stones can break your bones, but names can never hurt you" but of course with the sensitivity and desire to fit in it fell on deaf ears.

Mavis was always under pressure to have meals ready promptly to avoid provoking her husband Ray's swinging moods. Frustration with his lack of prosperity and life's enjoyments meant he could exhibit ugly moods at times, usually associated with drinking. On occasion, the frustrations swelled to the surface and he physically hit out.

The farmhouse was old with peeling weatherboards and a rusting corrugated iron roof. It was run-down. The ramshackle appearance was not enhanced by a dirty old Holden ute parked (always sloppily) beside the house.

The house was close to the road, with a short concrete pathway from the front door to the letter box. Unkempt grass edges meant the 'garden' looked much like the rest of the farm, where long grass grew around farm fence posts. The sheep paddocks were all of a similar size, each separated by rusted wire gates to keep in the 50 to 60 sheep and to protect around the Bills traditional concrete water trough. An equally run-down shed and derelict stables that in the past had been used for shearing and shearers' accommodation completed the dismal picture. Fringe farmers of this type were assumed to be cruel to their dogs and farm animals. Water reticulation was always an important and ongoing problem. With little timber or shrubs the scenery was drab, and bushfires were not a high priority to be concerned about. The entire property was considered 'scruffy'.

School transport for Cliff was either via the school bus from the front door, or sometimes by pushbike. He did not like school and never tried. Ray had always preached it was a waste of time but Mavis tried to help. At sixteen years old, Cliff was comparatively uneducated and non-skilled, and considered a real 'boof head'. He wore mainly hand-me-down clothing and his employment prospects were almost nil.

Ray was not averse to handing out physical violence on occasions. Most often it was around supper time after having consumed a beer or two, or after returning home from Friday night drinking sessions. Sometimes he hit out at Mavis for unknown reasons, and sometimes at Cliff for perceived insolence or simply a lack of response. Open-handed wallops were the usual method accompanied by a torrent of language— that no one else in the family was allowed to use.

Sometimes, in a really ugly fit, Ray—clearly the worse for wear— would storm in the door demanding "Where is my steak and chips? Where is my beer? And why is there no music?" Totally ridiculous questions. If Mavis and Cliff smiled or scoffed, that could send Ray into a violent assault on Mavis, raining blows down on her body and head until she slumped down on the floor. Shock and horror from Cliff before he would sometimes receive a backhander. These incidents were not reported but they left permanent damage to Cliff's psyche.

Some months after Cliff's sixteenth birthday, Ray had laid Cliff low with two strong blows to his solar plexus. It really hurt and Cliff had screamed between the pain and tears, "Never do that again, you old bugger!" When he stood upright, he looked down on Ray, who now realised his son was much bigger than him. Cliff added, "And while I'm at it, you never whack Mum again, or I'll report you, or I'll hit you!" It did seem to Ray it was time to back off.

Cliff had his own bedroom that he could retreat to, close the door for privacy and have some solitude. His favourite pastime was riding his bike, as that gave him an element of freedom and escape. He would climb out his window and go for a spin in the dark. As soon as was allowed, Cliff left school and got a menial job in the timber store in Creswick. His job was mainly loading and unloading heavy products of all shapes and sizes. He was paid the absolute minimum wage but the job added to his evolving independence. It allowed him to mix with some locals and to occasionally enjoy a beer, and otherwise to be pretty much left alone. Some of his mates worked in the Wool Store and were better paid than him but there was an enjoyable underlying sense of being part of a group.

As time went by, the boys started to travel further from Creswick for their Saturday relaxations, and some had acquired body tattoos as a badge of honour. Daylesford was the best and brightest town to frequent. His group all thought Cliff was a bit thick but they took him along to provide some 'muscle and persuasion,' if needed in any altercation. "Don't argue with us or we will ask Cliffie (or 'Montie') to straighten you out!" That was usually the deal breaker. Behind his back, he was referred to as 'the Neanderthal' though most of his group had no idea what it meant—maybe it meant the skull shape?

The group was known to be a nuisance and to be into petty thieving. The police had tried to get the boys involved in a local club and even playing AFL or Rugby League. To no avail, as Cliffie was simply badly coordinated. He had grown into a very big and belligerent, formidable-looking young man. He was clearly overweight and his habit of wearing over-tight black singlets or T-shirts just exaggerated the formidable look. Add to this his black lace-up ankle boots and very short black hair, and he looked like someone to be avoided. Although he could drive a car, he had never bothered to get a driver's licence.

Daylesford, which was only twenty kilometres from his home, was the favourite social destination. Considered quite a 'flash' town by their standards, with good camping facilities, hot spa pools and regular tourist attractions, and home to The Old Daylesford Hotel and Bar, the town was renowned for its ambience, cold beer and budget accommodation.

The group now consisted of five or six local boys from around Creswick, plus two or three added locals from Daylesford. They often became boisterous and a nuisance inside and outside the pub. Between them all, they only had two cars. Most of the group were paid weekly in cash, so it was always planned to have fun on a Saturday. The usual routine was to have a few beers in the pub before walking down the road to the fish and chip shop close to where they parked the cars.

One day, as they were leaving the pub, they got into a verbal stoush with several very well dressed and groomed young men, who they loudly referred to as "nancy poofters". These young men were in the twenty-five to thirty age group, and stood their ground in the foyer, telling the 'country bumpkins' to "bugger off home to your pigsties". This did not go down well, and the shouting continued outside on the footpath, where it fizzled out as Cliff and his mates headed off for their fish and chips. It was then that Cliff remembered what he had in the car: a brand-new set of Spear and Jackson hedge clippers that he was taking home for his father.

Full of beer and bolstered by the noisy support of his friends, Cliff insisted they go back to the car so he could retrieve the hedge clippers, still in their wrapper.

He bragged, "I'll cut their fuckin' hair off with these and see how good they look then!"

Egged on by his mates, they headed back towards the hotel at the top of the hill. They soon found the three guys looking in the window of a men's outfitters. Without any ado, Cliff barged up to the man in front and jabbed the pointy end of the clippers right into his stomach. He went down in a heap yelling and screaming, and from somewhere blood appeared, but it turned out to be from Cliff's hand. People gathered, and others ran in every direction. Police and ambulance were called and of course there were plenty of witnesses.

The outcome was one man taken off by ambulance with a non-life-threatening wound to his arm and bruising to his ribs, plus damaged clothing. He wanted to press charges for attempted murder. Cliff was arrested and taken off to the Daylesford Police Station and held overnight. He was eventually found guilty of an unprovoked assault and given a stern warning by the Magistrate never to appear before him again. All it really did was add to Cliffie's notoriety, and the police 'suggested' the boys socialise anywhere other than Daylesford. Ballarat would now become the bigger target for their activities.

Only one of his group turned up at the police station on Sunday morning to take Cliff home to Creswick. That was Glen Robertson. Viewed as 'smooth', Glen was a bit of a mystery. Now in his early 20s, nothing much was known about him or his past. He was small, very neat and tidy, and owned an older car that was fastidiously maintained. He seemed somehow to have become attached to the group, but no one knew how or from where. Behind his back some called him 'Flash Gordon'. Apart from being the best dressed in the group he had no obvious shortcomings. An unusual member of this group!

Do still waters run deep? A bit of a stroke of luck for Cliff, as the boys were as different as chalk and cheese. All they had in common was that they were roughly the same age, lived in times of hardship in a regional area, loneliness, and the courage that comes with being united in a social group. For Glen to pick up Cliff from the police station and deliver him home to Creswick was surprising and unexpected. Even the police noted it with interest and with an element of hope.

When Cliff arrived home, the little information he passed on to his parents brought gasps of disappointment from Mavis and derision and contempt from Ray. No threats of a good whacking though; those days were well over. Cliff still had his job at the Timber Shop, so he had his own income, but Ray made it abundantly clear that it was time for Cliff to look for digs elsewhere.

The boys group still met regularly but gradually their activities mostly moved on to Ballarat, Daylesford now being less welcoming. Perhaps Cliff had learned a lesson, or even the growing influence that Glen was having as a regular companion and mentor was keeping him calmer and more restrained. It seemed a very unlikely companionship—even strange, but opposites can attract. The big question of why Glen was taking an interest in and helping Cliff was never considered by Cliff.

Eventually Ray made the home atmosphere so toxic that Cliff did move out, much to the distress of Mavis who feared a resumption of physical abuse with Cliff gone. In his later memories of home life, Cliff never remembered it with nostalgia.

With the help of Glen, accommodation under very favourable terms was found in Ballarat. It was a two-bedroom unit in central Ballarat that belonged to Glen's Aunty Polly. What an unlikely pair to share accommodation. This had all evolved within a year of the "hedge clipper" incident. It was well known that Cliffie's use of the English language was limited and often incorrect. His response to a stuffup was often, "I know I didn't do nothing wrong."

Cliff's hair, though short, always seemed unkempt and he was in need of help with personal grooming and behaviour. A slow contributor to some improvement was Glen occasionally taking him to visit his parents, where he began to appreciate a more normal family home and culture. The relaxed and supportive happiness associated with Robertson family life and discussions around the family business gave Cliff insights into other lifestyles. He wasn't necessarily aware of what was happening to him by osmosis. The 'normal' relationship he witnessed between Glen, his father and brother and other family members was an eye opener. He commented to Glen, "You don't know how lucky you are to be able to chat away to your family as if they are friends!"

5

Australia – Lucky for Glen

In contrast to Cliff, Glen was polished, smooth, well-groomed and always on time. Some of the mystery surrounding Glen gradually cleared in social chit chat. He was the second son of a blacksmith/farmer from a middle-sized Victorian country town. A happy, successful family environment where the business was run from a large shed almost next door to the family home, set on two acres. The forge and furnace and associated equipment required to create products through heating, bending and shaping iron and steel were on site.

Work clothes for Glen's father were tough dungarees, black singlet, large black leather apron, and leather gloves of all sizes for different needs. The workplace was not well lit, so the glow of heated metal could be easily seen. It was usually a noisy environment as hammer and anvil were in constant use. Metal filings could fill the air. As a blacksmith, Glen's dad was big and strong, and physically resilient.

Glen's older brother had joined their father in the business and quite quickly the dust and clothing created a lookalike family. It was a financially strong, successful business, respected and used by the local council, farmers, horse-owning residents and builders. Glen's mother was different in looks and temperament. Small, blond and blue-eyed, she had always presented a contrast to her blacksmithing husband. She ran a happy, clean home for the family, and supplemented their income and her independence by running a 'Buy and Sell' business from small premises just off the main street. She fringed into antiques and sometimes purchased from deceased estates. Sometimes she took Glen as a child to carry out inspections up to sixty kilometres away. The help of her husband and his ute was often enlisted to make pickups and deliveries. The family was involved in the town community.

As Glen grew up, he did well at school and was an excellent athlete. He was popular. He did not wish, and was clearly not destined, to join the business, so he was sent off to boarding school at Ballarat. Clarendon College was the chosen school for years 10, 11, and 12. The college was co-educational and run by the Uniting Church of Australia. Over 100 of the students were boarders mainly from country Victoria, New South Wales, and a few from overseas. The school was founded in 1876 by Presbyterians. It became Ballarat Clarendon College in 1977 when the Presbyterian and Methodist churches combined as the Uniting Church. The college was proud of its history. Learning was paramount, and the culture aimed to produce results that spoke for themselves. Glen's parents had done much research on options for the final years of his secondary schooling and had carefully chosen the core values provided by Clarendon. Ballarat Grammar they considered to be 'too tough' and St Patrick's College of lesser standards.

Glen fitted into Clarendon College like a hand in a glove. He was an excellent student with little interest in rough physical sport. Always happy to be a part of a team but with no apparent leadership aspirations. Smallish in stature, and polite and popular with staff and fellow students, both male and female. They liked his quiet demeanour, respected his intelligence and humour. Somewhere along the way he had developed an unusual hobby of bird watching. That made him a little different with an additional range of interests. He learned to mix happily with a range of different personalities without prejudice. Glen had a healthy curiosity and liked talking to all types of people. He advanced through his three years without angst, rancour, or punishment, much to the delight of his family.

Ballarat liked to be known as Australia's largest inland city and was famous for many notable bluestone buildings. After the Gold Rush subsided, growth declined and many facilities were underused. The fully fledged University of Ballarat resulted from amalgamations of various tertiary institutions. Only an hour or two from Melbourne and with tourist attractions such as the living museum of Sovereign Hill and the historic Eureka Stockade, it was a lively and developing city. The retail precincts were fresh and colourful, which served to emphasise the incongruity of a small local shop owned by Glen's mother's elder sister, Aunt Polly.

Rail connections from Ballarat to Geelong and Melbourne added strength to the city. Lake Wendouree, with its scenic waters covering more than six hundred acres and stocked with fish, was a popular picnic area. A very pleasant and newly vibrant city with population steadily growing to 60,000.

With no family traditions to influence his ambitions and with guidance from his school vocational sessions, Glen enrolled at Ballarat University to do a Bachelor of Arts and an overlap into a Bachelor of Education course. Accommodation was easy to arrange with his Aunty Polly, a spinster who owned an unknown amount of property in and around the centre of Ballarat. The concessional rent Polly asked for from Glen was paid for by the family blacksmithing business.

Glen and his Aunt Polly had always been close and 'favourites' with one another, so Glen quickly and seamlessly fitted into his new status and home environment. Ballarat became his home and he fitted well into a small group of friends from school days, plus some new associates through University. Year one at Uni went by like a dream and he enjoyed the intellectual challenges and kept up with all the credits and exam passes needed. He developed an appreciation of art and his favourite painting was 'The Golden Fleece' (1894) by Tom Roberts, depicting shearers at work in a timber shearing shed. Aunt Polly was a big influence in his life even though they did not meet regularly. She did not seem to have a great range of friends but she occasionally introduced him to acquaintances. By coincidence, Polly, a little like Glen's mother, was a trader in second-hand goods. In fact, she had a licence as a pawnbroker and her small shop was on the corner of Pleasant Street and Don Place—not far from the main street called Sturt Street. Polly was 'the family mystery woman' even though she and Glen's mother were sisters. They were as different as chalk and cheese. Polly really was a trader in all ways, in all goods, and strayed into gambling on horses. Glen's mother was totally traditional.

Polly wore outrageous clothes and apparently had never had a lover. To Glen she always seemed wealthy. She enjoyed alcohol, had a high level of freedom, and never attempted to impose her opinions on others. She was an irregular visitor who Glen adored. When she visited, as a special treat she would take him for a meal at a restaurant and order food on his behalf. Usually something he had never heard of, which was often outstanding. Polly could be outrageous in her behaviour to waiters with her flirting, but more often was just polite. Glen had to admit to himself she was 'different'. He loved her inconsistencies and the discussions they had and always looked forward to her next visit. She could surprise him by saying, "When I get thoroughly sick of someone, I tell them to 'F___ off'." He always blinked at the use of the 'F' word by her. Polly encouraged and taught him to always be curious about others; to try to understand them, and to get to the bottom of obviously different opinions. He was fortunate indeed to have her influence. Polly called her Ballarat shop an 'Opportunity Shop' and it was managed by an ageless, wrinkled man of unknown heritage. Glen got to know him very slowly as he infrequently accompanied Polly to the shop. The manager was called Frank or Frankie. That was all Glen knew as Polly did not often speak of her business. To Glen, most of the products in the store looked like old furniture and junk of no value. Each time he went back it looked the same, as if nothing had moved! Sometimes he wondered how much had been paid for the rubbish. There was a special area that had shelves and glass doors that were closed and locked. Polly said those were her favourites. Lladro, Toby jugs, Royal Doulton, Waterford crystal, other commemorative plates, and various silver spoons and pieces. All clearly priced and Polly knew where she had obtained them. Glen never went into the shop without being accompanied by Aunty Polly.

6

Australia – Benefits from Aunt Polly: Glen

Cliff seldom went to Polly's shop in Ballarat but he was well aware of it. Although still socialising together on a Friday or Saturday evening for drinks, he and Glen were now housemates rather than close friends. Glen did call him 'Montie' on occasion, in recognition of the special relationship. No one else used the name. With the bedrooms situated at either end of their unit, it allowed them privacy and space. Glen roamed and romped with his university friends, including chanting loud and crude songs and ditties. There was the occasional semi-orgy and some very mild taking of so-called party drugs. With little concentrated effort, Glen progressed through his second year at Ballarat University.

When he occasionally did visit the shop, always accompanied by Aunt Polly, Glen found it all quite confronting and formidable. He was not sure why. Was it because of the unusual manager Frankie? Or was it because it was always packed tightly from floor to ceiling with old, dated tables, chairs, lounges, and with the tables covered by miscellaneous crockery, glassware and knick-knacks. It always seemed to be exactly the same as it was on the last visit. How valuable could all the rubbish be? How important was Frankie in the greater scheme of things? Polly never referred to his role or his importance, but Glen did observe on occasion what he assumed were wages in a brown envelope. Maybe a commission on profits? Whenever Glen tentatively tried to question Polly on the value of what seemed to him to be excessive and valueless stock, she would joke that perhaps "a little harmless arson could always fix the problem!" As a single person, Polly appeared to be very well off, always with a reasonably new car and, despite her flamboyant sense of style, always extremely well groomed. Glen had no idea how old she was but as his mother's older sister, he could get close to a figure in his head.

At the beginning of his third year at Ballarat University, Aunt Polly died. She was not young by his standards but had not been obviously unwell. It came out according to the medical report that she had been ill for some years with cancer but had not disclosed her illness to friends or family. No one had known. Her passing was a surprise that no one in the family had anticipated. Most of all it was a shock to Glen, who had thought her indestructible. Quietly over a beer at their local pub, Glen in distress tried to explain her to Cliff.

"You know I really loved her for her sense of fun, she was so different; she was sometimes difficult to understand, but she made no judgements, always curious, and quite irrepressible! I miss her already," Glen lamented sadly.

Cliff sat there with him in sympathy and listened, coming to the realisation that he had no similar personal relationship with any-one else.

An even greater surprise to Glen, and to all and sundry, was that he was the sole beneficiary of Polly's will. A final, massive, surprise was what was included in her estate: Two residential properties in Ballarat, the shop and everything in it, her car and a sizeable share portfolio. There was also a substantial amount of cash in three different bank accounts, one of which was designated the 'Opportunity Store'. As would be expected, unravelling and explaining the intricacies of it took many tortuous discussions with solicitors and 'advisers'. It was suggested that some time by Glen should be allocated to discussions with the shop manager, Frank Camorra (aka Frankie), to get to know how the business operated.

Over slow and deliberate conversations, Frank informed him as best as he could how the business operated and the role he personally fulfilled as manager. It was mainly gibberish to Glen because most of the transactions bordered on 'barter'—and was Frank being deliberately unclear or misleading? In fact, it seemed the business was a 'front' for a wide range of activities covering all the small activities associated with second-hand furniture and bric-a-brac, but also involving short-term financing, illegal betting and card games in the back office, some drug-dealing activities, and also strong-arm collections of overdue debts.No direct physical application of the latter, but using the 'co-ordination' of a family of young Lebanese men who dressed in black and drove a black Zephyr car to the offender's premises. They used extremely heavy persuasion!

Glen had been transformed overnight into a wealthy young man. The finalisation of the will went along surprisingly well even though it took time. Glen was to learn much about his Aunt Polly and how she had accumulated her wealth. A smart business person, she had made few enemies and had operated just below the surface without ripples over the years ... well off the radar of officialdom. The challenge was how to deal with it all? Being young, energetic and intelligent Glen decided to "get to know it all". Now often accompanied by Cliff, he began to seriously inspect the assets. The houses alone were in good order and contained many pieces of quality furniture. Their rooms were bigger and better than Glen and Cliff had appreciate. The shop was a labyrinth of rooms, corridors and cupboards that had a range of uses. No doubt some of the spaces had been used for both legal and illegal storage purposes. Gambling and 'sly grogging' had taken place, and even scantily dressed dancers at special events had all apparently used the premises. Glen's question: "Was it a long time ago, as I was not aware of it?" Frankie just looked the other way.

Glen began to understand more about his departed Aunt Polly. He began to recall some of the partly forgotten incidents quoted about his Aunty. One of the more famous was when she had gone out and bought a motorbike. She had never ridden one previously, but the basis on which she made the purchase was that the motorbike retailer had to give her lessons and guarantee she would pass her driver's licence test. It all went well and she also bought the necessary gear for safety and to make her absolutely anonymous when on the bike. This probably also allowed her to carry out some nefarious operations that no one knew about. Inevitably she had an accident and finished up in a hospital, from where she famously announced "I'm not ready to go just yet!" and simply took her own leave by signing herself out. Back to mainly using her car which was usually driven by an unofficial chauffeur. She had style!

Cliff did not have the mental sprightliness of Glen but he too was becoming used to Glen's new inheritance. Glen was now wealthy, but socially he still enjoyed his University cronies, who had no idea of his changed circumstances. He liked the on and off-campus fun activities with them. He was able to maintain the necessary level of studies with minimum input to graduate at the end of the year. That side of his life was simple and easy.

7

New Zealand – Growing up: George

In another country, in New Zealand, there was a boy with quite a different evolution of circumstances.

George Barnes lived with his mother in a decrepit boarding house on the fringe of a small rural town in the Waikato area of the North Island. His mother ran the house which had five bedrooms available to let. There were three more or less permanently unemployed welfare recipients, and the two other rooms were available for casual passers-by, who were mainly scruffy elderly men. Rent was cheap and so was the quality of the accommodation. There was a shared bathroom and separate toilet down the hallway.

George and his mother had their own accommodation through a substantial doorway down the hall from the rented rooms. The premises were all under the same roof. Their accommodation had a big open kitchen/dining/lounge area, with two bedrooms and a bathroom/toilet for the exclusive use of Mother and George. The plumbing was old and noisy and the kitchen antiquated, with electricity supply intermittent: A cold, draughty and very basic establishment. There was often drama and sometimes minor assaults occurred among the tenants, with George's mother required to threaten to call police from time to time. George was used to irregular hot water for a just adequate shower and although he was never smelly, he was teased about having a dirty face and ears. Some teachers cruelly offered a facecloth for him to go and wipe his eyes and ears.

His mother tried hard to run a decent place and looked after her boarders as well as she could in her limited circumstances. It was difficult to make any profit at all and George had ordinary clothes. He did well at the local State School, but did not like rugby, or indeed any other sport, as he had no means of acquiring sporting gear needed to learn to play hockey or tennis. George progressed through Secondary School and achieved excellent marks in mathematics, history and English, and other subjects as needed. He passed the School Certificate and University Entrance exams in regulation form. No problems and nothing outstanding.

His absent father was a barber and tobacconist in a nearby town—and it had been suggested maybe other smoking material— and a bookmaker on the side. His father contributed nothing at all to George's upbringing. The boy's relationship with his father was neither close nor antagonistic. Dennis Barnes ran a profitable business, kept a low profile and well out of the way of local police. He participated in community affairs by sponsoring events. George spent some school holiday time with his Dad and got to understand a little about betting odds, 'men's talk' and sport. Dennis was a neat dresser, even a bit slick. He never ever denigrated his wife, in fact he admired how well she had provided for George. Hypocritical perhaps, when examined closely.

George's mother had provided a sound and supportive base, but the family economics were tight. In spite of the boarding house experience and its diverse inhabitants, there had been little or no personal violence or perverse behaviour towards George. Thin walls had provided overheard conversations. Some dishonesty—no guns— and a cat had had its ears cut off, illustrating the basic quality, or lack of, of some of the tenants. It didn't seem to overly distress George or his mother, nor was much reported to authorities.

At seventeen years of age, George passed his university entrance examinations with good marks, and was then employed by the ANZ bank in his rural town. It was a good job with prospects for advancement in other towns and even to nearby bigger Hamilton where the ANZ district head office was based. Very quickly George adapted to the dress standards and behaviours of his work companions. He became noticeably better groomed, and some of his attitudes modified as he closely watched and listened to his colleagues, and learnt.

He was a tall, thin, intelligent young man, prepared to listen to suggestions from senior colleagues, and well-liked by his male and female work associates. He had no real outside friends and did not play any sport but was an avid follower of rugby—and sometimes cricket—i.e. the main sports, but not horse racing. George was good at his job and had good prospects and quietly became a good conversationalist.

After a little over eighteen months, he was offered a new and more senior position by the bank at Frankston Junction, which was really a suburb of Hamilton. This meant he needed private board and represented a huge change to his domestic life. He was fortunate enough, with the help of good references from the bank, to procure accommodation in a family home almost within walking distance of the bank. He occupied what had been a veranda converted into a spacious bedroom, with side door access that added to his independent coming and going. Down the hallway he shared a bathroom with the family's two sons. Mr and Mrs Leader were around forty years of age and turned out to be generous and friendly landlords. Mr Leader was known by everyone as 'Boy', and worked as a guard on the Railways, working irregular hours and long shifts. Mrs Leader (Beryl) did part-time sewing, and provided a stable home and better meals than George had ever had in his entire life. The family welcomed him into their home just as if he was family.

The let room provided extra money into their home and almost immediately he was never again thought of as a tenant. Not only did Beryl provide great food but also did his washing, ironing and full laundry services. As a rail guard, 'Boy' was always clean and neat in well-pressed rail uniform. A few extra clothes for George created no problems.

The rent was reasonable and George was able to save enough for his first modest car, an old Hillman Minx. The car gave him opportunities to go home at weekends to visit his mother, and he began to socialise for the first time. His mother was delighted as she loved him dearly, and she observed him becoming a handsome, well-rounded and sophisticated young man. It was, however, his other 'parents' who were really widening his horizons.

'Boy' had a small unofficial arrangement to supplement his income. He irregularly carried unauthorised luggage in his Railway guard's van. They were generally small, well-wrapped parcels that were mysteriously delivered to his train carriage shortly before departure time and equally as mysteriously picked up at a distant station by a wordless stranger. Boy's trains were all freight trains. He did not know the contents of the parcels and did not want to know. His service was rewarded by a handshake and a cash payment. Family betterment, with better education and prospects for the boys, was the prime motivator for the parents and if that required some on-the-side imaginative activity to achieve, then so be it, was their attitude.

George was the ideal young bank employee. He loved his job and was conscientious and flexible. It was known that he regularly visited his mother on the weekends in the Waikato, where he contributed to her financial welfare and also the gradual upgrading of the small and very ordinary boarding house where he had been brought up. She could see and appreciate that he was now a smooth dresser with a good job and a nice motorcar. The bank rewarded him for hard work, and he had prospects for future management opportunities. He was sent to out of office seminars and training conferences to build up his skills, and was becoming a very typical 'bank man'. Fellow staff members liked him and there were no bad vibes surrounding him. He was seen to be an up-and-coming cleanskin.

Promotion was inevitable and he was offered another position in a big branch in Newmarket in Auckland, where he would be exposed to a greater range of the services and products that banks offer. The world of high finance, bonds, mortgage loans, importing and exporting, and all the back office methods of transactions. The Assistant Manager took it on himself to be George's mentor and teacher. The new job meant that George regretfully left his happy home and family in Frankston Junction. It had been one of the real joys of his life. The new job in Auckland also meant new accommodation, and he secured a small flat in Mt Albert that allowed him to train into work, thus avoiding the hassle of heavy traffic in the 'big smoke'. Initially, he socialised mainly with other bank staff members as they generously invited him to meet other friends and family. For the first time, George realised that women seemed to be attracted to him - and he to them and the prospect of their company. He was at ease with himself and had progressed from the struggles of being a 'second rater' in a small rural country town to exuding the confidence of living and working in the city.

Part of his extended education was provided by one of the tellers, Mary Petrovitch—who saw him as a challenge to seduce! He thought she was really gorgeous. She was of Yugoslav ethnic background, with big brown sparkling eyes, heavy black brows and black hair that she usually wore pulled back into a short ponytail; she had a radiant smile that could defuse any disagreement. She was slim, with the advantage of a well-proportioned body and long shapely legs. It was known to all that her favourite song was Neil Young singing 'Heart of Gold'.

At the first branch social function attended by George, she began a subtle programme to get to know him. The dazzling smile whenever their paths crossed no doubt helped. He was inept with progressing a female relationship and was both a virgin and sexually naïve. That was not a total handicap, and after many months of flirtation she finally had him home at her small flat in close by Epsom. After a glass of sauv blanc, it seemed as if she had rather mysteriously partially disrobed, and then she started taking off his clothes piece by piece. She was delighted to observe his excitement and healthy body reaction and even more delighted when without further ado, he entered her. No sophistication, noises or preliminaries—just straight on with it. No need to consider 'mutual consent'. It was just a great event; particularly so for George as a first experience. They became regular lovers and began to meet out of office and out of Auckland. Trips to meet some of Mary's friends and family became weekend events. They ventured as far away as Waitangi, in the Bay of Islands in the far north (Northland), and Coromandel in the east. They enjoyed learning more about Maori culture and history, and on another visit to the Bay of Islands enjoyed a Maori 'Hangi' at Russell. Maori history was a subject they appreciated as part of their country's heritage.

They were getting to know one another and exploring common interests. Her family were keen for George to become more aware of Yugoslavian pioneering in New Zealand's history and particularly in Kauri gum collection and Kauri tree farming. Northland was rich in fascinating history, and the opening of the Auckland Harbour Bridge in 1959 had made trips north quicker.

As young lovers, the two were able to spend much of the weekends together as the bank had little or no overtime requirements. They explored local areas such as the ferry boat across Auckland Harbour to Devonport or to Waiheke Island, and sometimes as far away as the hot springs in Matamata, south of Hamilton. Overnight stays were one of the added enjoyments for the relationship. Their lovemaking became more intense and exploratory as their trust and happiness grew. Like most young Kiwis they joked and laughed about the superiority of New Zealanders over 'common' Aussies!

Their togetherness inevitably led to discussion about the future and how that fitted with anticipated future promotions and lifestyle. They agreed that being a bank employee was safe, sound, and full of good prospects for bigger and better remuneration and a sound future career. There were, however, a number of well educated, bright bank employees in Auckland. Aspirations were fine but George had his rural background and family that could be regarded by some as 'baggage'. The climb up the bank ladder was also long and perceived by some as perhaps uninspiring.

In between wonderful lovemaking and hours and hours of discussion and theorising, they eventually decided that George would be better off leaving the bank for better career prospects, so he quietly entered the job market. Soon, without many trials and tribulations, he was offered what to him seemed an excellent position—Assistant Manager/Buyer to a NZ-owned import/wholesaling company called Paramount Enterprises Trading Pty Ltd. Conveniently, head office was in Kingsland, Auckland, and they also had a small branch in Australia, in Melbourne.

It was a successful business and most products were sourced from India, Taiwan, Japan, some from China, with a few exclusive boutique products from NZ manufacturers. Products were sold to garden centres, hardware stores and country general stores. The owner (Joe McFadgen) considered that George, with his banking experience, age and natural charm, would fit in well with his thirty-plus local employees including the sales staff and representatives. The remuneration package included an A40 Austin Van, and salary forty per cent higher than his bank pay. A future relocation to develop the Melbourne branch was a specific target that had been offered to George as an incentive to move from the bank.

George immediately fitted in well with the full support of the owner who knew he would need some help. He fitted seamlessly into sales and marketing as he appreciated the importance of the relationships with customers and their methods of distribution. Purchasing was of prime importance to the business, so cost prices, and what customers wanted and could afford, required in-depth understanding. He went out regularly with the Sales Manager and spoke to customers on every possible occasion to be assured products were more than competitive. Intuitively, he became a 'retail horse trader'. Clearly not like his father.

George and Mary were becoming closer, and intimate friends as they no longer worked together. It seemed the intensity grew more urgent in the time actually spent together, as their jobs took them apart for longer periods. Weekend visits to Oneroa on Waiheke Island became their favourite lovers' destination. Memories of the ferry boat trips back and forth to and from Auckland mounted up.

At the same time George was moving deeper and deeper into the management of Paramount Enterprises, and carrying more responsibility. After nearly a year, owner Joe had developed full trust and respect for George. They began to evolve in depth the future plans, with the permanent inclusion of George and the suggestion of his becoming a director of the company. "How about we appoint you Manager for Australia, and get on with the development of our specific plans to expand into the much bigger market there?" asked Joe McFadgen.

Hundreds of questions arose from that exciting proposition. Timing, increased remuneration, authority and responsibility, share-holding, vision and mission, budgets and targets, company financial status, and full confidentiality, etc. etc. George did not discuss much of this with Mary as he knew the job would require mobility and flexibility of him in the early stages, even just back and forth between Auckland and Melbourne. Though they were clearly in a serious partnership he had always stopped any discussions on permanent home sharing. Was this a case of his ambition overriding his personal integrity?

Joe and George had long and detailed discussions in order to implement the final agreement. They wanted to incorporate a formal arrangement that included flexibility and fairness, that was reasonable to all concerned, including staff members. The appointment of George as a director of the company aided the acceptance of his status and was formally announced at a staff meeting with the company lawyer present. It was applauded and accepted with harmony by all.

Immediately, George was off to Melbourne to become acquainted with the branch there. This involved a repeat of some of his early actions in the Paramount Enterprises organisation in Auckland, and working out how best to plan for expansion. Joe met with him regularly as they discussed finances and personnel. George spent time looking for an apartment as well as surreptitiously exploring the businesses of the main local customers. Fact-finding of the local scene.

George selected a small unit in Williamstown, close to the Scienceworks building, almost under the Bolte Bridge. It was an easy fifteen-minute car or train trip to the Melbourne CBD and he really liked the village feel and friendly, easy-going social atmosphere of that area. The company's branch address in City Road, Southbank, in the CBD was ideal, and the rent and facilities were adequate. No changes would be necessary even to accommodate future changes and anticipated growth.

George's Williamstown unit was completely self-contained in the back of a stylish old weatherboard period home. It gave him privacy, and came with an off-road semi-covered parking area for the new Commodore car that his new position had provided. George was now deep into major changes, both in his personal life and in the revisions of job descriptions, responsibilities, and the lifting of morale of his Australian team.

Back in New Zealand on a company update visit, George needed to address his relationship and responsibility to Mary. He chose to be unable, or unready, to fully discuss the situation and the conflicts that were bedevilling him. It was, at that stage, in the too-hard basket. Ambition versus personal courage and integrity? So he kept putting off broaching the subject and by omission behaved very badly. It was crystal clear that Mary was aware of bigger things going on. She could not be unaware nor disappointed as she had given her all to the partnership.

George began to slip away from decent behaviour, hoping the solution would sort itself out. He genuinely hoped that his new position would be appreciated as the greater event in his life. Perhaps in the bigger scheme of things in life, and with his complex and sometimes ugly childhood experiences, he enacted avoiding personal commitment and expectations as the easiest. His own assessment and reflection of his behaviour towards Mary was that his shallow emotional response had been contributed to by his experiences as a child in the ordinariness of the cheap boarding house. No one had ever suggested that some form of therapy might be beneficial.

None of these emotions affected or handicapped his daily commercial decision making, or his ability to embrace the challenges associated with his new business responsibilities. The decision making, the implementation, the rewards, the successes, the importance, and new friendships, all awaited him in Australia.

After many discussions in Auckland with Joe, legal advisers, and a senior financial executive, George's official permanent move to Melbourne was fulfilled. George was still surprised how much bigger it was than the NZ business. It was more diverse in the product range of imports and countries of origin. He needed to diligently appreciate the roles, activities, and responsibilities of existing staff. He spent hours inviting input from all staff and initially putting them at ease by admitting he was no expert in their areas of expertise. His broad and friendly smile, his boyish face and easy demeanour helped smooth the way.

Regular telephone calls came in from Mary in New Zealand, but he let her leave messages. He was extremely busy, but his behaviour was ordinary to say the least. He completely 'ghosted' Mary. He justified it to himself by constantly telling himself how very he was.

His accommodation in Williamstown was comfortable, and he allowed himself Sunday morning walks along the foreshore to the local cafés. On these occasions he could feel contentment sneaking in.

George tried to enact his work habit motto based on an accounting acronym: 'FILO' for him meant 'first in, last out' of work. It was easy with his single-minded attitude to enact this as he was young, fit, single and living only fifteen minutes from work. Some of the staff resented his intrusions into detail and there were inevitable changes, as a 'new broom sweeps clean'. George was smart to single out for a generous remuneration increase the existing Melbourne manager Bryan McKenzie, to retain him. Back in New Zealand it had been agreed that to retain Bryan and make his position comfortable, an attractive and well remunerated package would be ideal. Easier said than done, but he was an important cog for current success and was needed for the future. Finally, it was worked out.

George went to great lengths to befriend Bryan, his wife, Barbara, and his family. It was not difficult as he found they were decent people whom he respected. Bryan was an efficient executive and seemed to have accepted his new role and George's position. He did not yet know of potential plans to put him on the board of a new subsidiary company being discussed and plans for him to run the expanded Australian operation.

The McKenzie family found that George, as a single person, responded quickly to invitations to join their family for an occasional picnic. He was socially pleasant and never 'big noted'. They liked him and he fitted in well with his supply of Australia versus New Zealand jokes, which he used with discretion, as he well knew that laughter could quickly turn to resentment if someone was offended! "How do you make an Aussie laugh on a Monday? Tell him a joke on Friday!" "An Aussie is proof that God has a sense of humour!" Socially, the Aussie jokes usually resulted in retaliatory jokes that could add to the fun, "Why did Kiwis stop making ice for drinks? Because the old lady who knew the recipe died!"

Bryan introduced George to his friends even though George had indicated from day one that his attitude to the general staff was, "Be friendly but not friends," i.e. he would not be fraternising with staff.

One Friday evening outside work, at the Williamstown pub, Bryan and Barbara introduced George to a friend of Barbara's. It was all very relaxed and casual and George was immediately attracted to her. Melanie Ortega was probably a little older than George; very slender and tall. She looked like a model with high cheekbones, a slightly long, fine nose, full lips, dark hair with highlights, and smouldering dark twinkly eyes that sloped slightly upwards at the edges that seemed to be laughing both with him and perhaps at him. Some arrogance there that was helped by her attractive easy laugh. George was smitten!

Melanie had been married previously for four years, was now divorced and had no children. She was well groomed and had a mature look about her, even a 'no-nonsense, I've done it all before' look. Over many weeks, and encouraged by Barbara and Bryan, their friendship grew. They had exchanged telephone numbers and they began to meet outside the patronage of Barbara and Bryan. George was feeling 'as free as a bird' in this new stage of his life. He had rosy prospects all around. Without the historical restraints he could adventure into new fields. His sex life accelerated in leaps and bounds as Melanie's experience and lack of inhibitions opened his eyes to many new pleasures. George's faded childhood memories of the boarding house had mainly shown him only a rough and ready side of sex. His own adult experience had mostly been accompanied with love, care and attention but was not greatly imaginative. He still retained strong emotional ties with Mary back in Auckland—even guilt for the unemotional way he had treated her. Melanie encouraged George to be sexually creative and explore and use all parts of his and her bodies—and to enjoy the activities with abandonment. It was truly wonderful. Occasionally, Melanie took him to meet her friends and acquaintances in more secluded and private areas where George became aware of the selective use of recreational drugs. Dark corners or separate rooms at parties where these new and casual 'friends' were sexually active were normal. It was all very new and seemed sophisticated to George.

The business of Paramount Enterprises was progressing well in

Australia as it was in New Zealand. Good growth and profits were the base from which the imagined future could proceed. With plenty of guidance and preparation from Bryan, George went off on his first overseas buying trip for products for both Australia and NZ, sourced from Taiwan and Japan. In Taiwan, he was fortunate to be hosted by a representative appointed by the government to aid exports. Tall and angular, Takeo Shee's English was excellent. After George explained to him the range of products wanted, Takeo took George to multiple manufacturers up and down Taiwan along the main tolled freeway and even into remote small businesses using what looked like under-age girls packing hardware products into blister packs.

Then on to Japan, where more sophisticated and expensive products were sourced, in particular leaf blowers which were then very new on the market.

Takeo Shee turned out to be a great help over several visits to Taiwan. Interestingly, on the first trip he met George in the airport arrivals hall and they headed off in a really battered old Toyota taxi with the driver sitting on a single seat made of beans. Very basic. Over the next two visits, Takeo had clearly increased in status, now having a car of his own—albeit very small, as only very small cars were allowed, and then he moved up to a small-medium car with a little flag on the bumper. This gave him official recognition for his contributions to exports. He certainly helped George to source new and better products in Taiwan as well as explaining how the Taiwanese regarded mainland Chinese. Taipei was a bustling energetic city, full of noise, music and laughter. Its people were well aware of their own history and the precarious future that relied on support from the USA.

Japan was totally different in business practice and society, its people being more stilted and formal in all walks of life and showing little or no sense of humour. There was one other factor involved in how they viewed international interactions and the world. Business was conducted in an extremely formal manner and product quality was never doubted. George made no personal relationships in Japan but Takeo from Taiwan became a friend and even sent gifts home for his new partner, Melanie. Life seemed to be working well for George and he was content.

8

The Melting Pot: Australia

Almost by osmosis, Glen gradually found out more about the size and significance of his inheritance from Aunt Polly Gamble in Ballarat. There was no guidance or advice in the will about how he was to operate. There had been no challenges to the will and probate had been granted within the usual time frame. Perhaps it was just as well that few, if anyone, knew or realised the size of the Gamble estate.

Ballarat was notorious for its freezing cold and wet winter, and conversely its heat and dryness in summer. It was equally famous for its beautiful historic buildings. It was a substantial and vibrant town, big enough to be self-reliant, and with a direct railway line to Melbourne.

Glen, usually accompanied by Cliff, took input from shop manager Frank regarding his part and contribution to the shop and its activities. Glen was unsure of the real relationship that had existed between Frank and his Aunt Polly. How long had they known one another? How long had Frank run the shop? Was he just an employee or were there other special agreements? No documents had surfaced and none were referred to. From discussions with the accountant, who over the years had prepared and submitted the annual tax returns, it seemed the amounts of wages paid had been small and intermittent. The name Frank Camorra did not appear in the shop's books.

The discussions did not result in more empathy between

them but did expand the type and style of language that was more commonly used by Frank. On a few occasions an acquaintance of Frank's was included in discussions and their style of discourse was more confronting, e.g. "Butt out, dummy," or "don't be a f__wit." This was all a bit extreme for Glen, but Cliff took it in his stride when it was clearly not directed at him. His best reply usually included his favourite adjective, "strewth". It gradually became more obvious that Frank and Aunt Polly had not just been active in furniture sales.

Glen and even Cliff were aware of a culture that used marijuana in its different forms. The cultivation and possession of cannabis was acknowledged as a punishable offence but was not greatly feared. Heroin and cocaine were a different category. 'Coke'—a strong stimulant, was used in theory as a 'recreational' drug. Taken, snorted, smoked, or injected, it was addictive. Called blow, charlie, crack, or toot, it was used by some in the local community. It was known that you became euphoric, talkative, and that the drugs lowered inhibitions. And what about 'opium dens'? Glen's education included knowledge of opium use by the Chinese in the goldfields and suggestions that some dens were known to exist as late as 1950. Opium could be smoked, eaten or converted into a pill. It could also be advanced into heroin. Used to create a sense of euphoria, for relaxation, as an analgesic and to lower the heart rate, but it also impaired reflexes. The latex liquid that came from the poppy seeds had historically known multiple uses.

When Glen raised the subject of exactly what many and varied purposes the shop had been used for under his control, and Frank had given only a completely bland reply of "not much", Glen had exploded. His responsive pejorative was intended to illustrate to Frank that the days of bullshit were over. Trying to get Frank to elaborate on these subjects was like pulling teeth, but when Glen's patience wore thin, he raised his voice and robustly asserted that cooperation was needed for any relationship to continue, and that included staying employed!

Under continuing pressure from Glen, and no doubt in an effort to distract attention, Frank decided that there could be value in his taking Glen to see a legitimate wholesale company with whom the shop did occasional business. "And what sort of business would that be?" enquired Cliff somewhat flippantly.

"Well, it's a small importer of giftware from Taiwan that customers buy when they are desperate for a small purchase," was the response from Frank.

It had previously occurred to Frank that it might divert attention from himself if he took Glen (and Cliff) to Paramount Enterprises in Southbank, Melbourne. Frank had been made aware of some management changes there and was uneasy that it could upset one of his 'friendly' relationships. An appointment was arranged and the three of them went off to Melbourne in Glen's brand-new Holden Commodore VB. This vehicle was definitely an upgrade from his dark-blue Kingswood. Cliff, sitting in the back seat on the trip to Melbourne, thought it was a little small for his bigger frame. Glen thought the strong shade of red really suited his new vehicle.

Parking at Paramount Enterprises had been arranged, and Glen was grateful as he did not want any marks on his new Commodore and, being a bit of a country boy, he was timid about city traffic. Frank was thinking that his only connection with a Holden was through a twenty-year-old male acquaintance who had a Sandman panel van that was used for mainly nefarious purposes.

It became quite clear even before they entered Paramount Enterprises premises that it was very unlikely that Frank had been there before. They were greeted in the foyer by a young receptionist who indicated that manager Bryan was expecting them, and as she asked them to follow her, offered "tea or coffee?" A mumbled mix of replies, as they were not sure how to handle the meeting.

In the large office, they were greeted warmly by Bryan McKenzie, who should have been recognised by Frank. An awkward pause was smoothed over by Bryan saying "Frank, I think we may have spoken on occasions over the phone?" and then looking to see which was Frank.

Frank responded and introduced first Glen Robertson as his boss, and then his associate Cliff Richardson. In turn, Bryan introduced George Barnes as the newly appointed MD (from New Zealand), to whom he now reported. George hastily commented that Bryan was still very much in charge as the planned expansions relied heavily on Bryan's expertise and experience. Coffee came and was consumed as progress was made.

What followed was a 'round the houses' discussion, with contributions from Frank being evasive, and the other people present not establishing any value or purpose for the meeting other than general introductions. Bryan was keen to tell of the plans for growth that they had, but even with that, it could not really be established how they could increase mutually beneficial business. A small comment from George about new products from Taiwan and Japan added no new light on the prospects. With the exception of Frank, they all wondered "What the hell is this all about?" All the way home in the car there was an awkward silence, imitating the uncomfortable atmosphere at Paramount Enterprises.

It turned out not to be a complete waste of time, as George had at least been impressed by Glen, and was curious about past business. And why not? A week later George telephoned Glen and invited him to a light lunch in Williamstown. He was still getting to know the overall business and had found Glen to be interesting. Even more, he was curious about Paramount Enterprises' past. A nice lunch in an attractive café on the Williamstown waterfront allowed them both to be able to chat amicably over present and past experiences. They were both well-educated young men with a surprising number of things in common, even if from different childhoods and countries.

One of the topics for discussion was exactly what business the two companies had enjoyed together, and what were the future business opportunities. Glen was understandably careful as he simply did not know what or how business had been previously conducted (by Frank) in the shop, and George was equally ignorant as he had just arrived in Australia. It led to smiles and laughter by them both as it really seemed to be the blind leading the blind. They enjoyed the lunch and one another's company, and resolved to investigate the background and meet again soon.

9

Tough Being a Police Officer: Linda

Linda had to battle her way through prejudice associated with her being female and the perception that she was perhaps a bit 'snobby', because of her South African accent and the fact that she had a Uni degree.

Luckily, Senior Sergeant Sean Walsh was enlightened enough to recognise where the police force in Perth was heading with its new recruitments and new policies, and took it upon himself to be her unofficial mentor. Sean was a respected officer, and he could be formidable. Aged around fifty, a long-serving policeman with a family of five, he had no perverse motives or intentions. His support was welcomed by Linda as she often felt insecure and out of depth in her new country and new role. The constant 'Aussie style' ribbing sometimes became more than tedious. Sean was steady, calm, clear-headed and cautious, but a big police station needed those attributes among many of the younger ambitious cops. In addition, he had no hang-ups about female police officers.

There was one other female officer at the station but she had accepted a subservient role, doing as she was told. There had been a case of women going missing in the area around a popular drinking hole and night club, and the police had hatched a plan to use a woman as a lure. The other officer had declined to be the bait in disguise, and so did Linda. They were alluded to as 'pussies' by some of the male officers but got great support from their Sergeant. Linda was living at home in Claremont, in Perth, with her parents, so received plenty of family support as she battled through pockets of prejudice and slowly became more and more a young Aussie. Now not quite so respectful as she may have been in South Africa, the idea of being planted as bait did not appeal. She was also reflecting and widening herself and her horizons, and recognising that certain attitudes she had held previously in South Africa were changing within her.

She entered into a relationship with a policeman from the station. He was Aaron Naidoo, a second-generation thirty-year-old Australian-born Indian who, like Sergeant Walsh, treated her with respect and encouraged her to express opinions. With a european mother and a broad Aussie accent, he was also a uni graduate and widely read on global affairs. Over a period of time they became secret passionate lovers, and began to seek out each other out on every possible occasion. With her family history, it was ironic that her first tempestuous love affair would be with a non-European man, but all was possible in a fast-changing social environment.

Over time the relationship became known by some of the staff, but was not openly commented on. Rebecca, the other female officer, inadvertently brought the subject to a head one day, when she was provoked by what she interpreted as preference that had been given to Linda within the duty roster. The stakeout at the hotel where they were trying to catch the sex offender had Linda in a warm safe position, and Rebecca outside in a cold area. She raised her hand, waved it around, and in a strident voice pointed out that she had enough of the 'wrongs' being fostered and tolerated to allow Aaron, a married man with two children, to carry on a sexual relationship with the "little blond harpie who has just arrived from apartheid South Africa!" Anger and bigotry had bubbled to the surface. That really set the cat amongst the pigeons, but most surprised of all was Linda, who had not been aware that he was married with children, or was that he was living at home with them all!

When she confronted Aaron, he was quite offhand; he apologised and expected that the relationship could continue, or simply come to an end! Linda experienced a gamut of feelings and emotions. They ranged from heartbreak over what for her was a relationship of serious depth and significance, to betrayal and humiliation. In her calmer moments, she could acknowledge to herself that it was ironic and perhaps was for the best.

Reaction within the police station was that this was a one-day wonder, and everyone mainly dismissed Rebecca and attributed the outburst to her being bitter and twisted. Linda's mentor, Sergeant Walsh, urged calm and adult behaviour and to simply let it fade. Linda requested a few days' leave while she licked her wounds. With the resilience of the young, she realised that plants would no doubt flower again tomorrow, and she resolved to seek a transfer to another jurisdiction, at her own pace. This took time and patience, looking and filling in applications, even pursuing opportunities interstate. Eventually, with some help from family and friends, she secured an appointment as a trainee constable/detective in Footscray, Victoria. She was hellbent on becoming Detective Constable Linda Alexander.

Her farewell from Western Australia was low-key as far as the police were concerned but of concern to her parents. However, Linda was now a much more mature young adult than they recognised or gave her credit for. With enthusiasm, she set about finding accommodation in Melbourne. It had become a very real possibility that brother Brendan would be transferring to Australia from London shortly, and Melbourne was the probable destination for him. His imminent arrival provided several advantages to Linda. Socially and personally, having her older brother as a companion strengthened her wellbeing in a new town, and if they shared accommodation, costs could be split. She also looked forward to getting to know better her big brother as an adult.

With his approval, Linda was able to look for bigger and better premises than she had previously envisaged. Brendan was now a polished senior executive who stopped off in Perth to see his parents on the way across to Melbourne to take his promotion. Parents John and Prue were delighted to see him for a few weeks and they brought him up to date with all the local news, and a full description of the experiences that Linda had had to endure. They thought that might be useful to aid the siblings living together.

Linda found ideal premises, a unit within five kilometres of the Footscray Police Station, which was also not that far from Bourke Street in the Melbourne CBD where Brendan was to be based. That worked well and took only weeks to organise.

Linda's introduction to the Footscray Police Station was much less traumatic than had been her experience in Western Australia. A bigger and more organised police force with much clearer lines of authority, districts and training. Detectives had to undergo field training and regularly attend training at the Police Academy. Detectives could be allocated to regional areas where they could be involved in investigations not exclusively in their own base. Part of Linda qualifying as a detective included field investigations on which judgement was made and recorded. It could be onerous. In her own mind Linda became 'a learning leech'.

With the arrival of her brother in Melbourne, and the sharing of the unit in Footscray, she became much more confident and assured. Brendan was also a beneficiary in his new position as he occasionally included Linda in some of his social activities. Having a detective as a sister aided status and interest. Her work experiences ranged widely from the very mundane to an ugly murder where she had her first face to face meeting with an actual murderer. Linda later commented to her brother, "how could anyone look so evil!"

The killer was a woman of around thirty years of age, riddled with drugs, with a pale taut face, almost no teeth, and pale blue merciless eyes. She had an aggressive, challenging attitude that Linda had never previously encountered. Linda hadn't needed counselling following this case but it was certainly a new experience.

Unlike the unfriendly reception she had received in Perth, Linda was smoothly integrated into the whole team and given every opportunity to work as a detective. There was no antagonism, and other constables and the other ranks treated her with respect. Detective Sergeant Robert Accardo was her boss and he was not only skilled and respected, but blessed with a sense of humour.

One of their first investigations together in Footscray was a call to a tiny room up some narrow stairs in a dilapidated apartment, where it had been reported there was a terrible stench. DS Accardo, accompanied by Linda and another constable, with handkerchiefs covering their mouths, entered the airless room and Linda had to hold back from vomiting. The other constable was a little less successful. The naked woman was lying in a crumpled heap, amongst rotting half-eaten food, urine and other unidentifiable liquids and congealed blood, some of which was splattered on the filthy bedlinen. A truly ugly and foul-smelling scene. As soon as the pathologist had finished and steps were taken to remove the body, DS Accardo made a point; they were to respect the fact that no matter how the dead body had looked, she was first and foremost a human being. It was good to have her brother at home for support and counselling.

Field investigations of minor and a few major incidents contributed to the greater skills and intuition that Linda's superiors had stressed were necessary along the way to make for a top detective. She was loving the atmosphere and her chosen vocation and every day she was maturing as a person as well as a police officer.

10

A Trip Home: Linda

Family news back from South Africa was not good. Linda's favourite grandmother had been diagnosed with a particularly virulent stomach cancer from which she was unlikely to recover. This greatly distressed the whole family. Grannie Alexander had been Linda's closest, dearest, and best confidential friend for all her life. "Grannie" was number 1 for everyone and she had been unmovable when the family emigrated, so for the last years and months she had been living in an excellent quality, safe and gated community accompanied by Linda's mother's sister (i.e. Linda's Aunt Jean).

The potential passing of this family stalwart and most senior member rattled the family. It was almost too much for them all to contemplate, particularly from so far away. Without hesitation Linda sought an appointment with her boss in Footscray, Victoria, and requested three months sabbatical leave, acknowledging to him that she realised it may set back her career path. DS Robert Accardo listened with great empathy and sympathy, saying the application would have his support and he would forward it on to his District Superintendent. The speedy response of approval on an official form won 'for ever' thanks and respect from Linda.

Without delay Linda booked her flights to Jan Smuts Airport in Johannesburg, where she was met by Aunty Jean and Grannie in a wheelchair. Linda brought with her additional news about when other family would be arriving. It was almost too much for Grannie and she broke down and cried with joy. She was clearly frail but feisty as she asked Linda if she yet had a decent Aussie boyfriend with an accent. She did comment how gorgeous Linda looked and how proud everyone was of her new life being carved out in Australia. That brought tears to Linda's eyes. Linda was to stay with Aunty Jean and Gran in their townhouse which clearly gave them heaps of time to chat.

It was quickly clear that Grannie was far from well and that a tight regime of medication and almost daily visits from carers and experts was helping to ease and lengthen her coping with the illness. Linda caught up with other family members and was happy to extol the virtues and challenges she was meeting in Australia. Many of them were envious and had plans to follow if at all practical. Linda tried to put aside at least an hour a day simply to sit with her beloved Grandmother and talk away, even aimlessly. Gran put her through the hoops about growing up and maturing, in particular what her vocational aims were and how they could be achieved within a police force. She often got tired and suggested an extension of the discussion for the next day. Linda loved it. Many of the happy moments when Linda was a child were reminisced over together as Linda pushed the wheelchair through the beautiful, well-kept gardens of her grandmother's home.

"Remember when I used to call in after school and you and Poppie always had chocolates and Licorice Allsorts hidden in a cup! she recalled with a laugh. "I was not supposed to have lollies."

They talked about birthday presents and how Brendan once had an accident in the garden. The time just flew by. In some ways sad, but also significant as they appreciated the transitioning taking place with genuine love. Strength was also being transferred. Linda felt a new level of maturity being added to her wisdom.

It seemed strange coming from South Africa that her grandmother was keen to examine women's rights, and urged Linda not to sell herself short! Be treated equally and with respect, she told Linda, her major recommendation being to keep up her level of education. She even urged Linda to lead the pack by being out front. Lively discussions followed this urging, as Linda asked her if that was what she had done! That got quite a giggle as Grannie told her to behave herself and respect who she was. They had lots of similar jokes. Sometimes early in the day when Gran was brightest, she would ask more personal questions, which in the main Linda answered honestly, even confessing about the unfortunate affair she had with a fellow policeman who turned out to be married. Grannie smiled at that, expressed sympathy and added "A little spice in your early life probably did no harm." She quickly added "But regretfully for me it never happened." Linda went tut, tut, and they both giggled.

Gradually over several weeks members of the family arrived to stay for varying lengths of time and although it was a gathering brought about by a sad reason, it served a great purpose of bringing together in one embrace a family who by virtue of a splintered nation now lived in new places with new endeavours. Linda met cousins, uncles and aunties and old friends, most of whom she would not see again in the near future. It was a sobering thought that had to be assimilated with any new life challenge. Another step in maturing and pressing on with resolve while yet acknowledging the pain. She did not catch up with her first love Harry, who leaving had originally seemed such an agonising and impossible thought. They had kept up fervent communications for a while after Linda's family arrived in Perth, but as the two matured and stepped on in their separate adult lives they naturally grew apart, and contact became more spasmodic before dwindling away to nothing. While maintaining a warm affection for her first young love, Linda did not feel the need to re-establish contact.

The intimate discussions with Gran, Aunty Jean, and members of her own family who were visiting broadened her appreciation of family importance. Grannie did quiz her about any current special relationship but Linda said there was no such person and her concentration was on her career, which she loved! She added that thanks to Grannie urging her she thought she would, with approval of her bosses, enrol at University to upgrade her qualifications and study for an MBA. That would be a three or four-year part-time slog but she had the ambition to do it. Grannie clapped her hands and reached up for a cuddle. Memories are made of this. Maybe to some people's disappointment Linda often reiterated that Australia was definitely home.

Linda's father John and brother Brendan had arrived separately later than Linda just in time for a final farewell. Grannie passed quietly one evening, at peace with herself having clearly done enough.

Linda arrived back home in Australia, saddened but stronger, with her ambitions intact. She was back two weeks earlier than the time off that had been approved but she used the time for a holiday.

11

Ballarat Shop – Commerce: Glen

Glen knew he had to delve deeply into the 'Frank situation', as he called it in his own mind. He invited Frank to have a light lunch at the Ballarista pub in Lydiard Street, Ballarat. The invitation included Cliff. The Ballarista was comparatively new and had an interesting menu, and Glen asked for a table by a window so it could be private. Both Frank and Cliff were a little nervous about the formal setting but Glen felt he needed to know and understand more.

It started tentatively, as Glen explained that there were little or no records of Frank's employment in the enterprise, and no records of his relationship with Polly. Could Frank explain that, and what his expectation was of the ongoing situation and future? A silence ensued, as Cliff had been told not to enter into the conversation.

Frank took his time as his features tightened and he took deep breaths, then swallowed twice, before, "It's none of your fucking business, Mr. Robertson!"

Another silence. Glen tried to placate him by asking if it would help to have another colleague come to a meeting, as it was important that Glen know all the businesses details in proper order.

Frank replied, "I don't know what a colleague is, and I'm sure I don't have one; I just want to continue along as I have been!"

Glen indicated that would not, and could not, be allowed. They proceeded to have lunch in comparative silence, mumbling along with meaningless observations about the weather and passers-by. It had been a total waste of time, but Glen insisted they meet again next morning at 9am at the shop and if possible, Frank should bring an associate as matters were going to be resolved.

Glen genuinely hoped that would happen and said, "We want you involved, if possible, but it must be on agreed terms."

Frank left without a thankyou or acknowledgement. Glen and Cliff lingered awhile over a second cup of coffee and tried to evaluate the discussion. Cliff's opinion was that Frank was in a no-win position and that he would need to modify his behaviour and attitude to be treated with fairness, if in fact he was entitled to be treated fairly. Glen thought that to be insightful. They did some preparations of questions for the next day and Cliff even had some pertinent input to be put to Frank, e.g. 'Are you an Aussie? What is your real name?'

Promptly at 9am they met again in the shop, now with the addition of Frank's young 'helper' Tony, who had parked his Sandman panel van right outside. Glen started with a clipboard with foolscap lined paper attached. He made a show of it and indicated he was going to record the answers to his many questions, as in formal notes of a meeting. Firstly, he wrote down everyone's name with a flourish, until he got to Frank, who he asked to spell his surname out.

"C-a-m-o-r-r-a," replied Frank.

Tony, when asked, was hesitant about speaking and looked to Frank to see if it was OK. Finally, the answer came: "Tony Lombardi".

They were still only at the front door! From then on, the questions were all directed to Frank. They ranged over a wide area of subjects and Glen insisted that they would not move on until there was a satisfactory answer to each question, or he noted down that 'an answer would be provided by the next day'. It was like the Spanish Inquisition!

"Who had keys to the shop? Who were staff? Full bank account details. Who controlled and checked the account? Who were signatories for cheques and the bank account? Where is the cash kept, and show us the secure safe? Is it a cash-only business? Full description of all activities held and permitted on the premises. Who controls these activities? Is there a basement? What 'exactly' do you consider was your role and responsibilities to Aunt Polly? Are you aware of substance abuse on or around the premises?"

The latter brought a scoff from Frank and Tony and the response that they had no understanding of the terminology. Glen couldn't resist a Churchillian quote, replying to them that it must have been "a terminological inexactitude"—which went right past all three of the others.

Now a physical walk-through of the premises, with progress slow and interesting to everyone except Frank. There were many rooms, some of which were locked, and one or two which when opened contained only a table and chairs, but were mainly in good order, dust free and obviously used. Frank had to promise he would find keys later for two locked cupboards and a little back room (bedroom). The kitchen was surprisingly modern and well equipped, as was an adjacent area set up like a study which had a TV, computer and fax facilities. The back door led to a sealed parking area for three cars. The tour and questions included a coffee break in the kitchen from where it was possible to see through an internal window into the cluttered store. Glen had hoped that Frank might relax a bit and open up about his role in the business, and in particular how he related to Aunt Polly. That turned out to be an unfulfilled expectation.

'Come for your inheritance and you may have to pay for the funeral' was a Yiddish proverb that Glen thought of then, and it seemed it might be possible as the meeting broke up with little satisfaction for him. It was apparent that unorthodox and most certainly illegal activities had been condoned and approved under Aunt Polly's auspices. What the hell was the next step, he thought to himself?

12

The Mysterious Aunt Polly Gamble

Serious investigation was needed, so Glen went back home to visit his parents. He asked his mother to elaborate on everything about her sister Polly. The sisters had grown up together harmoniously, Polly had gone off to Teachers Training College and on graduation had been appointed to a primary school in Ballarat. The sisters had always been close and when Glen's mother got married, they continued their close relationship with telephone calls and regular visits. Polly eventually decided that much and all as she enjoyed teaching and was happy for the life choices her sister had made, she needed to widen her own horizons.

Polly had no close relationship with anyone else so, with some spare cash and time, planned overseas tourist trips by sea. On one such voyage, she was befriended by a similarly single American woman of around her age. Their friendship grew as their discussions developed more deeply into religion and philosophy. The American was exotic and mysterious to look at and her name, 'Mikaela' Kennedy, added to her presence. She was the self-appointed high minister of a religion called 'The Church of the Golden Sight'. Over several years the two corresponded regularly and Polly was a guest of Mikaela in her home in Missouri, USA—with dire warnings from the family in Australia that it must be a con.

The friendship developed and Mikaela suggested that a branch of her 'Church' should be opened in Australia. Investigations seemed to show that the only practical method to do that was for the Church to be founded and financed from within Australia. Polly did not want to invest in such an idea, but Mikaela was by now a close friend and confidante, with an apparent aura and very persuasive powers. Maybe there was even more to the relationship?

The idea was progressed through the necessary legal steps, again against dire family warnings and with questions about what obligations Polly would be accruing. Mikaela went to Ballarat briefly, looked at a few potential properties and agreed that an existing shop site could be easily converted for the new Church's purposes. A small villa close by would be needed for staff. The money necessary for the purchases was remitted to Polly from the USA, and the purchases were made in Polly's name with signatures from Polly and Mikaela attached. All local legal requirements were met.

For many long months nothing more eventuated. Correspondence went back and forth with great warmth, and many plans for the future were exchanged. Polly continued her school teaching. Glen's mother occasionally inquired about any developments but was not enlightened. As a Presbyterian she was suspicious of any 'new' religion. So, it was never really discussed.

Polly owned her own home outright, purchased with savings from her schoolteacher salary. With the purchases through the Church, she now had a cluster of three properties within a five-kilometre radius. The two Church properties were interesting. The shop was a very small opportunity shop operated by a traditional religious organisation. The small house, or villa, at the time of purchase was vacant and in good condition; suitable for immediate use or for reletting.

It became obvious that Mikaela's health was slowly declining, and with it her fanatical drive to expand the influence of the Church of the Golden Sight. Polly was invited for one more, and what turned out to be a final, visit to Missouri. It was sad to see that Mikaela, the inspirational leader, was dying without having achieved all of her dreams. The ownership and operation of the cult, like many in the USA, relied on the drive and vision of its leader. Polly returned to Ballarat and could only sadly await the inevitable outcome. In due course, Polly became the unencumbered owner of the properties that had been planned as the basis for the new Church of the Golden Sight. She had no such vision or energy and with no follow-up from anyone from the USA, she replanned her existence.

Polly had always been a little eccentric and now began to wear at almost every opportunity a hat. Not overly noticeable but it led her to look more closely at the op shop that she now owned and which was leased and run as a fundraiser by the Anglican Church. Polly often discussed the shop with her sister, who still ran her own business from home. Polly suggested to her that she help run it. That was declined with thanks.

Polly put on hold the necessity to address a rent review while she took financial planning advice from her solicitor. It all took time but Polly gradually began to enjoy some of her new wealth. She became a frequent visitor to the shop and became friendly with the volunteer staff that ran the business. She had undertaken tours encompassing all of the nooks and crannies in the building and became aware of how little quality stock was available for sale, and how little real cashflow the shop was generating. It was obvious that changes had to be made so with all of the parties' consent, it was made known that the business, or even the overall site, was available and 'open for discussion'.

What eventuated was an arrangement for a new anonymous company to take up a rental contract and pay Polly an agreed price for the existing stock, fixtures and fittings. They apparently planned to increase the stock dramatically and be more of a traditional pawnbroker business. Perhaps a Cash Converter-style operation. The new business began with a fully registered and qualified manager and a fresh façade and appearance. This lasted less than a year before Polly was approached by manager Frank Camorra, apparently on behalf of the lessee, to modify the lease back to a traditional contract at a higher rent, and some public trading involvement that could include Polly. That would make the appearance of the shop more friendly and non-controversial. The arrangement quite suited Polly from an ego point of view, as she would have a manager on site whom she did not need to pay and she could indulge in her own small trading. Details of lines of demarcation were vague but initially it did not seem to matter as systems evolved with great harmony. Frank initially had a young female assistant but that ceased after six months as the business was quiet.

Polly and Frank both had sets of keys and Frank controlled the day-to-day running of the shop, including the finances. Polly did not like the man but tolerated the arrangement. To herself, she theorised that he was from a southern-European background, probably a loner, had had a dominant mother, did not relate easily to women, was maybe impotent, no children, and was divorced!

She certainly disliked him. Frank was clearly the front man for an unknown or unidentified lessee.

13

Business Prospects: George

George from Paramount Enterprises had found Glen interesting and as part of his 'getting to know' people and businesses, he invited him over to have a light evening meal on the foreshore at Williamstown. He suggested Glen might like to include Cliff, and he planned to bring along a female friend, plus his manager Bryan and his wife Barbara. He suggested it could be a pizza-type light meal with a red wine and no particular agenda. Everyone agreed and George hoped that Melanie would accompany him. She was delighted to accept.

The evening started quietly as they sat around talking in generalities. The two ends of the scale were the gregarious and sophisticated Melanie, politely waiting out her introduction and then in the appropriate time actively contributing, and the gauche Cliff—always just listening and hoping not to be expected to fully participate. Cliff was introduced as working 'with' Glen, but all there understood he was very much Glen's 'gofer'. Cliff could be underestimated as, now well into his twenties, he was becoming quite presentable under Glen's advice. As the food arrived and the wine was enjoyed, company business, histories, and future plans were explored. Paramount Enterprises' plans for expansion, using new products from Asia and a new emphasis on DIY products, made conversation and discussion of ideas very easy.

In a mild way, George tried to introduce talk about 'authority and responsibilities' but that got no traction, nor did organisational charts. That was all too formal.

Glen's telling of a joke, "What's the smallest room in Australia? The Australian Hall of Fame!" went down with loud abuse and raucous laughter. Everyone relaxed, and with another pizza and more wine, and input from almost everyone, the evening rolled on. Glen suggested that he had an underutilised property on a good site in central Ballarat that could be used for more than secondhand goods. That got the attention of everyone and initiated suggestions in many directions. For George, it was like a brain storming session at the bank but much more fun. Suggestions ranged from coffee, music, computers/telephones, hairdressing, real estate, escort agency, chemist etc. No one suggested an opium den or gang headquarters, as crossed Cliff's mind! The biggest problem for any of them was who had the expertise to run such a business. The idea of a brothel, of course, drew suggestions galore, and the quality of discussion deteriorated as the volume increased. The night was a lot of fun and achieved both social and commercial progress.

For George, it resulted in a closer friendship with Melanie who he appreciated very much for her sophisticated, mature attitude and wonderful, slightly wacky, sense of humour and easy laughter. George was finding he needed to keep a sense of his own reasoning, as he was getting more and more strident telephone calls and messages from Mary in New Zealand. These calls and messages were urging him to include her in their future together. George was busy both business-wise and socially and wanted to 'move on' in his new life in Australia. He was not handling the Mary situation decisively or well, though in his own mind he felt he was being kind as he did not want to hurt her by having the discussion. He clearly had forgotten or overlooked how they had first met at the bank and how determined she had been to befriend him.

Mary Petrovitch came from a pioneering background in New Zealand with family going back to Yugoslavia. She could not be fobbed off that easily! There had never been an unwritten or even half-acknowledged agreement between them but reasonable expectations could have been seen to exist by her. George had not yet made the critical and mature decision to eliminate her from his life by actually speaking to her.

He found it easier to ignore the pressure from across the sea as his relationship with Melanie blossomed, and that also worked well with the relationship he had fostered with Bryan and his wife Barbara. Melanie was naturally vivacious and her maturity helped her and George in particular, to see the funny side of events and life. Their uninhibited lovemaking was wonderful for George and her open unselfconsciousness seemed to lead to much more personal exchanges about past experiences and history. They were getting to know one another with greater depth. George confessed to Melanie the problem he had with Mary in New Zealand, and his own lack of courage to finalise the problem. Quick as a flash she gave him the correct answer. "Book a flight back there! Do some business with Paramount Enterprises, keep Joe McFadgen fully informed about Australia, visit your mother, and also sort out Mary," she responded.

For George, it was like a 'light in the night' illumination of how to resolve the issue; of not having realised in the past that he couldn't see the wood for the trees. With so much going on, he had needed some help to get there.

Off he went to New Zealand for a few days' work combined with a pleasant well-deserved holiday, with a potential sting in its tail if he did not finalise the mounting personal crisis. Business progress was spectacularly good so that was enjoyable to report back, and his mother of course was delighted to see him and took George to be shown off to friends and relations. That left only the Mary Petrovitch issue. George was not brave about the likely confrontation and was concerned about a potential escalation, perhaps involving a brother or family member. Finally, he invited Mary to a café in Newmarket that they had in the past frequented.

They clearly started with the intention of being friendly and sensible. It only took minutes for George to remember how gorgeous she was and to remember how they enjoyed pop music together and in particular Neil Young's 'Heart of Gold.' He was quickly reminded that she was a very direct person when Mary said, "What are your intentions?" George didn't need to ask for an expansion of what she meant. His typically indecisive reply of, "Well, I think we'll need time to let things evolve and perhaps agree to meet and discuss possibilities in a month or two" did not go down well. She exploded.

"That's as weak as piss, and that's exactly what my brothers predicted!"

He was taken aback by her aggression and also a little by the reminder that she had brothers, and was embarrassed by her anger and loud voice in a public café. Not sure if that was an implied threat, he gathered himself and more bravely said, "I think it is all over; my job and future is clearly in Melbourne, and I have a new partner of whom I am very fond."

Mary responded, "You're such a 'gutless wonder'; why couldn't you have said it all months ago? Good bye and good riddance!" and she gracefully, if furiously, walked out on him. George could feel himself sweating profusely from tension and embarrassment. He was intelligent enough to wonder if there was a lesson to be learnt as he arranged to fly home to Australia. In his own mind he claimed, 'mission accomplished'!

14

Possibilities: Glen

George and Bryan decided that they needed to formulate plans and policies to implement a possible commercial future with Glen and the Ballarat area.

Firstly, how genuine and commercially stable was Glen? Socially they liked him and as their knowledge of him was expanded they respected him. What exactly could the two businesses do together for their mutual advantage? Were they ready to be totally honest to investigate alternative, more lucrative, endeavours?

Secondly, was Paramount Enterprises clear in its own vision? Was there a necessity to consult Joe in New Zealand, and what about staff facilities and finance? The legality of new activities and the customers needed to develop them was evolving.

Coincidentally, Glen had reached the point where he had decided that the 'buy and sell' business issues had to be resolved. He contacted his lawyer and asked him to arrange a meeting with a fully authorised representative of the tenant, as the renewal of the lease was imminent. He rang George and invited him and Bryan to a meeting at the Ballarista pub. Cliff as usual was to attend with Glen.

Possibilities for any type of joint venture were on the unwritten agenda as a follow-up to subjects that had been touched on previously, both formally and socially. Glen had decided to be totally honest about the shop and how ill-informed he really was about the tenant, and the manager, Frank Camorra. He did not really know much about his late Aunt Polly Gamble and her commercial activities. The four men speculated again with imagination what the premises could be used for and whether or not the existing business could fit within the circumference of a joint venture. It seemed unlikely when little or nothing was known about the stock or it's supposed value. However the discussion ranged happily on, covering the possible conversion of the site to a retail outlet for mainly products from Paramount to maximise profit margins.

The brainstorming continued amicably until the first serious contribution from Cliff: "Why don't we import bicycles from China (or anywhere) and have our own retail business in Ballarat?"

Stunned silence as everyone considered the possibilities. George was the first to respond, "You know, that could be a bloody good idea, but who knows anything about bikes?"

Cliff was always reticent in this type of discussion but quietly added, "Just maybe I do."

That got the discussion rolling; more coffee was ordered and the shop-site was reconsidered. Would it be suitable and could other stock such as DIY products be included? Was there a demand for bicycles and were there any statistics on sales available? Did Paramount have an overseas manufacturer? If 'we' owned the site and managed the whole business, how much stock and finance would be needed to set up a viable business? All great questions to which only speculation was possible.

Other more speculative ideas included massage and gym combo, a club house for motorbike gangs, and a nightclub that could maybe feature pop music. Glen quite fancied being the disc jockey featuring Don McLean and Bruce Springsteen! He could see himself as 'The Boss!' His Uni pals would perhaps appreciate the gig.

After two hours, the agreed next step was to all go together and look at the shop and consider its suitability, and to observe strict confidentiality anywhere close to Frank. As expected, the shop was open, but freezing cold as it usually was in April in Ballarat. Upon entrance, Frank was not visible but he quickly appeared from the back office. Perhaps he had a heater there! He was wary of four men descending on him, only two of whom he recognised. The introductions were minimalistic and Glen simply indicated he was giving them a tour of the premises. Frank was clearly uneasy about it, so Glen glibly suggested "he should ring the boss". That didn't happen, so a brief walk of the building took place that gave the Paramount 'boys' an appreciation of the size and quality of the premises. Frank could not resist directing a couple of snide remarks to Glen who ignored them but said to himself 'he who laughs last, laughs longest'. Or was it loudest? One of his dad's favourite sayings.

They all adjourned and agreed to research different areas and to meet up again shortly, by which time Glen assumed he would have met the tenant's representative. He mentioned also to Frank that coincidentally, the lease expired on June 30th, and he was planning not to renew as he wanted vacant possession.

Eventually the meeting with the representative of the tenant was arranged in the office of their legal firm, with their lawyer, a Mr Needham. By then, Glen had established that the lessee of the shop was a company named Investment Co-op Pty Ltd, and shares were held by a variety of trust funds. The registered office was a medium-sized legal firm in Flinders Lane in Melbourne. The official representative was a Mr John Khoury, a well-dressed, well- spoken, pleasant man with a slight European or Middle Eastern accent. His attitude was relaxed and it seemed he had little knowledge of the circumstances but was prepared to listen. Glen and his lawyer were the only others in the meeting.

To get the ball rolling, Glen said he would not be renewing the lease on June 30th and that he required the premises cleaned and cleared for vacant possession. John Khoury hardly changed his expression and mildly asked, "Who do you consider owns the stock, fixtures and fittings, and goodwill?"

Glen had to admit, "That's a very good question. Relative to goodwill, there clearly is no goodwill attached to the legal retailing of secondhand and antique furniture."

John Khoury didn't even blink about the use of the word 'legal.' Glen's lawyer volunteered that there was probably no dispute about stock, fixtures and fittings, as there had been an agreement from Polly to 'hand them all over' when Frank Camorra had been appointed to manage the business. Mr Khoury seemed vague about such an agreement but not fussed.

Glen wanted to clear up any arrangements that could relate to Frank and in particular any inherent liabilities. Mr Khoury was more animated in this area and seemed anxious to have Frank retained in some way. Both Glen and his lawyer were adamant, to the point where in a semi-formal way the latter said, "My advice to my client is to sever all relationships with Frank Camorra, as there are historical and current matters under investigation."

That was clearly a surprise and even a bombshell to Glen. No elaboration was volunteered. On the side, it was hinted there was a name issue. The meeting rolled on for another thirty minutes exploring possibilities and timing, and then Khoury indicated he had to report back to the company directors' and would respond accordingly. The meeting finished. After they had left, Glen asked about his lawyer's bombshell advice, and was informed, "I think they are a gang of crooks using the premises to launder money or drugs and my few dealings with Camorra have truly frightened me. I think Ms Gamble and you have probably been very lucky not to be involved."

It was agreed to wait and see what the response would be. A week later John Khoury telephoned Glen to arrange a new meeting and asked approval to bring along his lawyer. There were no problems with that idea.

On this occasion, it was obvious that they were all prepared, and agreements were quickly arrived at and minutes recorded. The lease would not be renewed. The fixtures, fittings and most of the stock belonged to the tenant. Clean and vacant possession would be handed over on August 31st, which was a two-month extension at the current rate.

There would be a joint operation to sell the stock (except for any that had been established as belonging to Polly Gamble) with all proceeds going to the tenant. This subject was a little contentious as no doubt Polly had historically purchased some when she had been actively involved. It was agreed that a small amount of china, glassware, crockery and antiques that were readily identifiable were to be put aside.

The marketing and selling of the stock would need more than the narrow skill set of Frank Camorra, so Glen agreed to arrange for some sales staff, and including himself, Cliff, and others, at no cost to the tenant. Glen would arrange closing down advertising, signs and marketing, which was seen as a goodwill gesture. Frank was to organise and be responsible for necessary operational items, including dump bins, rubbish clearance, electricity etc. The joint effort was not to begin before July 15th, with a completion target of August 15th. Insurance cover was to be taken out to cover all possible liabilities on the stock up to August 31st, and to be the responsibility of the Investment Co-op Ltd. Full evidence of the insurance coverage to be sighted before work commenced.

It was agreed that a new meeting would be necessary to clarify the roles and responsibilities of Frank Camorra. It was further agreed that the liaison necessary would be through John Khoury, who seemed to be aware of some of the connections. Glen and Cliff wondered what surprises might yet surface from this den of iniquity.

15

Investigations – After the Fire

The day after the shop fire occurred, an Incident Room was established at the Ballarat Police Station which included files, cabinets, white boards, tables, chairs and two extra telephone extensions. As soon as all the police officers had arrived in Ballarat a meeting was convened by DS Thomas including the local police constables who had been involved the previous day, and with DS Wilson visiting again from Footscray.

After all appropriate introductions were completed the most senior detective, DS Thomas, began proceedings with the obvious, "Where are we at, and what do we know?" In effect, 'the who, what, where, why.' And what don't we know?

DS Thomas led off by confirming that the old wooden shop building was now completely burnt out down to ground level. Two, probably three survivors, had been interviewed and details recorded and they had been sent home. Two males and a female.

"How can there be a 'probable' third?" asked DC Linda Alexander.

DS Thomas responded, "We are not yet sure whether the second young male had been in the building or was just sheltering in his van around the back of the building."

He went on: "There are two deceased and badly burnt bodies, and from information from Ms Barbara McKenzie, we believe them to be a Mr Frank Camorra, the shop manager, and a Ms Melanie Ortega, both known to her." Next question was who owned the building.

The local Ballarat constable answered quickly, "A local kid named Glen Robertson."

DS Wilson, who was used to conducting this type of session, asked, "What do we know about any of these players?"

Surprising to some, the answer was that Cliff Montgomery Richardson was found to have an old police record, but nothing at all was known about anyone else, particularly the owner or the manager. In fact, no information could be found or seemed to exist at all about Frank Camorra.

Quick as a flash, DS Thomas spoke, "DNA report, please". The team was starting to work like a big co-ordinated police organisation.

"What is currently happening on the burnt-out site?" was the next question. The local Duty Constable thought that a team was assembling to work their way through the still hot ash, dirt and rubble for anything that could be useful evidence.

DS Wilson and Linda almost simultaneously asked, "What is the theory about how the fire started?"

It surprised almost everyone when the local constable volunteered, "Local witnesses reckoned there were at least two explosions and maybe even four."

DS Thomas leapt to his feet and said, "Get an urgent message to the team on site to be super careful as there may be booby traps or other explosives still in the debris." Some thought he might be being dramatic but accepted and passed on the caution.

It was only much later on Sunday that a report arrived at the station that the search team had discovered where the explosions emanated from. Almost in the middle of the building there was now a large hole that had splintered the floorboards to smithereens and exposed, amongst other things, what looked like burnt bones of a long-dead person. A cadaver! Another, totally unexpected element to add to the investigation.

In what would become a regular event, DS Thomas said, "Let's summarise where we are at, and actions to be taken now. Right, the owner of the building? Do we know anything about him, and have we contacted him?"

The answer was that the owner, Glen Robertson, was a Ballarat Uni graduate who currently lived in Ballarat. He had been at the uni campus attending a hockey match and then drama classes. That had progressed on to an onsite Uni party before Robertson had been delivered home to bed around 1am, rather inebriated according to friends. It was agreed that Linda should conduct an interview with him urgently.

Next question: "Who managed the business and was in charge of current trading?"

It was thought that Frank Camorra, whoever he was—and now deceased—had been employed to run the business on a daily operational basis. There was no real information as to whom he reported to. It was to be checked out.

Other questions emerged. "What about a man called John Khoury who represents a legal firm?" "Who is, or was, Melanie Ortega?"

It seemed Melanie was a close friend of Barbara McKenzie, the female survivor, who was the wife of a business associate of Glen Robertson, the shop owner. A local constable was to follow through on the connection.

"Who is Cliff Richardson, who witnesses state seems to be a hero for helping to rescue Barbara McKenzie from the inferno?" The group was told he was known to be a close associate of the owner Glen Robertson, and Linda was requested to make urgent contact with him.

"What witness statements do we have?" All the neighbours had signed off on statements that broadly agreed with one another.

In summary, it looked like a normal shop stock clearance sale was on when the afternoon was shaken by at least two explosions, with debris flying and heavy black smoke coming from the middle of the shop. Maybe, there was an additional explosion? A scream or two was heard before any action followed.

According to witnesses, a strong smell of rubber (tyres?) burning, and an acrid smell a bit like sulphur had drifted across. It seemed to be at least fifteen minutes before the first Fire Brigade truck arrived, by which time the building was an inferno. DS Thomas and his team would check it all out.

Were any additional experts needed and expected? Agreed needed were fire and arson specialists. DS Thomas was to coordinate and to hurry up the pathologist. Was the reported wound to the head of Frank Camorra critical? Was it an accident? Or was it a murder?

When would the media or the insurance assessors descend on Ballarat and who would deal with them? DS Thomas, in full uniform, was to be the head spokesperson, aided by DC Linda Alexander in plain clothes.

Late on Sunday, DS Wilson said farewell and wished everyone good luck in solving the mysteries involved. He quoted one of his favourite professional sayings, "Nobody ever forgets where he buried the hatchet," (Kin Hubbard), and returned to Footscray Station.

Monday morning dawned to an icy, clear-blue sky that allowed full forensic actions to proceed. Urgent invitations to ring the station to make appointments for interviews were issued to all known persons as lists were drawn up. Police experts of every description were on-site early and a special tent was erected to gather and accumulate any possible evidence. Interim preliminary reports and a visit from an insurance inspector/assessor added extra interest.

The police expert opinion reports were the most interesting of all. It seemed that Melanie Ortega had been killed instantly by an explosion that had probably been triggered by her touching a tripwire that led to a bomb. It was likened to those that had been seen to occur in Vietnam.

What on earth had the tripwire been protecting? How had it been set off? It was now known that Melanie Ortega and her friend Barbara McKenzie had been looking for bargains, and were probably individually scouring the nooks and crannies in the shop. The explosion had also opened up the floorboards to reveal a safe buried in concrete and a human skeleton three to four metres away.

The vestiges of a burnt-out collector's Indian motorcycle remained, its tyres completely gone. Cliff Richardson had been with Barbara at the time of the explosion and had hurriedly helped her through the dust and the noise out of the building then had bravely rushed back into the flames looking for Melanie, whom he hardly knew. A real hero, said some!

More interesting was that the remains of Frank Camorra were some distance away in the building, and although his body was badly damaged by fire, it was theorised that he was already dead, possibly sometime before the explosion and fire started. He definitely had received a blow or blows to the head. Also extremely interesting was that where he was found had probably been his office, and in the rubble was an assorted range of weapons, e.g. knives, machetes, a hand gun and a shot gun. Also found were a small assortment of valuable antiques, mostly still intact.

"What we desperately need now is more information," was how DS Thomas addressed the full police meeting in the Incident Room. "Someone please get a locksmith to urgently open the safe, and is there any suggestion about drugs?" he asked all and sundry. "Most important of all, I want to know who is/was the shop manager Frank Camorra, and also who are these other people; John Khoury and Tony Lombardi—and what are the connections? Get Khoury in here quick smart!"

Two hours later, John Khoury was in the police station accompanied by his lawyer, Mr Needham, and ready to talk about the Investment Co-op Pty Ltd. Khoury confirmed that this company was the lessee of the shop, and the lessor was Glen Robertson, who had inherited it from his aunt, Ms Polly Gamble.

"That's all very well," exclaimed DS Thomas, who was accompanied by Linda, "But we want to know exactly who was Frank Camorra, who was his employer, who did he specifically work for, and where does Tony Lombardi fit in?"

Mr Khoury responded after he had given the question some thought, "The answer to the last part of your question is Tony is not part of us, but perhaps he is distantly related to the late Frank Camorra, who seemed to treat Tony as little more than a semi-intelligent bug who did occasional tasks," he said.

Linda interjected, "Was he possibly a 'mule' making deliveries?"

Khoury raised an eyebrow and protested a little before returning to his commentary, "Frank Camorra was on the payroll of the Investment Co-Op under a different name, and had been an employee for many years. He possibly was a small shareholder."

Khoury and his lawyer Needham agreed that they would supply full and proper further details, adding at the end of the conversation that Camorra was a Vietnam veteran with a dishonourable discharge. DS Thomas quietly added that Tony Lombardi was known to police as he had minor misdemeanours against his name. Assaults, minor burglaries and traffic offences. He also appeared to be unemployed.

Linda asked, "What are the major products that Investment Co-op trades in and can we see the accounts and annual reports for the past three years?"

The answer to both questions was, "Perhaps" from Khoury.

Linda added with emphasis, "On the surface there seems to be a suggestion that the company is indulging in a range of nefarious activities."

Very carefully, Khoury said, "I am not a direct employee of that company."

DS Thomas then very deliberately said, "Mr Khoury, we will be referring this matter to our Major Crimes Division as we feel your attitude is one of non-co-operation, and we have a murder investigation to deal with."

It was made clear to Khoury and Needham that full details of Frank Camorra, his real name and history, were required forthwith to try to establish a reason for his likely murder. While the meeting was on, a constable brought in a note to say additional information had been received from pathology that Camorra may have been poisoned.

DS Thomas then gave the two men an unmistakable message to take away with them, "We are going to investigate every single aspect of this murder and interrogate everyone and everything involved." He went on to state that much more was needed about 'Camorra', his friends and associates, his history, and his responsibilities within the Investment Co-op. Information they were seeking included all who had been employed, any possibilities at all of who the buried bones may be, all possible family connections, and any company records of buying and selling stock for the shop. The first thing demanded was the name and address of anyone known to be a close personal friend or relation, and the proper name of 'Frank Camorra'.

As some information had been gleaned from the insurance inspector, a final question was posed, "Why and by whom would the stock, fixtures and fittings insurance have been increased to an inflated level just three months ago?"

DS Thomas made a note to remind himself to pose the same question to owner Glen Robertson, and also enquire about the current value of the building.

It had been left to Linda to follow up on Tony Lombardi, as he was the least mysterious of those involved. He was invited to the police station, with Linda fully informed of his history and past misdemeanours. Linda was very relaxed as she was now on 'official loan' to Ballarat station and they had arranged accommodation for her at a motel almost in the university. She was pleased with that and was enjoying her new role.

Young Tony Lombardi strolled into the station with an exaggerated swagger, having parked his red 1976 Holden Sandman panel van almost at the entrance door. It needed a paint job but was very noticeable. A constable led him into the interview room which was set up very simply with only a table and two hard, straight-backed chairs in it. He was invited to sit, and the constable left the room and closed the door behind him.

Linda let him sit there by himself for ten minutes, then hurried in. His first request was to have a smoke.

"Definitely not, and no cup of tea until this is over," she answered aggressively. She noted with interest his 'hippie-looking' facade and began the interview. Some of Tony's bombast fell away as she weighed in with her knowledge of his background. It was quite sad really, his having left school early and now barely literate, a skinny young man with a complete absence of charm. His greatest attribute was that he was of the extended Lombardi tribe, of whom there were a large number of cousins, uncles and aunts. It was both a protection and a handicap as the Lombardis had reputations both good and bad.

Linda was probably only five years older than Tony, close enough in age to be able to communicate on the same wavelength. Her plan was to establish where he lived, who his close friends were, where he socialised (alcohol and/or drugs?), where he worked, and how much he was paid for the work he did. How could he afford to run his beloved Sandman van?

Still feeling a bit cheeky, Tony asked Linda, "Where does your accent come from?"

She paused a moment, looked at him as if he was a worm and coolly responded, "Australia, where does yours?" and the interrogation really began in earnest.

Having established the ground rules and cut through any balderdash, Linda set about encouraging a free flow discussion to gather new information. Did he know Frank's 'proper' name? No. Was he closely related to him? No. Where and with whom did he live? With his mother in Clunes, where he also regularly had drinks with some 'friends'. Thinking to show off, Tony further volunteered that he often had drinks with other 'friends' at Craig's Royal Hotel, Ballarat. Details please, he was asked.

Linda had informed Tony that the interview was being recorded and would be converted into a witness statement that would need to be signed. No problem.

Linda, now looking for more relaxed answers, went on to express admiration of the Sandman and caught Tony by surprise by calling it a 'shaggin' wagon'. He was clearly impressed by her knowledge of the local idiom, but not embarrassed. Tony volunteered how plush the interior was and how proud he was of all the extras in the vehicle.

From Linda, "Here is an important question: do you do drugs?" An emphatic "No!" from Tony. "We know you do deliveries for Frank, family and friends in your van, do you think you have ever delivered or picked up drugs for Frank?" asked Linda. Tony responded emphatically, "Probably, but I do not personally use!"

Out of the blue Linda asked him "Did you know Frank served in Vietnam?" Tony did not answer her.

Linda began to like the simplicity behind his façade, although that seemed to be cracking a little.

"How about that cup of tea now?" he asked, thinking that Linda was being a bit more friendly.

"Not a chance! Now on your bike—and I will need you back here tomorrow to sign the witness statement, so don't go far away!" She escorted him off the premises.

Tony went home feeling both energised and deflated at the same time. He telephoned John Khoury and reported most of what he could remember, adding, "Yeah, I had to dodge most of their smart-arse questions but you know what the police are like—stupid bastards!" What he didn't appreciate was that John was also part of the larger Lombardi tribe. Trying to sound 'educated' before he hung up, Tony added, "You know, I was told a coroner has been appointed and forensic something will be involved."

Routine door-knocking by police of neighbours and locals known to be regular walkers only revealed two cars that were remembered as regular parkers in the street. They were Tony's red and noisy Sandman, and Glen's shiny red VB Holden. No one could recall any other regular visitor to the shop except some references to small silver Japanese cars. The order went out to have both vehicles forensically run over. Had anyone searched Frank's lodgings?

Senior DS Wilson, now back in Footscray, undertook to follow up on a George Barnes and a Bryan McKenzie (husband of Barbara) from Paramount Trading Enterprises. As DS Wilson was based in Footscray, he thought it a good tactic to invite them to an initial interview in his Footscray Police Station, with its bigger facilities. In addition, he invited Barbara McKenzie (who had now recovered from the shock of the fire), and Glen Robertson to a second planned interview of all of them at Ballarat Station. DS Wilson's main aim was to establish the relationship between Frank Camorra and Paramount Trading Enterprises.

The first interview in Footscray was conducted in a friendly fashion over coffee and biscuits in DS Wilson's large and plush office. Bryan McKenzie went straight to the point and said, "I don't think I ever met the manager, Frank Camorra, personally, and as far as I can ascertain only two small orders were ever delivered to the shop at the Don Place address in Ballarat. The invoices were made out to the Investment Co-op and were paid promptly by them. When Frank visited our premises, he clearly did not know who I was."

DS Wilson asked, "Full description of the goods please, and speculate what they may have been for?"

That turned out to be interesting as they were tubes and pipes for scaffolding and more tubes and pipes used in kids' play equipment. Bryan added that when ordering, Frank or his assistant Tony had been very helpful about a possible supplier in China.

On arrival, the goods had been cleared through Customs and forwarded straight on to Ballarat. DS Wilson immediately and aggressively asked, "Are you or any of your staff implicitly involved in what stands out to me to be illicit importation of drugs?"

Hurriedly and emphatically, Bryan denied any such implication or to accept such an accusation.

The second, bigger interview took place in Ballarat, with all four together. The invitation to Barbara was at this stage mainly just a courtesy, and she was invited to leave early as and when it suited her. She left after having a coffee. That left George Barnes, Bryan McKenzie and Glen Robertson at the interview.

DS Thomas, with some calmness to try to achieve the information he needed, asked, "OK, it's a long bow, but probably it's drugs they were experimenting with. The whole business in Don Place seems to have operated without notice and under our radar for many, many years. We will want much more input from you later, Glen, even about your Aunty Polly."

In his skilful way, DS Thomas proceeded. "Now George, I know you have recently arrived from New Zealand and that there are plans to expand the Paramount Enterprises company. (How did he know, wondered George?) What new products did you have in mind?" This was all accompanied by a smile. George answered that planning was very much in its infancy but discussions had taken place about garden and hardware products and the possibility of using some sites for retailing.

"OK, I'm fine about that, but what was your relationship with the now deceased Melanie Ortega?" asked DS Thomas.

Tears welled up in George's eyes as he looked across at Glen and in a strained voice said, "She was Barbara's close friend, but had become my very close companion."

DS Thomas responded, "I can see the relationship between Bryan and George, but how did things develop with Glen?"

Bryan answered, "Glen started out investigating the relationship that existed between Paramount Enterprises and Frank Camorra—which didn't really exist—and a new friendship just grew from that."

The Sergeant added, "Possibilities for commercial growth!" The meeting wandered on with pleasantries about City Road, Williamstown, and New Zealand. Finally, to conclude the discussion DS Thomas added that no doubt Glen would be needed again for much greater detail, and the sting in the tail was that it was probable that 'Frank' may have died more than once! He indicated that he was happy with the outcome of the interviews and most of the future inquiries would be funnelled through Ballarat. He considered Paramount Trading Enterprises innocent of any misdemeanours and wished George and Bryan well for the future and a speedy recovery for innocent Barbara.

On returning home, Glen received a phone call that he would be required to attend another interview at Ballarat Police Station at a time to be agreed, and that Cliff Richardson would similarly be required to attend.

It had come to light from ongoing investigations that witnesses had provided opinions that Tony and Frank had on one occasion been seen at Craig's Royal Hotel in Ballarat having a heated argument. It had been some time ago but they positively identified Tony, as he was easy to remember.

16

More Police Probing

DS Thomas and DC Alexander welcomed Glen and Cliff to the interview room at the Ballarat Police station in quite an informal fashion, but also indicated that as this was the beginning of a murder investigation, what was said would be recorded.

Linda was building a reputation at the station for being competent, pleasant and fair. Her Sergeant was happy to let her lead the interview as he admired her professionalism. No coffee or biscuits on this occasion. The two men were informed that the police had basic information about both of them and elaboration was required, not the least of which related to their relationship with Frank Camorra. If they didn't know previously, they were now informed that that was not Camorra's real name.

The first question to Glen was, "Do you know if there was a special relationship between your Aunt Polly Gamble and the man known as Frank Camorra?"

Glen took time to think about that and responded, "I'm pretty sure, no, as I think she was scared of him, kept her distance, and left him alone." He added that Camorra was employed by the Investment Co-Op Co to "run the shop" and that Glen had found out that Polly received rent from them.

From Linda: "Can you throw any light on who John Khoury is and his relationship with Frank Camorra?"

Again, thoughtfully Glen responded, "We met with him and a Mr Needham from a legal firm and they were not very forthcoming, but it seemed that Khoury was the main communicator of instructions from the management of the Investment Co-Op to Camorra. There was no obvious indication of a close or friendly relationship—almost the opposite, as Khoury seemed to indicate that dealing with Camorra was a bit below him."

Linda pressed on, "What exactly do you think was going on at the premises, conducted legally or illegally under the tutorship of Camorra?" and she hastily added, "On his own, or with help!"

Another long pause and Glen turned to Cliff seeking some input from him. DS Thomas and Linda, separately in their own minds but at the same time, noted how different the two men looked. Glen was medium-sized, very compact, tidy, well-groomed and assured. Cliff was tall in stature and looked too big for his very ordinary but clean clothing, with a slightly masked and almost shy look to his face and body language.

Cliff took them by surprise by volunteering, "He was a nasty piece of work who was undoubtedly breaking the law and using standover tactics to dominate." He added to these words his huge winning smile.

Sergeant Thomas was first with, "Elaboration, please Cliff."

Quite briefly and in a low voice Cliff gave examples where he had observed them, and the two were advised that they would be checked out. Glen then added that he was not aware of that information and added that Camorra was clearly a liar. He had told lies to Aunt Polly and even in front of the lawyer Mr Needham had been misleading or simply refused to answer. No doubt he had used the premises for illegal activities.

"Can those accusations be proved?" asked Linda.

"Probably not," responded Glen.

"Glen, we have a few more questions and they do overlap to Cliff, so please feel free to mix the answers," said Linda clearly leading. "Firstly, we know you seriously increased the insurance on your property just a few months ago, and now it has burnt to the ground. Are you psychic or did you have some inside knowledge?"

Glen was seriously offended by the question and clear implication of wrongdoing. His face flushed as he replied a little loudly, "Clearly Aunt Polly was under-insured, and as the building owner, I had concluded that with it being an old wooden building full of old and antique furniture that I had no control of, it was prudent to increase the insurance." He was angry enough to almost add that he was also well educated and had a brain, but only added that he also paid the rates and water accounts but not the electricity usage.

"OK, OK," Linda said, as she could see she had struck a nerve. "Now to you, Cliff," she moved on. To ease the tension, DS Thomas volunteered, "You know Cliff, we refer to you as the "Spear and Jackson Man!" All credit to Cliff as he responded in very mild fashion with, "Aah! the hedge clippers," and with another big smile that lit up his whole face.

"A long time ago now, and no doubt the record is correct," Glen interjected, "But that's a bit unfair under the circumstances as it was years ago!"

The Sergeant said, "We are aware that you two live together—is there any significance in that?"

Quite deliberately, now recovered and with a smile on his face, Glen retorted, "I believe DC Alexander lives with her brother, so is there significance in that?"

Linda interjected with a protest to stop the silly sparring so that common sense could prevail. Glen and Cliff went on to make the point that they lived in separate rooms at either end of the house, and although they were good mates, they also had separate social friends. Cliff even added an invitation, "Come round home for your own inspection."

To restore the equilibrium, Linda posed another question with a hint about where she wanted it to go, "You have both indicated that Frank was, to say the least, 'unfriendly and unlikeable.' Have you any thoughts about who may have done him in? It now appears that he may have been killed three times!" Glen and Cliff both showed similar signs of surprise and asked what was meant by that?

Linda added for greater emphasis, "Burnt, poisoned, and axed!" No real need for greater emphasis.

In a calm voice Cliff said, "He was a rude and uncouth bastard who probably deserved to be done in, but who was he really?" The Sergeant agreed, "That really is important and that's one of the things we are concentrating on. Thank you, Cliff."

DS Thomas then gave the men a summary of their own history, including how they met and with whom they fraternised. Even some details of their parents and in Cliff's case some rather unflattering opinions about his father, Ray. They were both a bit gobsmacked about the depth of knowledge the police had. However, surprisingly little information about Glen's Aunt Polly and no indicated connection from her to Frank Camorra.

"Do either of you know anything useful about Camorra, such as where he lived, what type of car he owned, who were his friends or associates?"

The answer from both Glen and Cliff was an emphatic, "No!" They did suggest that he must live close by as it seemed he walked to work.

They were thanked for their co-operation and told further questioning would probably be needed. After they had both left, DS Thomas and Linda summarised the content of the meeting in a report. They agreed that there was more to Clifford Montgomery Richardson than met the eye, and that he was maturing into a presentable young man. Glen Robertson was assured, well educated, wealthy. They were not gay but comfortable companions.

Back in the incident room, part of the routine was always an ongoing summary of where they were up to. It was agreed that they needed to concentrate on Frank Camorra and John Khoury. Real pressure was applied to find Frank's lodgings, his car, and of course his real name and history. Police have amazing investigative powers, data sources and connections when they really try. They allocated personnel from different sections, divisions, and areas for details.

In a preliminary telephone call, Khoury provided Frank's real name of Francis Lyons, and that he was a Vietnam War veteran. More importantly, on investigation it was established he had been dishonourably discharged from the Army for unjustified violence. Then on his return to Australia, members of his family had helped to re-establish him using the name Camorra. Interestingly, he was a distant relation of a known Sydney-based, Australia-wide criminal family named Lombardi.

Francis, (aka Frank) had lived a short walk from the shop in a place where it seemed he was almost invisible. His equally anonymous car was an oldish silver Datsun registered to the Investment Co-op Pty Ltd. A police instruction had immediately gone out to secure and inspect his premises and impound the car, both to be searched in detail for traces of drugs, explosives, records, or anything incriminating.

Linda, using her full name and rank, made a formal telephone call to Khoury and asked (demanded) that he attend a meeting at the police station at 2pm that afternoon. It was not even a polite invitation. She had approval to conduct the meeting on a one-on-one basis to extract full details.

"No mucking around now," she informed Khoury after he had arrived, and the meeting had commenced. They knew who Francis Lyons was and his background. She made a show of recording in her notebook each subject mentioned.

As previously, Khoury adopted his, 'I'm above all this' attitude, and somewhat disdainfully muttered, "Nothing to do with me."

Linda leant across the table so she could ominously whisper to him, "Oh yes it is; we know your wife was a Lombardi before she married you, and we are just getting started on you!"

Sitting back, she added, "My advice to you is, cut the belligerent attitude and volunteer all the information about your role at Investment Co-op, your responsibilities, your relationship with

Camorra (aka Lyons) and full disclosure of everything about the shareholders." She added, "The police will be informing the regulators and Tax Department, and I respectfully suggest your help would be a very good idea!"

Khoury looked shocked and, still recovering from her verbal assault, became obviously attentive. But still he pleaded, "Nothing to do with me."

Linda now came on really strongly, "Mr Khoury, cut out the crap! We know who you are, where you live—which is a substantial home that you own—and that you are the 'message boy' and maybe the 'implementer' for The Investment Co-op Pty Ltd. Now, we want to know exactly where you were on Saturday afternoon of August 15th. Minute by minute from twelve noon onwards! We also want in detail who your boss is, how you're paid, and do you have any other employment. Please appreciate this is a full murder inquiry and a Coroner has now been appointed to investigate the fire."

In milder tone she dropped in, "You are no doubt aware of our ability to subpoena witnesses, and we certainly will!"

Linda didn't add that the Coroner had extra powers of investigation, but wondered aloud if Khoury had any knowledge or experience with poisons!

His attitude had most certainly now changed and the interview continued. Without too much more questioning, Linda then unceremoniously accompanied John Khoury off the premises.

Meeting the Press was scheduled for later in the day, and DS Wilson had again arrived in Ballarat from Footscray to accompany DS Thomas, Linda, and the two station constables at the meeting. The presentation was professionally run and controlled by DS Thomas, and Linda admired his accurate precis of the situation.

His summary was that the house had caught fire after an explosion, and two bodies—a male and a female—had been retrieved from the scene. There were suspicious circumstances and the victims had been identified. The remains of a third body suspected to have been long buried under the building was also discovered. The owner of the shop had been informed and was helping with the inquiry. DS Wilson was friendly and at ease and had clearly conducted similar presentations. He welcomed questions and introduced all his staff. Linda was watching and learning.

The most expected question was the first one, "Do you have anyone in custody, or do you have a suspect?"

With a smile, DS Thomas said, "No to both, it is too early in our investigations but there is no need to be concerned about any likely associated violence."

Further various inane questions from the media were followed with an assurance that they would be kept informed. What was expected to be the final question came from a reporter from the Ballarat Times, "Was the shop owner one of those killed?"

Linda responded, "No, the shop manager was the dead male, and the female was a customer. The identity of the third body is unknown, so we will be searching records of missing persons, but it appears to be quite old."

The reporter persisted, "Do you know who the owner is and has he or she been informed?"

This time Detective Sergeant Thomas responded, "It's a little complicated, as the owner of the building did not run the actual shop. But we know who they are and they have been informed."

Persistent reporter again, "Are they locals and can we have details please?"

DS Thomas considered that, looked to Linda then cautiously advised, "Yes, they are locals, a male and a company is involved. We can release their names after this conference."

Some negative muttering from the Press followed.

DS Thomas continued, "Relative to the bones found, we do not have any more information at this stage, other than it is obvious that they were buried and very old. Enquiries will be ongoing using data and forensic skills to search for answers."

He added, "In case you are not aware, a Coroner has been appointed and we will work closely with that official, and an autopsy is being carried out on each of the deceased persons."

In an effort to conclude the meeting he then said, "I'm not going to pretend that innocent people do not suffer in a murder investigation, so I ask you not to leap to conclusions nor to publish misinformation." An appeal blatantly ignored, as several days later, two pages into the Ballarat Times an attention-grabbing headline read, "Man stabbed in alleged drug deal"! The story included a vague town address and carefully using the word 'alleged' several times said that a stash of cash and a variety of tools that could be used in burglaries had been found. No reaction or contribution was issued from the police.

The gathering of further information led DS Thomas to request renewed concentration on those who were the friends or relations of Tony Lombardi. This was easy enough for a local constable to do, and a serious dig into information on Frank Camorra, aka Lyons began. This needed some additional help from DS Wilson, who had now returned to Footscray, with a special official enquiry by him into Camorra's past Army experience and qualifications. It was asked if he was SAS? What were his close relationships and full details of his Army discharge? Any drug associates or known criminal associates after the Army? Who might want to kill Francis Lyons/Frank Camorra? Had he become a nuisance, or a liability to some old or even new acquaintances? Any update on any findings relative to his car or where he lived?

17

Interviews – First One-on-One: Cliff

DS Thomas and Linda Alexander were now a close team functioning well together with confidence in each other. Delegation where necessary was automatic as was exchange of information, opinions and theories. It was obvious that there was not a maniac loose in Ballarat about to commit further mayhem, so now there was the small luxury of being able to be very thorough.

DS Thomas offered that he knew he shared with DS Wilson the opinion that it was part of policing to be 'scavengers'. He added, "We trawl up everything we can gather in our nets, then throw away what is useless. In the process we learn many secrets, some of which we have no right to know, and that can be unfair to those concerned."

They called in Glen Robertson and Cliff Richardson again, this time to be interviewed separately. They were formally cautioned that their statements could be used in evidence, and emphasised it was a formal murder investigation.

In the interview with Cliff, DS Thomas reminded him that he had a police record but that it would not count against him. Cliff quietly smiled but did not respond. In her own mind, Linda admired the assurance of this young working-class man, who was physically quite plain and who had a troubled upbringing, but whose presence she found quietly enjoyable.

She asked, "How old are you now, Cliff? Do you have a girlfriend?"

His response was, "Mid-twenties, and I have both girl and boy friends."

Linda admired his restraint; he was behaving in a likeable and sensitive manner. She asked him to summarise his experience to date with Francis Lyons aka Frank Camorra. Cliff had nothing pleasant to say at all.

DS Thomas then asked, "Does anyone these days call you 'Cliffie', Cliff? How well did you know Polly Gamble? Did you have any direct conversations with Frank Camorra?"

It took Cliff a moment to recognise the name Polly Gamble but he quickly recovered when he realised it was Glen's Aunty Polly. He responded that the only person using the name 'Cliffie' to him these days, was occasionally his mother when being silly, and Polly he really hadn't known well—he had met her on rare occasions when he had accompanied Glen to the store. He had never had any direct conversations with Camorra, as Camorra always treated him like a common bug. And he didn't need that in his life!

Both DS Thomas and Linda were surprised by the fullness of his response. Linda sensed that Cliff was confident enough to express his own opinions and she asked, "We know Glen 'rescued you' from the police station after your assault charge in Daylesford, and also financially helps with your accommodation, so could he be described as both your rescuer and protector? Are you his physical guard, or just his 'gofer'?"

Quite ingenuously, Cliff responded, "Maybe, maybe not; and under the right circumstances I could be, and I'd probably get my dad to help me," Delivered with a big grin. The two police officers realised how Cliff had matured into a likeable man. They were not yet at the stage to ask if he would murder for Glen.

Linda changed direction and asked Cliff what he was doing at the shop on the afternoon of the fire. Cliff gave a very simple explanation that he was there to accompany Barbara McKenzie and her friend Melanie Ortega to look for bargains in the clearance sale. It was no more than a 'Saturday outing for the girls' and as Glen was involved elsewhere, and the women's partners were working in the city, Cliff had been asked along to keep them company.

DS Thomas finally asked, trying to exert more pressure on Cliff, "When the explosion happened, where were you and Barbara McKenzie, who we believe you rescued?" He followed up with "and where was Melanie Ortega?"

Cliff answered "Mrs McKenzie and I were just inside the front door, and I have no idea where Ms Ortega was."

Linda then offered thanks for his help and, signifying it was her last current question, asked, "Would you punish Frank for his evils, and have you or do you use coke or crack or any drugs?"

Cliff's expression hardened and he uttered a one-word terse reply, "No!"

Interview finished, Cliff left the premises.

18

Personal Development: Linda

As snippets of information filtered back and were accumulated, a clear picture of Francis Lyons/aka Frank Camorra was evolving. He was never a commissioned officer in the Army, but had been in the action in Vietnam with a reputation for being fearless. On a personal basis, he was a bully and dominated a small group of malcontents. A range of adjectives about him were included by most contributors; he was a liar, dishonest, had no loyalty, was called the "shortcut king", and was bone-lazy and unreliable. No doubt about it, he was as hard as rocks.

After he was transferred to the Army Quartermasters Store, he became less visible but the descriptions were even more concise. A real 'bad arse', scary, a real prick, a total sleazebag. No one seemed very surprised when they were informed that he had been dishonestly discharged from the Army. One added that, "Lyons would not have a friend on earth!"

"Did he have any close associates or friends in the Army?" was the first question asked.

A resounding "No," was the answer.

"Did he have any special skills relating to explosives, booby traps, guns, or security?"

"Almost certainly! He was formidable!" were among the responses.

As this information flowed in and the investigation was making good progress, Linda was able to sit back and indulge herself for a few minutes and reflect on her current status.

She was happy, she was thoroughly enjoying her job, the status associated with it, the team camaraderie, and the challenges involved in trying to solve a most interesting crime. On a personal level, she was enjoying the limited spare time she and her brother Brendan shared together in their unit. Mainly catching up over short breakfasts, as they then each hurried off to their wildly different workplaces. Occasionally they enjoyed a social evening in Melbourne together, sometimes in the company of Brendan and his long-term partner, and sometimes just by themselves, exploring the narrow streets and eateries, particularly in and around Flinders Lane in the CBD.

Sometimes Linda's current boyfriend Jeremy—a friend of Brendan—joined them. Jeremy was also a banker, tall and handsome, and carefully dressed with expensive informality, and had none of the typical police occupational hazard of drinking too much alcohol. In fact, he was a very pleasant and lively companion and there was discussion about current topics, and politics, which Linda enjoyed immensely. She had not made a deliberate decision to keep him out of her professional life, but did appreciate that he resisted the temptation of most other men to question her on why she was a detective and what was she currently involved with! Socially, she just wanted a non-police break.

She had an interest in his commercial banking world of finance, ratios, risk management, the price of the dollar, gold and oil etc. Linda was genuinely interested to become more rounded, in order to pursue and grow her own career. Jeremy's self-assuredness, almost hubris— common amongst most of Brendan's friends and associates—was sometimes annoying. A 'balance' of confidence combined with a healthy fear of failure was one of the many things Linda had been alerted to try to achieve in her police training.

All in all, life was looking very good for Linda and the only small thing she was trying to overcome was a recent habit acquired of eating lots of takeaway pizza with one or two glasses of red wine that had crept into her long work days.

She was looking forward to the time when she could have the odd weekend off to explore the outdoors and to enjoy Jeremy's opinions, and coffee and biscuits in a seaside café. Something for the future when the immediate crime had been solved and some of the frenetic pace of a police officer on a serious active case had subsided.

The adage, 'Once bitten twice shy' was never far from the surface in Linda's psyche as she recalled her catastrophic friendship/affair in Perth. Jeremy was a great companion with whom she found she could discuss a range of subjects without ever needing to be over-cautious. Together the friendship quietly grew without expectations and without any pressure to delve more deeply into her personal or family history. Sexually, it was good for her too.

It was also time to re-establish her ongoing rapport with brother Brendan, now they were both adults, and to recall with nostalgia some of their childhood memories. A renewed 'getting to know you' and to appreciate their status. Linda also, for some reason, had fleeting moments wondering about how Glen Robertson was going.

19

Police Work: Dig, Dig, Dig

Almost a week had gone by when DS Thomas called another meeting and started by announcing the Chief District Officer had asked for an update. He then asked for input in turn from everyone on all possibilities.

He announced that pathology had confirmed that Camorra/Lyons had died from a heavy blow to the head with a blunt instrument, and perhaps almost simultaneously, asphyxiation, followed by incineration! Tests indicated that there was also significant poison in his gut. Quite a choice. The main point was that he was one of the victims. The other two were Melanie Ortega and the still as yet unidentified skeleton. With regret, DS Thomas confirmed that Melanie was a totally unconnected, random innocent victim, and expressed sympathy to her family.

He returned to the main subject by asking, "What do we really know?"

Francis Lyons. Almost anonymous to the main population and community of Ballarat. He continued, "At this stage we don't know who is responsible so let us first consider—who could be beneficiaries from the event. Ideas please?"

They were listed and speculation ensued. Glen Robertson—owner of the property and building insurer? His close friend and house mate Cliff Richardson? Discounted. The Investment Co-op Pty Ltd—the contents insurer? Maybe a long shot, the Paramount Enterprises Trading Co—for a potential trading site?

John Khoury and his associates—to be rid of Frank, seen to be an embarrassing nuisance?

What about other unknown enemies, of whom there may be many as Francis Lyons was not a well-liked man?

General discussion ranged over these possibilities. Linda suggested they try to be more specific by dropping people into groups.

Group 1: Glen Robertson and Cliff Richardson, house mates and friends—even though of different styles. Yin and yang. Their additional new friends and associates, George Barnes and Bryan McKenzie, plus his wife Barbara McKenzie and her friend Melanie Ortega. All connected to Paramount Enterprises with ownership going back to New Zealand and Joe McFadgen.

Group 2: The Investment Co-op Pty Ltd and its associates. Full ownership details as yet were unknown, although rumour had it that both Lyons and Khoury could be small shareholders. John Khoury was clearly employed in some fashion by The Investment Co-op as the 'frontrunner' and main communicator. Tony Lombardi, a low-level helper, was seen as a general delivery operator only.

In the background there were perhaps other remote low-level family connections. The breadth of what had been going on at the shop had clearly been below the radar of authorities or neighbours.

DS Thomas asked, "Is there a 'most likely perpetrator' and are there any winners or losers that obviously stand out?"

They all agreed that Lyons/Camorra was a malicious, malevolent probable 'psycho' who had hidden himself well over the years. No one offered an opinion at this stage on the most likely candidate for his demise. One opinion offered was that he had caused his own incineration by booby trapping a hidden stack of illicit drugs and contraband, and that then uncovered the remains of an old enemy?

"And who might that be?" was the general response.

A constable entered the room and announced that the pressure being exerted through radio, newspapers and all other media was achieving results. Several anonymous members of the public had volunteered two new snippets of information. The first was that Frank had been seen on Friday evening in Craig's Royal Hotel in Lydiard Street, Ballarat having a drink and perhaps a meal, with an unsavoury-looking middle-aged character. Secondly, it had been volunteered that Frank was a regular user of prostitutes. It was easy enough to check out details and the names of any who had spent time with Frank. The best or worst they could offer was that he was smelly, active and seen to be very 'normal', preferring the missionary position. He always paid cash up front.

Opinion seemed to reinforce a growing awareness to all that Frank was a prize bastard that no one would miss. Additional leaked Army information about Frank/Francis Lyons was that he had early on been involved in 'black ops', and had been fearsome and decorated. He had been injured and fully recovered, but was 'hardened' and resented all forms of authority and in particular officers. He had two bank accounts, paid his taxes, had been married, maybe with a daughter.

This meant there were at least two more leads to be followed.

There was not much progress being achieved, so it was agreed that each individual in the two groups of interest would now be re-examined with a fine-tooth comb. Exceptions would be Barbara McKenzie and Joe McFadgen in New Zealand. Much more information was to be obtained on The Investment Co-op. Glen's lawyer might also be worth a word with also.

20

Number 1 Suspect

The police took a break, and then Glen was recalled to be interviewed on his own.

Linda commenced by asking him, "Where were you on the afternoon of Saturday August 15, and why were you there?"

Glen responded easily, "I was at the uni from about 1.30pm to play in a hockey match starting at 2.00pm, and then went on to a Drama Class group at 4.30pm, and followed on with a few drinks. All on campus." No details of how or when he got home. Glen's demeanour was, as usual, patient, calm and collected, with hands casually in pockets.

DS Thomas and Linda made mental notes of how assured and confident he was without being arrogant.

Linda asked, "Is it not reasonable to ask why you were not at the shop?"

"The answer is, it's not my stock on sale and Barbara and Melanie could report back to Bryan if any of the stock was of interest to Paramount Enterprises."

Changing tack, DS Thomas commented that Glen was now quite the remarkably well-off and lucky young man. Glen was not in any frame of mind to contest that. DS Thomas then asked another question that he hoped would promote a more general type answer, "Why was Polly Gamble so generous to you exclusively; and how well did you know her, and how did she become so wealthy?"

It was a big question, so Glen gave it his full attention and a very considered response. "She was my mother's sister. My Mum and Dad had a successful business in our home town, and my older brother was destined to join the family business, and everyone was happy about that. In school holidays I was often sent to stay with Aunt Polly for city experience and she spoilt me by taking me to the pictures and other places she thought I might enjoy. She thought I was the 'academic' of the family and worked on making me a little more refined than the rest. She was more like a friend and really helped me, and although I always was very appreciative and said thank you, we were not really close."

Linda joined in trying to encourage more, "Sounds to me like a perfect childhood! Were you ever bullied or teased by your peers?"

"Not really, even though I was a bit small for my age, but I stood up for myself and also had a bigger brother, and my parents seemed to be well admired."

In more general terms, Glen outlined that he had been good at sport, and as the family had been reasonably well off, he had always had all the sporting equipment he required and support to be well groomed and get to matches. Yes, he agreed that he had been given an excellent childhood. School-wise he did well and it was agreed by all he should go on to university to widen his career prospects. Where better than Ballarat Uni? He had not been sure which 'stream' he should follow at uni so after discussions with Aunt Polly, kept open both arts and commerce. He confessed he really had enjoyed university life and the wider social extensions it had offered.

That response gave Linda room to ask, "Have you ever been into drugs?"

A slight hesitation from Glen who then responded, "Yes, I have been to parties where there was common availability of marijuana in various forms."

Quick as a flash from DS Thomas, "Have you ever dealt in drugs or supplied drugs, or did Frank Camorra ever discuss supplying you with drugs?"

A terse response from Glen, "Christ no! I hardly knew the guy, and I certainly wouldn't have trusted him. He had no gravitas, and I think he was a bloody crook!" That made Linda and the Sergeant sit up.

Linda resumed, "Tell us about your friendship with Cliff?"

Glen replied, "It seems a lot of people have a lot of interest in us. You guys seem to know plenty about both of us and just maybe you are implying something that does not exist. What is your angle?" No response from either Linda or, just open-faced interest.

Glen took an obvious deep breath and added, "You know Cliff's family, his education, his mother and father and the fact that his childhood was somewhat violent, alcohol was an influence at home, and Cliff had little or no fun. He escaped that by going to work and to contribute to his mother putting meals on the table." Nodding heads.

Glen continued, "His major relief was mixing with a few local lads from around Daylesford on a Friday night for a beer and fish and chips. Some high jinks sometimes followed and that was my very first contact with Cliff. You guys know about the 'Spear and Jackson' hedge-clippers event, and that only started out as a bit of a lark!"

Linda encouraged Glen by asking if he had ever been to Cliff's home or met his parents?

The reply was, "No," although Cliff had sometimes referred to his mother Mavis with some affection.

DS Thomas asked the question which he clearly had been waiting to pose, "Cliff would now appear to be a mature well-balanced young man, whose appearance and demeanour could perhaps be attributed mainly to you? Is he under your spell?"

Glen replied, "Now that's a stupid question, go ask him yourself!"

They came to a halt and all took up glasses of water. Glen was determined to have a final word, "We are really good mates but not very close friends; we share accommodation and occasionally social events, and my greatest contribution to Cliff has been that I have introduced some fun and humour into his life that he had not previously enjoyed. I also helped him to get a driver's licence and he is always there as a good friend."

Linda was then quick to ask, "And what has he introduced into your life?"

The educated Glen emerged, "When we first met, the other guys and a couple of the girls treated him as if he was a bit thick. He wasn't, but he was awkward. To me, he was like having a big brother who was clearly 'always on your side.' More than that, he was always really keen to learn and to absorb new ideas and habits. I actually taught him among other things to play chess!"

Glen went on to quietly add, "and he can now beat me at chess and other games." It was interesting for the two police officers to see him smiling to himself.

Getting serious again, Glen added, "One of the good things that chess teaches is not to move too quickly because if you are not calm you cannot concentrate on the game in hand. We both absorbed that lesson early when dealing with Camorra, and it seems someone else solved our problem!"

Seeing Glen was now being more effusive, Linda asked, "Do you think that more than one person could be responsible for Frank's death?"

Glen immediately asked, "Are you telling me something I don't know?" Linda decided that some bluntness may not be out of order, "We are wondering if he could have considered his own suicide, or an unknown associate had poisoned him or someone had decided violent retribution was deserved."

That was clearly too much information all at once for Glen to absorb. Again, trying to be provocative, Linda volunteered that it was possible that Frank may have been poisoned the night before or he had tried to kill an old associate in a shared meal at Craig's Royal Hotel and somehow it had gone wrong. It was too much for Glen to accept all the obviously new information. He knew absolutely nothing about poison. Glen offered up that his education was in the arts and commerce. Definitely not science!

Linda asked, "Can you throw any light on any likely associates of Frank Camorra?"

"Regretfully, no!" was Glen's response. He then asked the two officers, "Well, how do you see my relationship with Cliff? We live together most of the time, and have mutual respect and trust, and are great mates. There's even loyalty, and that's enough!"

In conclusion, DS Thomas and Detective Linda Alexander agreed that was all they wanted for now, and with some new respect for Glen, ushered him off the premises.

21

In the Clear?

Cliff Robertson was invited back to the station for another interview just by himself. Linda chose to use the same austere office with minimal furniture but with the addition of a station officer sitting simply as an observer. She went through the formal warnings to emphasise the seriousness of the occasion.

She started in a soft voice indicating that the police had now closely questioned all those people that they considered were associated with Frank Camorra/Francis Lyons and had come to the conclusion they were one and the same person. Did Cliff agree?

A simple "Yes," from Cliff was the reply. "An accident of pure association?" asked Linda.

Cliff just nodded his head. Linda went on to suggest the major part of her questioning would be about his friendship with Glen Robertson. She asked, "Are you OK with that?" Another short reply from Cliff, "Of course."

Linda assured him they were trying to be in a position to arrest the culprit of a major crime in which at least two people had been murdered and where some major criminal activities had taken place. She asked, "Please just assure me you are fully aware of the seriousness of the situation."

As on a previous occasion his response did surprise her.

"Yes, I am fully aware of the circumstances and appreciate how you are doing this, and you can count on my co-operation," he said.

Into the questioning, Linda posed several more questions, one after another, about drugs. "Do you use drugs, do you deliver drugs, do you know if Tony Lombardi delivered drugs for Camorra, and got paid?"

Cliff's face brightened and he answered, "That's easy, no to all of them and thank God I hardly know Camorra or Lombardi."

And with a light touch of humour, "I don't know God either."

Linda was quietly amused but wanted to move more into his childhood experiences that may have affected his behaviour. She asked about his relationship with his father Ray. She told him that police were aware that Ray had on occasions hit his mother Mavis, with his usual excuse of alcohol, and that she had needed medical attention.

That they knew this information clearly surprised Cliff. Linda went on to say that on Friday nights, sometimes Mavis or Cliff had had to go up to the pub to collect Ray from a fight when he was still drunk and abusive. Cliff was even more surprised that this was known and it brought back unhappy memories for him. He asked in a low, angry voice, "What is the exact purpose of this information, please?"

Linda said, "We know he had an attitude that he espoused of 'the working-class man against the rich and privileged'."

She was trying to establish if that was also a strong feeling of Cliff's—was he now in that category? Was she simply looking for flaws in either of them?

Taking his time Cliff looked right at Linda and said, with some dignity, "You know that is a stupid question and I'm not going to answer it."

He said he was surprised that at no time had anyone asked about religious beliefs. That surprised Linda as she considered it irrelevant. May have been more likely to be Glen because of Polly and her Church.

"Why did your family name you 'Clifford Montgomery Richardson'?" she asked.

Restoring his sense of humour Cliff answered, "Probably better than Sue."

Linda returned to her questioning, "I have been told that a day ago you took exception to a question from the reporter from Daylesford calling you Cliffie, and when you ignored her, she then called you 'Hedge Clipper Cliff.' Is that correct?"

He looked puzzled and said, "I am not aware of such a happening."

When later it was checked, it turned out the reporter had made it all up.

In further general discussion and in a more relaxed fashion Cliff was able to reassure Linda that he was still very fond of his mother and had an 'OK relationship' with his Dad who was not in great health. He reassured Linda he would not kill on behalf of Glen with whom he had a great friendship, and that Camorra probably got what he deserved. In even more relaxed and friendly terms Cliff finally suggested his football team, the Cats, from Geelong were the likely winner of the AFL comp.

The interview was concluded and he left feeling quite comfortable with how it had all gone.

22

Who Employs Lombardi and Khoury?

The next to be interviewed was young Tony Lombardi and it was agreed that more serious pressure would need to be exerted. The same would later be applied to John Khoury.

They had little or no information on Tony Lombardi. He had previously denied any family connection to Camorra or that he had a police record. Not quite true, as he was in fact a distant second cousin to Francis Lyons and he did have a record for minor offences such as assault, traffic and burglaries. Tony was not employed by the Investment Co-op. He had no PAYE tax records and no tax returns. He was noticeable because of his rather extreme hair style, facial piercing additions, and colourful and tight clothing. As someone had observed, "He was full of bravado." The Holden Sandman was clearly his pride and joy, and instantly recognisable.

Tony Lombardi really was 'not the sharpest tool in the box' but was very over-confident.

DS Thomas, who knew a little about him, had decided that the time had come to shake him up. He reminded him formally that this was his third interview related to a murder charge and that someone would definitely be going to prison for life! There were other equally serious charges associated with drug trafficking that could and would be attached to him, as he had admitted he made deliveries for Frank.

This evinced a loud protest from Tony that was aggressively shut down by the Sergeant. DS Thomas went on, "You have been identified as making deliveries in your 'hot' van to locations known to be frequented by users of opium. How dumb can you be to use your bright red vehicle."

That got the crestfallen look wanted by the DS, who went on, "Now, I want you to admit that you are related to Francis Lyons (Camorra) and you did do work for him for which you were paid!"

Many deep breaths and swallowing by Tony followed. Then in stammering sentences, he admitted in his own words that he was distantly related through his mother to Francis Lyons, and in some ways, he felt quite important to be involved as 'a mule'. He had vaguely remembered Francis when he was still at primary school but could not remember the time or place. It was only in the past year that the relationship had been re-established, he said, and he added, "Like everyone else, I disliked him and was scared of him!"

Pressing on, Linda then infused herself into the conversation with another enquiry in an aggressive tone, "What about your smooth and friendly other relation, John Khoury?"

In an agitated voice, Tony responded, "No, no, I hardly know him and he may be some sort of relative but we have no connection."

Linda added in a sarcastic fashion, "That may be helpful for one or other of you!"

It seemed that Tony wanted to talk further—and did—but nothing he said was significant, as it was all about his favourite drinking spots and the names of his 'mates'. They warned him that they required much greater detail of his habits, his social contacts and his close family. The addresses to which he had made deliveries. The specific details required were written down for him to take away. The final question given to him was, "What gives you your kicks?" He declined to answer.

When he had gone Linda said that he seemed to develop verbal diahorrea towards the end of the interview; he just couldn't stop from burbling on and on!

They prepared themselves for the next scheduled interrogation which they anticipated to be much more intellectual. The smartly dressed Mr John Khoury had a touch of gravitas. As expected, he arrived at the police station right on time, immaculately dressed in a suit and tie and shiny black shoes.

John Khoury was well prepared with details of his involvement. Although he considered it irrelevant, he confirmed he was of Lebanese heritage, and also confirmed he had degrees from La Trobe University in Melbourne, in both law and commerce. That got Linda's attention and respect.

John brought with him his latest annual tax return which confirmed he was a very well-paid legitimate business consultant, and stated his home address in Carlton, in inner Melbourne. After that had been absorbed, he continued to impress them, telling them that he was a well-qualified and experienced senior commercial executive who had 'been around the houses' a few times.

Khoury stressed that he considered himself to be a hard-nosed commercial consultant who was employed to maximise results and profits. He certainly convinced them of the accuracy of that. They patiently waited for him to finish, to get on to their own questions.

Linda then asked, "We want to know all about Francis Lyons (Camorra), the Investment Co-op Pty Ltd, and your exact role there—duties and responsibilities please." Khoury confirmed that he had been employed by the Investment Co's managing director, through an employment consultant, to be the part-time supervisor of the secondhand/antique shop and to keep an eye on Camorra. It was a small business with few official transactions, most being 'off books' in cash. In many ways, he was little more than a 'messenger' for the Investment Co.

Khoury confirmed he was aware of the personal unique status of Frank Camorra and the protection that existed. Similarly, he knew how the business was structured and about the cash that was lodged in the bank. He was not so positive about any remuneration paid to

Camorra. He was the regular communicator with lawyer Needham from the legal firm that acted for the Investment Co. Khoury was keen to stress that he was not the accountant and had no responsibility for the financial accounts of the company.

Linda asked him if he was aware that enquiries had been made among the known 'low life' to carry out a hit on Camorra. The question did not faze John Khoury in the slightest as he enquired, "When was that, and how much was offered?" with a slight smile.

DS Thomas offered, "That's information that has just come to light, and apparently was many months ago, and the description of who was making the enquiry certainly does not sound like you!"

Khoury replied low key, "Well I'm pleased about that."

Linda, in a friendly tone, asked, "Was Camorra a nuisance or a well-respected employee who did his job well?"

The response was pretty much as expected. Khoury responded, "Well, I think he was pretty much a person inherited from an unpleasant situation and he exacerbated the result by being an unlikeable human being."

Quite a mouthful, to which he added, "Polly Gamble didn't exactly help, as she was not exactly Snow White!"

Linda, in her now usual fashion of keeping on, asked, "What on earth does that mean?"

Treading carefully, Khoury replied, "Certain 'authorities' have her name flagged for the money she brought into Australia from an unusual group called The Church of the Golden Sight."

Linda thought he may just be illustrating his contacts and access to certain information and how authorities worried about fringe religious groups.

DS Thomas and Linda knew they were trawling for information but it added to the mystery of how Glen Robertson had become a wealthy man. They continued to question John Khoury who repeated his low-level responsibilities and accountability in the Investment Co-op or involvement in the day-to-day activities of the shop. He had certainly never visited the premises outside of normal shopping hours. He re-emphasised that he had no close relationships with anyone at the Investment Co-op and he was not even really aware of their major activities. He no doubt could be clever at concealing details from anyone.

After he left, the police pair agreed that he was likely innocent of any misdemeanour but they urgently needed to follow up the new underworld snitch about someone shopping for a 'hit man' for Camorra. The vague description seemed to fit Glen Robertson!

23

Glen again

Back in the station Thomas and Alexander reviewed where they were up to and made a priority list of things to do, before holding the next police group meeting. This was to tidy up some of the loose ends before concentrating on establishing the culprit.

The group was advised that forensic pathology had now confirmed that Camorra had died from the heavy blow to the cranium before he was incinerated. Melanie Ortega had died from asphyxiation caused by the fire. The circumstances were agreed but the perpetrator was unknown.

The explosives experts from the Army who had examined the site where the bomb had exploded were adamant that it had been tripped off by a pressure device that would have been professionally designed and installed. This was no amateur hit and miss!

Did someone attempt to poison Camorra on the Friday night beforehand? And who was the mystery man he had a drink and supper with? Unknown and no clues.

Who was the corpse, and who owned the trinkets and small amount of drugs found? Unknown. To whom did the stack of valuables belong? Reasonable to assume it was Camorra. All loose ends!

DS Thomas and Linda agreed to the group that the Army may be able to cast some light on associates or even goods stolen and possible old associates. They decided to question Glen Richardson again informally about the possible 'hit,' so searched him out and hoped to catch him by surprise in a public café. They found him, strolled in on him and went straight to the point.

Glen was his usual friendly self and immediately said, "Yes, I did make some silly lighthearted enquiries among a couple of 'heavies' at uni but I think they thought I was kidding and when they mentioned a likely figure of around $5k that was the end of that!"

Linda agreed, "Fair enough, but did you discuss the subject with Cliff?" He thought he might have, probably not in detail but quite possibly just in passing. While they had him in the café, they changed the subject to his association with George Barnes and asked how far he had ever discussed the potential joint use of the site between Glen and Paramount Enterprises for trading?

"We flirted with the idea and how it could be accommodated. No details, no finance!" Glen responded. Another long lead and loose end, it seemed.

A quick check-up on George Barnes was easy, through the help of the New Zealand Police who responded, "Nothing adverse on record". But when further checking with his previous bank employer it came out about his relationship with Mary, and they were informally told, "He may be irresponsible as he left behind a cranky deserted girlfriend"!

24

Deep Enquiries: Tony Lombardi

Unbeknown to Tony Lombardi, the police decided to conduct a low-key inquiry into his background.

Linda, in particular, found the childhood background of Lombardi both fascinating and sad. She had found Tony to be perhaps 'needy' and had tried to empathise with his total lack of personality. He was part of an extended family of uncles, aunts, cousins and other relations. He was shuffled from school to school as his mother moved from one poor relationship to another, and lived in towns around the perimeter of outer Ballarat. His primary schooling was mainly in Maryborough where he attended St Mary's Catholic Primary School for a short time and Maryborough West School for longer.

Tony had short periods of time attending school in Daylesford, Stawell and Ararat. Needless to say, he did not do well at school. He was always small and skinny for his age and was bullied and teased. He was aware of various family members with whom he met occasionally as they gave assistance, but he was never close to them, and barely knew who they were. At Maryborough Primary school he was called "Lolly" because of the alliteration with 'Lombardi' and because, more cruelly, they said he 'sucked up' or was a sucker. He was often sworn at and told, "You are at the wrong school, you little 'Micky Doolan'." Occasionally he would hit back and he finished up with a reputation for bad behaviour and was referred to as needing mental support.

There was little or no loving support from his mother as she was otherwise distracted and desperately trying to put food on the table. School reports were mainly unsympathetic as times were tough. In amongst some records from Maryborough was an item where Tony, whilst quite young, had reported to a teacher that he had been sexually assaulted by his mother's 'friend'. The busy teacher took some time to question Tony's mother—who the teacher hardly ever saw—and was told not to be so silly. Being a responsible teacher, and because she felt Tony had 'some problems', she mentioned it to the local policeman.

Sometime after the alleged event, in a very low-key fashion the policeman interviewed Tony, accompanied by his mother, at the station. The description that Tony gave was that he had been playing after school in the back shed where the potatoes were stored, when Mum's 'friend' came out from the back of the house for a pee and joined him. He sat down on a bag of potatoes, opened his fly and exposed himself, and then got Tony to take down his shorts and play with him. The description was very woolly and the telling of it was clearly traumatic. Some of it was colourful and vague. Tony was not a clear communicator and, his mother advised, had often told 'porkies'.

The constable was inexperienced but had taken notes and wanted a full description of the man. Tony did not know who he was but quite clearly his mother would have known. She indicated to the policeman she would supply details after the meeting; not in front of Tony. Tony was too young or immature to insist on more detail at the time. Mother and constable agreed no further action would be necessary. His mother never referred to it again and never took any action, leaving Tony feeling let down and despondent.

Tony moved on but had behavioural problems for most of his school years. He was regularly referred on for both physical and mental therapy. When it came time to leave school, he was still only semi-literate and not a good candidate for any serious employment.

However, remarkably, two good things happened to Tony and they coincided around his fifteenth birthday. His mother seemed to have settled into a permanent, non-volatile relationship, and relatives had rallied around and offered a job to Tony working for one of the families, for their Co-operative company in the fresh food industry. It meant him getting up very early and being part of the team that attended the Markets, and delivering the produce to shops and businesses in the greater Ballarat area. Tony was pleased for the opportunity and really didn't have to do much, but he was very willing and kept to himself. He slowly but surely was accepted, and began to enjoy the routine. More importantly, he was paid regularly and could now pay his own way. Quite significantly, not long after he joined the business and after he had opened a bank account, an amount of $5k was deposited into his account. That was mysterious and when he asked his mother if she knew anything about it, she was evasive. Tony was simple enough to believe in good luck!

Her best effort was, "It seems you may have a benefactor."

25

Police Review

Time for a serious review of information gathered and to summarise the police position. A Saturday conference was called and scheduled to go for all day if necessary. The group meeting would initially be chaired by DS Thomas who quickly pointed out that the case was being run by DS Fred Wilson and DC Linda Alexander. Briefly in attendance was District Commissioner Yates (observing) plus three other constables from the Ballarat Police Station.

The contribution from the District Commissioner was brief, "Death is usually associated with the old, the infirm, the sick, the unlucky, or the very tired, but this is a murder so be inquisitive and conscientious, and good hunting."

After the introductions, DS Thomas gave an outline, "This is where we are at, and where do we go from here?"

The summary was: We have two deaths. The pathologist's report confirmed one female and one male were dead. The female had died from fire, smoke and toxic gas inhalation.

The death of the male was a little more contentious. He had been hit on the head with a blunt instrument which caused his death but there had also been traces of strychnine in his gut. Linda took a quick look at the assembled officers and reflected to herself, "What an Anglo-Saxon, male world!"—she being the only woman in the group.

DS Wilson brought every one back to attention by saying, "We need to concentrate on motives, beneficiaries, winners and losers, and do we know of any wills?"

Motives in the case of Ms Ortega were nil, and her will had left her assets equally to two adult children. In the case of Lyons aka Camorra, nothing could be found.

"Well, let us be wider and consider facts, opinions, and assumptions" from DS Thomas. Thoughts tumbled back and forth and the note-taker was hard pressed to keep up. The incident room already had many diagrams, photos and maps on the walls.

The background to the death of Camorra was that he was disliked, even hated, by everyone. It was more than probable that revenge was the motive for his demise. Ms Ortega was simply an unlucky victim.

Main possible beneficiaries from the death of Camorra were Glen Robertson, (from a business and personal tidy up?), and the Investment Co-op company, (from a nuisance point?).

Suggestions from other associated angles, considered also of interest: Cliff Richardson? (on behalf of Robertson)? Tony Lombardi? (sometimes partly employed by Frank), and George Barnes? (for business progression by Paramount Enterprises Trading).

Just before he departed, the District Commissioner asked the obvious, "Who is the number one suspect? And be well prepared before you talk to the Press!"

DS Wilson looked to the more senior DS Thomas, and then also to Linda before responding, "Thank you, Sir, for attending; we think the actual time and cause of death requires more definition as it may be that Camorra caused the explosion that led to his incineration; however, our main suspect right now is Glen Robertson."

As he left, the Commissioner complimented the police staff and urged them to be in a position to make an arrest soon. After he had left, opinions flowed more freely suggesting more aggressive investigation about Camorra and a deeper look into Robertson, who seemed to be 'extremely lucky, rich, single, good-looking and very smooth'!

DS Thomas said that Linda would now have to do the bulk of the digging as he had to return to running the Ballarat Police Station. He announced he was allocating a Detective Constable full time to her for assistance for ten days to 'dig, dig, dig.' The DC would be Beth Jenkins.

26

Explanations: Glen

Media pressure was now being leveraged by the police. Editorials, photos, radio and TV articles, opinions, and even suggestions of financial rewards for information leading to a conviction.

Linda and DC Beth Jenkins were given a special office with their desks facing one another, so they could share telephones and all incoming information. They were wonderfully compatible and their investigations got cracking immediately.

One of the results from the media pressure was a flood of information that came out of the woodwork about Francis Lyons aka Camorra—but not yet about the probable culprit. More and more it became obvious what a despicable person Lyons had always been. He had always been rebellious and nasty, but a rebel without a cause! His best-known saying was, "I hate everyone!" A real hard case.

The local underworld simply added to his infamous reputation by confirming that the premises had been used for purposes other than that which was obvious. Most of the 'facts' were volunteered on the basis of guarantees that they remain totally anonymous. All it really confirmed was that Lyons was a 'total scum bag' to whom the local crooks could to go for illegal gambling, fencing of stolen goods, minor drugs, and the supply of explosives.

After thorough preparation, Glen Robertson was invited in to the station for another formal interview. It was held in a specially prepared room with minimal furniture of a table and three bare chairs. A sound recorder plugged into an electric lead was the only adornment.

Linda began by stating date, time and who was being interviewed and by whom, informed Glen of his rights, introduced Constable Beth Jenkins and stated Glen was entitled to legal aid if desired. Glen was informed that he was a suspect and more research had been done. That did not seem to surprise him. The two police then both aggressively verbally attacked him. They concentrated on his childhood and family relationships, his sexuality, and his ambitions. What did he know about the history of Aunt Polly Gamble? This was all quite easy for Glen to answer even though he was reminded that the truth was compulsory. The two police women tried to give him a hard time.

In summary, he confirmed a happy childhood, closer to his mother than his father, but no problems there and all OK with school and siblings. His mother may have taken some small advantages when dealing with deceased estates and maybe Aunt Polly was quite 'sharp.' He had had a simple, uncomplicated time in boarding school, where he was happy with the rough and tumble with the other boys. It had taken him a little time to enjoy the new freedom that went with university life, and a new learning curve to enjoy the company of female friends. Low level sport, academic achievement, social songs and ditties, and drama club were his main enjoyments. He felt he certainly had been fortunate.

Linda asked him, "Do you have any plans or ambitions to utilise your newly acquired wealth?" She observed that the tone and bluntness of the question did trouble Glen.

It took him a moment to respond, but he did so with aplomb, "Yes, well, I'm glad you asked that, because I'm making good progress there!"

He then proceeded to succinctly outline to them the plans he had underway. Back at the family home he had discussed at length with his family the setting up of a trust to be called the 'Pollyanna Animal Welfare Home' for old or injured dogs or horses. This seemed to be in keeping with his Dad's business over many years, the family attitudes and values and the Polly connection. The fund had been established and property acquired. The other 'project' he had underway was at his own university where he was lobbying the senior staff to create a specially fenced open area where students, tutors and admin staff could exercise their dogs in safety. Discussions had included members of the public also using what would be a new uni facility. He added that progress was being made there, and that he had also donated funds for university research.

That astounded the police officers. Beth then took it on herself to change the subject and pointedly asked, "Are you gay?"

Glen looked very pained, and responded with a sigh, "No, I'm not, but I do have friends who probably are, and more questions like that and I will be telling you to piss off!"

A quick comment from Linda, "No offence meant!"

With a small smile Glen added, "Your research probably does not show I'm a member of a bird-watching group and am considering building an upmarket 'hide' for them." No one was sure if he was just kidding!

Eventually they asked Glen about his friendship with Clifford Montgomery Richardson.

Using Cliff's full name brought a real smile to Glen's face, and he volunteered, "Now isn't he the success story! You probably don't know this, but he has enrolled to resume some studies!"

They chatted on in generalities for a while before Linda said, "We know all about him and your rescue and friendship, so would he be grateful enough to you, or could you manipulate that loyalty, to carry out actions on your behalf?"

This time the reaction was really hostile, "That's really stupid!"

"Please just confirm for us your whereabouts on Saturday August 15th, from 1.30pm to 5pm," asked Linda. He answered he was at the university campus attending events. Glen then stated that he had given them his undivided attention and honesty for over two hours, and unless they had anything of significance to add, he reminded them he was educated in the law and knew his rights. He rose to his feet to leave. He added a parting shot, "If you plan to charge me with something unimaginative, let me know and I will certainly bring some 'heavies' with me!"

A quick response from Linda to placate Glen and to request co-operation in solving the murder was how the meeting concluded. Linda and Beth sat back together in the office to consider all the information just gathered. What was their assessment of Glen Robertson?

Their opinions coincided. Either, he was a very good liar and actor, or was as clean as newly fallen snow! Even more, he was totally attractive, and they blushed a little together.

27

Reluctance: John Khoury

Linda and Beth went to Sergeant Thomas's office to report on progress. They indicated that they both agreed that Glen Robertson was an unlikely culprit. By association, they added they believed Cliff Richardson was also an unlikely killer. They reported what they considered was good news about Cliff taking on new studies and mature relationships.

DS Thomas, in very thoughtful mode said, "There is something really bugging me about this inquiry. I don't know what it is or what we may have missed. Let's relook at all the notes and evidence gathered." Then he asked for any added special input and for them to reconsider who was the major beneficiary from the elimination of shop manager Frank Camorra.

Back and forth they all talked it over, and finally agreed that probably there was an Investment Co-op link. Research had established that it was a properly constituted and registered company, with all records up to date. The directors were named and seldom changed. Tax returns were regularly filed, if a little late, and indicated small but regular profits.

It was agreed that if there was a direct connection to Frank Camorra, he was probably seen as little more than an embarrassment and an irritant to the company, as he was in no way publicly identified as a formal associate. It was discussed whether the MD or Chairman should be subpoenaed, to query if it was possible a hit man had been employed. That seemed to be too ridiculous, so John Khoury was summoned for another formal interview.

In came John Khoury again, his usual immaculate, assured and confident self, a little taken aback by the small, cold and austere office in which the interview took place. All the necessary formal warnings were read to him and the obvious recording device in place. First up, the police officers insisted that he give them the full name of the director to whom he reported.

He offered, "Mr Dane De Angelis, Managing Director and a major shareholder."

Linda, leading the questioning, offered the opinion that the company would be the major winner from the demise of Lyons, aka Camorra.

"How would that be?" questioned Khoury.

Beth chimed in, "The insurance cover, still requiring an explanation; the irritation of an irresponsible and out of control rogue employee; illegal activities—any one of these are ticking bombs that could surface at any time."

They went on to theorise that therefore, the ongoing association could only be an embarrassment, and as such an elimination as a remedy could be very attractive. Khoury was being treated as an accessory to a major crime.

Linda made an accusation, "We believe a professional assassin was employed and we have evidence of two attempts being made to kill Frank Camorra. One by poisoning and one with a blunt instrument. Furthermore, we believe you may have played a part in the plan."

A strong body reaction and alarmed response from Khoury, "God almighty, No!"

Beth added, "We will subpoena the telephone records of both the Investment Co-op company, your own business and all personal telephone calls to see who you have been talking to."

Khoury did seem to go pale.

Beth, being an avid young student in all matters of law and order, was reminded of an aphorism, 'To many people, virtue consists chiefly in repenting faults, not in avoiding them' (Lichtenberg).

Linda repeated several points from the previous interview and the need for 'truth' and suggested further co-operation was being requested. She added that they had confirmation of where he had been on the day of the explosion, so no need for further detail.

Khoury confirmed that Camorra was employed by the Investment Co-op company, but the terms and details of that employment were deeply buried and confidential. He was not privy to them, as it was considered to be on a 'not needed to know' basis. He relayed messages and instructions and he thought that Camorra occasionally had telephone discussions with 'Admin'.

The Police officers kept clearly exerting pressure and finally Linda asked, "Any ideas about previous associates, extraordinary behaviour, possible revenge, or a long shot, who may be guilty of killing Frank Camorra, aka Francis Lyons?"

Clearing his throat, John Khoury answered, "I really don't know, but don't imagine it would be suicide!"

Linda then asked, "Why is that?"

Khoury succinctly replied, "Because he liked being a prize prick!" and added, "Excuse the language, officers." That pretty much concluded the interview.

Linda and Beth were growing into an efficient, happy team. They even looked somewhat alike, being about the same age, and some of the station staff had labelled them 'The Terrible Twins'. Both had blonde hair and blue eyes, and wore neat pony tails pulled securely back to give off a no-nonsense professional look. One was in full police regalia, the other in neat and conservative day wear.

They discussed whether there was merit in using subpoenas and did they think a 'hit contract' had actually been put out on Camorra? It did seem highly unlikely that the Investment Co-op or Khoury were guilty of much more than questionable, over-protective commercial behaviour. Blackmail was not uncommon as a motive for murder. Personal revenge seemed a much more likely motive.

Dig, dig, dig, and more! Previous life and records, in the armed forces? Urgent requests were sent with the full authorisations for the release. Even with the request for urgency, they knew it would take time and needed patience! The unrelenting attention and pressure on gathering information resulted in new details surfacing. An example was the safe. It had survived the blast and was intact. The first local locksmith called in to open it said it was out of his league. It was a Chubb, a sophisticated partly electronic, high-tech, fire and waterproof model. He passed the opinion that all documents inside it would be undamaged. The Chubb expert from Bendigo was requested.

The safe had been installed in concrete and well bolted down and the Chubb man expertly opened it with obvious care in case it had been further 'protected' in any way! The contents were immediately confiscated and included a small stash of drugs, a handgun, a few pieces of jewellery, what seemed to be three detonators, and a large amount of cash.

The Army had responded early on by sending their explosives expert, who confirmed the evidence of a not very complicated trip mechanism had been used in the shop, and the use of standard army regulation detonators and explosives. Definitely not electronic or remotely activated.

There was also an initial response back about the Indian motorcycle, that it had possibly come from an Army museum? A newer report from Army administration confirmed that Francis Lyons had been a soldier in Vietnam and had done active service against the Viet Cong. He had been dishonourably discharged from the Army back in Australia. He had been in the Australian Army Ordinance Corps concerned with supply and administration, and demolition and disposal of explosives, and salvage of battle-damaged equipment. The Ordinance Corp's motto was Sua Tela Tonati, "To the warrior, his arms".

The Corps included clerks, operator supplies, petroleum operators, parachute riggers and ammunition technicians. Members of the Corps were nicknamed "Roaches".

In 1973, the Royal Australian Army Service Corps ceased to exist and was divided into sub-groups. Royal Australian Corps of Transport (RACT) and the provision of foodstuffs and petrol and oil lubricants were given to the Royal Australian Army Ordnance Corps (RAAOC). It was a time of change and disruption for responsibilities and personnel. Francis Lyons had been mixed up in these rearrangements and he had one close associate known to the senior staff. No further information was given on that person.

The Indian motorcycle, as yet to be confirmed but probably ex-Army, may have come from Army Reserve? Clearly a collector's item, the Indian was badly damaged by the fire but not destroyed. It was of great interest to the Army, the police and the insurance company. Built in Springfield, Massachusetts, from 1901 to 1953, Indian Motor Cycles had survived two World Wars and the 101 Scout was well known to everyone who knew motorbikes. The 'Scout' was produced from 1920 to 1949 and was used by the British and Commonwealth forces. The WW2 model was mainly the Scout 741 and over 30,000 units were produced; probably the damaged model was a 741, which was very valuable, even without tyres. Adding to the value was the famous legend associated with the Kiwi Bert Munro who had modified in his back yard shed a 1920 Scout to set a 'Flying Mile' world speed record at the Bonneville Salt Flats in US. His best speed record was in the 1000cc class at 183.586 mph (295.453kmh). Francis Lyons was not known for breaking records or for owning a motorcycle, or ever having been seen on a bike! Why was the bike there?

Lyons did use an oldish Datsun car registered in the name of Investment Co-op company in Ballarat. It had been confiscated by the police but no drugs, explosives, or other suspicious material was found. A detailed search of his house had turned up little more than alcohol and small traces of marijuana: not much to be found.

28

Reinterview: Tony Lombardi

Linda and Beth decided to reinterview Tony Lombardi. They agreed such an interview would probably not take long, even though Tony had been at the scene of the crime. To add emphasis to the occasion, Linda invited DS Thomas to sit in on the interview. It was arranged to be at the Ballarat Police Station at 10am and Tony was instructed to 'be there'.

Before the formal interview, DS Thomas had expressed an opinion, "Don't hold your breath for answers, because he is a gormless little prick."

When Tony arrived, he was escorted into the same austere office where John Khoury had been interviewed and that interview was referred to, as was all the assistance he had given.

As part of the casual opening preliminaries, Beth said, "Nice car, I like the colour, that goes with your clothes!" There was no obvious smile back, so DS Thomas got straight to the point and read Tony his rights, that he could remain silent, and could ask to talk to his lawyer, stressing he was not yet under arrest, however it was a formal recorded interview.

Linda started off by stating that Tony was on the site of the crime on Wednesday 15th August at around 2.30pm. She asked Tony to confirm that. He nodded agreement. Linda asked, "We want you to tell us what you were doing there at that time and had you been there some time?" Before he could answer, she added, "We have plenty of time for you to answer our questions. You have given us previous answers and we ask you to tell the truth, clarify previous points, and if necessary, we can give you time to think carefully about what you say. This is a murder case."

Beth asked, "Just for a break, would you like a coffee while you consider how to do the right thing relative to decency and fairness?"

Rattled, he gasped, "Yes, please."

DS Thomas signalled for coffee and quietly added words under his breath, "Agonise and search your bloody soul!"

On resumption they reminded Tony that other suspects had been interviewed, including John Khoury, who had been extremely helpful. This given with a look of anticipation. Then the preliminaries before the real attack began.

Linda was the main inquisitor. She fired off questions, "Do you believe in God? Were you called 'Lolly'? Have you had experience before with the police? Was your mother promiscuous? Was Frank Camorra your uncle? If not, how did you know him?"

Very slowly and deliberately, Tony answered, "Yes" to the first four questions but tried to be evasive about Camorra. DS Thomas beat Linda and Beth to it by verbally jumping on him and demanding, "Honest elaboration please!"

Tony was now sweating profusely. He went into a long and rambling answer, "Well, you probably know I left school at 15 years old, and then worked in a family related business in the fresh fruit and vegetables area. The police occasionally seemed to be around checking things but I was just doing lifting, moving and packing work. It was a happy, friendly and easy place that I enjoyed. I was paid regularly every week. My childhood was not so great, as my Mum kept moving, I kept changing schools, and she had regular changes of boyfriends. Some were OK and some very rude. Some stayed for a few days and some a lot longer. I don't remember most of their names. Most of them ignored me, a few told me to get lost, and a very few gave me some money! One very ugly and awful man grabbed me in the back shed and showed himself to me. When I told my teacher, it was reported. But nothing came of it and the man disappeared. I think a policeman did ask about it."

In a slightly hysterical voice, he almost shouted "You know I really hate my mother. She was a real fat slag, and mixed with the pits! She didn't even care much about me!"

He went on with, "These days I have a couple of mates I enjoy a beer with, mainly at Clunes, and have fun with my Sandman van. It attracts notice and people admire it and I spend money on upgrading it."

Linda interrupted the long response by asking Tony, "So where and how do you get your money for all these indulgences? What is your current work?"

That started him off again on his longwinded personal reflections, which he seemed to be enjoying. DS Thomas looked bored and passed a covered note to Linda and Beth, "Pathetic little prick."

Tony finally answered Linda, "Well, I am well paid these days because I deliver stuff as well as pack the fruit and vegies, and that gets me round in the company van."

Beth asked, "But do you need more money to pay some rent to your mother, some for the car and other things?"

After some hesitation, Tony added that Frank in recent times had been paying him in cash for some deliveries. He was obviously uneasy in the conversation moving on to Frank Camorra.

Linda suggested a short break as she said that right now, they wanted to concentrate on Camorra—aka Lyons.

After a ten-minute break, the questioning was restarted by DS Thomas asking Tony to reconfirm that he was discovered at 2.45pm on Saturday 15th August, at the back of the burning shop building on the corner of Pleasant Street and Don Place, holding his head in his hands and clearly in distress. The Sergeant asked, "So what was that all about?"

Surprisingly and hesitatingly, Tony answered "This is a bit of a long story but you said you had plenty of time. Frank Camorra is not, was not, my uncle. He may have been some distant relation but only came into my life in recent times."

Linda questioned, "How's that?"

Tony was clearly getting tired and irritable, and aggressively responded, "Do you want to know or not?"

Pacifying him, they then requested him to carry on. Tony carried on with the same theme about Camorra, "Someone in my family told me I should make contact with a man recommended by a Mr John Khoury, as someone needing a person to do miscellaneous deliveries in and around Ballarat. Payment would be in cash and I was given a telephone number to ring during the day. He was simply known as 'Frank' and I made an appointment to meet him in the Antique Shop in Pleasant Street. He said to park around the back and come into his office through the back door."

The three police officers found all of this intriguing. More than that, they could hardly contain their impatience for more.

Tony went on, "In my first meeting with him, I was intrigued by his office which was very clean, tidy, and well lit." He went on to comment that Frank himself was very untidy and had a grey stubble and longish hair. Frank had just said hello and explained that the deliveries would be small packets, mainly to non-commercial premises and payment was not required, but the delivery must be made in person to the person on the label, or bring it back. Simple enough!

For each delivery made Tony would be paid $20 in cash. To Tony that sounded too good to be true but that was the deal! Reflecting on things after his first meeting, Tony added he had had the strange feeling that he knew Frank from somewhere.

Beth interrupted the flow by saying, "In a previous interview you admitted that Frank was a relative and you quite enjoyed the status of being a 'mule'!"

Hastily Tony said, "That was a bit of a lie because I never really knew who were relatives or just 'business friends'."

He was keen to get back to his disjointed explanation about Frank, "The first deliveries went well as the names and addresses were easy to find. The more I met Frank, the clearer the recognition became! He may have been a distant relative, but he was definitely the one who had groped me in the back shed. The dirty old bastard himself! The memory was vague because I had buried it deep, and no one had seemed to want to help me way back then!"

DS Thomas asked if a break in the interview would be a good idea. Tony assured everyone he was fine and he wanted to continue on. So, as his definite positive recognition had set in, Frank had actually asked him one day, 'Do you remember me, from years ago, when we were in the back shed one day, when your mother was away?' Tony went on, "If I had any doubts, that was confirmation I needed that he was the evil bastard who had spoilt my youth."

The interviewers were sympathetic but remained quiet.

Tony emphatically added, "It got worse when Frank in the mildest fashion asked if we could perhaps do it all again and he would pay $50 each time and was I familiar with 'blow jobs!' Tony was sweating and very agitated, adding that he had bolted right out of Frank's office without a further word to him.

Linda suggested a coffee break should be taken, and that was agreed to by all. Tony offered to continue after the break as he had more to add.

The interview restarted with the police officers full of pent-up curiosity. To get the ball rolling Linda asked, "Please tell us what you were doing at the back of the shop at around 2.45pm on Saturday 15th August?"

Tony took some deep breaths and then away he went, "Well, I was actually there at 2pm for a meeting with Frank to discuss some deliveries." Frank had made the specific request for him to come in, following the hasty exit by Tony the day before from the unpleasant historical reminder. Tony confirmed he had parked his Sandman van at the back of the shop and gone inside to Frank's office, that featured some antiques, guns and other weapons. He confirmed that Frank started off as if nothing unusual had taken place the day before, and tried to assure Tony that a new relationship could evolve. He had started to outline the deliveries to be made and Tony said, "I just exploded and told him I would not help his dirty little business that no doubt corrupted many young and innocent people! You know he actually just laughed at me, right in my face!" Tony was again agitated and fuming.

Linda put her hand on his shoulder and half expected him to withdraw, but he didn't. Encouraged, he began again, "You know what I did then? I picked up off his desk a 25-pounder field artillery shell that was his pride and joy, leaned across his desk and belted him right on his miserable bloody head!"

You could have heard a pin drop in the interview room. DS Thomas had the presence of mind to ask quietly, "Tony, and then what happened?"

The answer was probably significant in a number of ways. Tony replied, "You know I really hated him. He crumbled like a weak little doll, with a look of complete surprise on his shit face. There was quite a bit of blood. He staggered around, muttered swear words at me and passed out."

Tony admitted that he was frightened at what he had done and cleaned up some of the blood before bolting out the back door, pulling it locked behind him.

"I don't know how much later it was when the officer found me, after the explosion and after the smoke and fire had covered the building."

There was a stunned silence as the two women silently looked at each other in triumph. Linda looked across at Beth Jenkins, and then very quietly directed her words to DS Thomas, mouthing "Congratulations, Boss!"

Immediately, DS Thomas realised this had created a whole new set of facts that needed fast action. He swung into gear and thanked

Tony for his honesty and told him he was now going to have to arrest him, and that he would be held in the cells in the police station whilst charges were finalised. He could make a telephone call and he should consider getting legal aid. The Sergeant then helpfully suggested that he ring his mother as he thought Tony may not be quite up to fully understanding the process. Tony was clearly overawed by it all but seemed to be relieved. He just kept nodding his head in agreement or understanding.

A constable was called to take him away and a booking with a magistrate was made. Bail would be contested even though Tony was not regarded as dangerous.

29

Result!

The news spread like wildfire and soon everyone knew that Tony Lombardi was the person arrested. The media was onto the arrest and quickly formulated their speculative opinions and headlines. A short, sharp press conference was called and although Detective Sergeant Thomas was the opening speaker, he handed most of the questions over to Linda Alexander as the Senior Detective, and she in turn gave praise and acknowledgement to each of the team she named.

Information released simply said that a young local man had been taken into custody to face charges of assault and possible manslaughter, associated with the shop fire at Pleasant Street on 15th August. The small number of reporters in attendance pushed questions to Linda thick and fast. Linda handled them well, stressed that the team work had been wonderful, and added that more work was now needed and that new pathology reports and the involvement of the Coroner were anticipated. That all seemed to go well but the headlines were bold and aggressive.

Examples were, 'Local boy embroiled in sex scandal! Local young millionaire cleared of guilt in shop fire! Young hoon locked up! Case cracked wide open!' and some less welcome headlines — one 'Blonde bombshells crack it'. Tired but thrilled, discreet police celebrations followed as the publicity was allowed to disperse. The police were pleased to note that there were no direct quotes from them. Almost everyone agreed that the world was a better place because of the demise of Camorra, aka Lyons.

Tony was found guilty of manslaughter. He definitely had been provoked. But he had assaulted with intent. The Court agreed on the inclusion of 'diminished responsibility'. He was given a sentence in a psychiatric facility to be treated for 'clinical depression'. He progressed well physically and medically and there were discussions on how best to rehabilitate him and even to prepare him for a new identity.

The Ballarat Police were showered with praise and recommendations from on high. DS Wilson from Footscray and DS Thomas were delighted to present individual awards to both Linda Alexander and Beth Jenkins. They took pleasure from the applause, Beth because it was her first award, and gave added weight to her upward career, and Linda because it emphasised her seniority and maturity.

As Linda was returning to her own station at Footscray in Melbourne, DS Thomas made special mention that Linda was also being nominated for a District Award for excellent detective work. Everyone clapped and all enjoyed the special morning tea.

Linda and Beth began a lifetime friendship and agreed on regular future socialising. Their careers within the police were not parallel but the look-alike young women had established one of many common interests. Beth was fascinated by the Southern African history and big game animals, and Linda valued the social maturity that Beth volunteered so freely. Linda was gaining appreciation of the value of the companionship that could exist between friends of a similar age and vocation.

Linda was working hard on her ongoing career plan as a Detective. Jeremy the banker was still in the picture. Linda was now identified within police as a 'hot' detective on the way up. The very old saying, 'Nothing succeeds like success' did apply.

Glen Robertson and the Investment Co-op company went on from strength to strength, arguing with their insurance company over the payouts for months, even years!

Cliff Robertson found romance with a fellow student at College and she quickly became part of the wider group of friends that included Glen and some of his more and unusual Uni friends.

The skeleton found was an unknown soldier. Unofficial advice from a source within the Army advised that the possible acquaintance of Francis Lyons previously alluded to, could not be associated with bones that had been buried in Pleasant Street, Ballarat, as that person had died in prison over four years ago. When the DNA arrived, it was confirmed that the skeleton bones were the remains of a different, but former companion of Lyons from his army days when he was known to deal in hard drugs. It was reasonable to speculate that the skeleton which the explosion had exposed had been killed by Lyons and buried under the house with the small cache of drugs. Lyons really was an evil man who was not missed. Rather a pity that such a harmless individual as Tony Lombardi had got caught up in the saga.

The drinking companion who tried to poison Lyons remained unknown.

The excellent Police result helped Linda's promotion and her identification as a talented detective.

case 2

double jeopardy ˎ

Prologue

Detective Inspector Linda Alexander was sitting at her desk puzzling over the next step to be taken in her current case.

Her telephone rang and she could see the call was from her Superintendant, Ronald Brunton. She picked up and said, "Good morning, Sir."

"Hi Linda, you know it's me, Ron Brunton, here." Quite formal, yet friendly as usual.

"I was just wondering how busy you are as we may have a case that would benefit from your experience and talent," he said.

Not totally at ease with with the comment, she respectfully asked for more information.

Superintendant Brunton launched into his reasons.

"Whether it is a coincidence or not, we have a double murder in the Macedon Ranges involving two adult children—twins—of a highly respected family from Woodend," he said. "The bodies of the twins have been dumped in separate locations, but with similar single gunshot wounds to their heads."

Stopping to take a few breaths, Ron Brunton then continued that not much more was yet apparent, nor were any obvious motives being theorised. The bodies had been found within an hour of one another several kilometres apart, by people walking their dogs in the early morning.

"The plan is to centralise the investigation at the Gisborne Police Station as there are adequate facilities there and some staff as backup. I'd like to appoint you as the detective in charge of the case and have you based at Gisborne until the case is closed. What do you think?"

Linda was excited by the offer and quickly expressed her thanks. She followed up with questions about to whom she would report and other details of the role, and added with pleasure, "I am flattered by the offer; I could be on the job tomorrow."

The Superintendant, in his usual laconic way, commented, "What's wrong with right now?"

1

The Moretti Family

Beautiful Woodend. Only an hour from central Melbourne, huddled in a little hollow on the edge of the Macedon Ranges bearing all the confidence that goes with an established town with its own identity. The conductor of the regular V/Line passenger service jokingly refers to it as 'Timber Finish'. A central pretty clock tower adds style.

A cold winter town that takes pride in warm open fireplaces, scarves, gloves and beanies, it has developed recognised business support facilities that attract executives from far and wide to attend courses and events. It boasts 'The Bentinck' offering meeting facilities for daily or weekly training and education, and even as a venue for Friday night drinks. 'Campaspe House'—another famous conference centre, with an equally famous Edna Walling garden—is an additional attraction. Both centres offer accommodation for participants from out of town.

This is the home town of Alessandro and Corina Moretti, third-generation Australians with a strong Italian heritage of which they are extremely proud. Alessandro—a well-liked, respected and successful business entrepreneur—had grown his several businesses from small beginnings in the Macedon Ranges, in company with Corina and their four children.

Woodend had progressed from the days when it had a traditional single main street through which all traffic drove, to show the footprint of more recent times where the addition of a major supermarket and eighteen support shops had created a large bulge off the main street. This created some traffic problems for vehicles and pedestrians alike until the inevitable highway bypass was created. Opportunities for some and costs for others.

Alessandro had begun in the family tradition of fruit and vegetable retailing, buying stock from the Melbourne Markets early each morning to sell from the shop in the main street premises that the family owned. Being astute and energetic, he and Corina had quietly purchased other main street Woodend properties as they became available. They were fair and generous landlords. On the fringes of Woodend, they had invested in land that in time was acquired by VicRoads for the new freeway that was built to cater to increasing Melbourne to Bendigo traffic. Small additional property purchases were made in nearby towns.

Alessandro was very community minded and made regular and generous donations to church and local clubs. He was involved in the local football-netball club, where he was for a term club president and patron and always featured in annual prize-giving and tributes. His children had all participated as players, and oldest son Dominic had been good enough to be nominated to feed through to Hawthorn Football Club in the city.

The original family home was a small weatherboard house on the main road just over the railway bridge but close to Woodend Station. They retained that home, but as family and fortune grew, the need was created for bigger accommodation. All through these expansions and growth activities Alessandro and Corina built respect and genuine friendships. Alessandro followed a routine of regularly meeting for morning coffee with his old cronies at their regular coffee bar to maintain tradition and to keep up with all the gossip. As soon as Dominic was mature enough, he was included in the group. Corina was active in community affairs even more widely as a keen member of the Catholic Church and as a volunteer worker in the Salvo's retail shop, in addition to being a regular at the 'Big I' tourist information booth in nearby Kyneton. Financial donations were made regularly to a wide range of local causes. A family involved in the community indeed.

The pinnacle of their personal properties was a house they built on their five-acre block just outside the rural town of Tylden. An easy ten-minute drive from Woodend. The home was large—one level consisting of five bedrooms—with four-car garage, heated swimming pool and lighted tennis court. It had a grey slate-tiled roof, white rendered walls, and an attractive portico over the front door entrance.

The property was surrounded by a white post and rail fence and had a large black remote-controlled gate. The graciously curved bluestone-edged driveway led through immaculately trimmed lawn and tidy gardens to the front door and an extra parking area, which in turn led to a more remote large garden shed. It was the epitome of a beautiful family home. Two pet Dobermanns completed the picture.

Over the years the family business interests had expanded to include fruit and vegetables, farming, packaging and retailing, property acquisitions, and wholesale and retail liquor outlets. The newest project was a major enterprise in importing, wholesaling and retailing of fashion and high-quality bicycles and accessories. The manifestation of this was a large, high-profile retail outlet in Sturt Street in Ballarat. World-famous brands for which the exclusive distribution rights had been acquired were regularly featured in expansive media promotions.

Head office for the Moretti business interests was a well-preserved and attractive converted old bank building in the middle of Main Street, Woodend. Managing director Alessandro had his office in the building as did son Dominic, titled general manager as he was the day-to-day operations manager. His sister Bria also had an office in the building, where she had broader activities in control of the retail businesses that in particular covered the growing and evolving bicycle phenomenon. Head office was compact and efficient with a small staff of under ten employees. The family deemed communications important, so had developed a habit of the three family 'business executives' meeting every week in the office over coffee to make sure everyone was up to date. In typical Australian fashion of scaling names down to as short as possible, within the office Alessandro was sometimes referred to as 'Alex', Dominic, as 'Dom', and Bria as 'Bee'. Not always to their faces.

The children had all begun their education at St Ambrose's Parish School in Woodend, and the two oldest (Dominic and Bria) had gone on to Sacred Heart College in Kyneton. They had been exemplary students and Alessandro and Corina had been active and generous parents to the school. The younger twin boys, Luca and Giovanni, (eight years younger than Bria) had also completed primary school at St Ambrose's but for secondary schooling were sent to Salesian College, a co-educational Catholic College in Sunbury where Alessandro and Corina thought the size and variety of the campus and curriculum could widen the boys' horizons and introduce them to a new range of friends.

At St Ambrose's the twins had been a nuisance, always pushing against rules and regulations and thinking controls did not apply to them. They were labelled by everyone as "spoilt brats" and people felt it would be good riddance when they were gone. Their parents were aware of some of their behaviour and hoped Salesian College, with its attractive old-world looks and respected culture, would improve their attitudes. They hoped and prayed that the tradition, culture, pride and excellence associated with the Salesian Society would add to the boys' aspirations. The Salesians of Don Bosco and the Society of Francis de Sales had a deserved reputation for quality education. The "Preventive System" as practised by the priests and brothers was to understand reason, religion and kindness and to help avoid the development of dysfunctional ways.

Teasing of the twins along the lines of "Who the hell do you think you are? Mathew, Mark, Luca or John (Giovanni)" was common and repetitive and did not help the boys' ongoing maturity. For many reasons, opinions about Luca and Giovanni lumped them together rather than the two being judged as individuals. A quote about them that was reputed to have come from a priest was "if an angel were to tell us something of his philosophy, I do believe some of his propositions would sound like two times two equals thirteen".

In their very early years they shared a bedroom and as the family fortunes grew, they graduated to separate but adjoining rooms. Dominic and Bria were years older and more like cousins to them. The younger boys began calling themselves 'Team M' and could almost communicate in their own language. They referred to one another as 'LM' or 'GM'. Dominic and Bria grew up immersed in the old-fashioned 'strive hard' regime of Alessandro and Corina. Not so the twins! They displayed unfounded optimism and arrogance without any input or basis. Jointly or singularly, they had no real sense of purpose or humour.

2

Carry-On Courier Company

Unfortunately, in their formative years Luca and Giovanni had been spoilt silly. They graduated high school with an attitude of irresponsible adventure and action, although there was a wish from both parents for them to go on to higher education at university. They fooled around for over a year doing very little. They eventually asked for parental help and financial support to start their own courier business which they cleverly called "Carry-On"—a fledgling freight-carrying unit.

They purchased two second-hand white Toyota panel vans that looked totally anonymous. By persistently calling on old 'friends and acquaintances', new-found friends and associates, and almost anyone else they came across, they built up a customer base. Customers wanting parcels or products of any size or shape, at any time of the day, moved from or to destinations within an eighty-kilometre radius of Woodend could be given a very competitive price, particularly for a cash payment with no receipt required. It was attractive to a surprising number of 'businesses'. Luca and Giovanni were the only drivers and shareholders.

Transactions grew and the Macedon Ranges base comfortably allowed deliveries from Melbourne City addresses to as far away as Bendigo. As the only drivers, Luca and Giovanni had total control of all activities. The only other vehicle they had was an old 250cc motor bike, and their personal doctrine was, quite bluntly, "we don't give a rat's arse what is being delivered, particularly if it's cash up front!"

Socially, Luca and Giovanni frequented Woodend and in particular the traditional old Keatings Hotel on a prominent corner in the middle of town. Here they met regularly with some of the 'young brigade', particularly on a Friday evening. The licensee treated them with respect as the building was owned by a Moretti company, and the boys conducted some of their transactions over a beer or two. On the odd occasion that Luca or Giovanni over-indulged, they were allowed to crash for the evening in a room upstairs. Alessandro was not informed. Neither he nor Dominic used the twins' Carry-On courier service.

Around this time, Woodend was still reverberating from the tragic death of a sixteen-year-old girl who had attended Sacred Heart College in Kyneton and was known to many of the local young brigade. It had been a stark reminder of the damage that can be done from drug use and how it affects large parts of a community.

It took time but the business grew in irregular leaps and bounds and although both boys mainly lived at home with all the associated benefits, including their mother Corina fussing over them, a move was inevitable. For a while they used some spare space in the Keatings Hotel as a part-time office and to accommodate the administrative work growing with the business. For many months they looked for premises that could meet their requirements, and finally settled on a basic shed on a property in the new industrial area close to the railway station at nearby Gisborne. This had many attractions including cheap rent, remoteness, some storage and vehicle parking behind a lockup gate. No identification of the business was shown nor required when taking on the lease. When or if needed, they could 'crash' there. The office space inside was minimalistic but comfortable and secure.

It took time and application and slowly the customer base grew, as did the encouragement from some customers to expand into new areas of operation. This positive response stimulated Luca and Giovanni to build the business more quickly. Their ambition led to their exploring the purchase of a semi-trailer rig that could be used for destinations further afield, and new categories of freight. Their personal motto became "Best not to enquire too deeply" into the legality or category of any products or the integrity of the customer. Carry-On simply pushed on with wild enthusiasm and irresponsibility.

As business owners the twins had ambitions that overrode common sense and practicality. They were doing a good volume of legal business, including some from Moretti companies, and had regular courier-type deliveries. Illegal work—much more lucrative— could be catered for with the semi-trailer purchase they envisioned. They were convinced that cigarettes in particular, and also liquor and drugs, would be easy. Some of their shadier customers had nodded in that direction. "Why don't you -------". No conscience required.

Steps were taken to make Carry-On a more regular commercial entity and to apply for registration and licences to do work at markets, wharfs, railyards and airports. Nothing spectacular involved. The purchase of a quality secondhand rig needed help, patience and support. But help of that type often comes with obligations!

The business continued to grow as did the number of employees and the responsibilities associated with legal commerce. Social activities scaled up at the same time, and the Keatings Hotel continued to be the preferred watering hole. Costs associated with the expanded group of regular 'friends' also escalated, as did the quality and type of stimulants indulged in. It was all becoming a bit of a roller-coaster. Some of the twins' acquaintances were drug-related, in usage as well as procurement, and added to the boys' supply of excess cash which was spent with great gusto at the casino in Melbourne. Members of motorbike gangs were often among the company they kept.

The search for a suitable truck finally resulted in the purchase of a curtain-sided, well maintained semi-trailer, including the tractor, with full history, fifth wheel, cab over and sleeper. It came with all history and warranties, and included the ability for rapid disconnect for easy loading and unloading. Armed with the full details, Luca and Giovanni needed financial help and some alterations. Hayes Trailers in Woodend were experts and, knowing the family, were happy to carry out modifications as ordered—mainly additional boxes and lockup areas. Finance took a while to organise but the last-minute addition of the signature of Alessandro on one of the documents as security, and extensive insurance guarantees, completed the deal.

For Luca and Giovanni and Carry-On this was seen as the achievement of a huge milestone demonstrating their independence and success. The twins held a champagne promotion on the new property in Gisborne to which they invited the local papers for promotional purposes. It was a colourful luncheon, and there was nothing humble about the colourful logo and Carry-On sign on the side of the impressive new-looking Kenworth semi-trailer. The two young men were as proud as punch. Notably, none of the Moretti family or business executives were present at the celebration. The papers did include some small reports and a photo or two of the event.

3

DS Linda Alexander

Detective Sergeant Linda Pretorius Alexander was a respected and popular first-generation Australian, having arrived in Perth as a young girl with her parents and brother after the family emigrated to Australia to escape the horror of apartheid South Africa.

Linda had graduated from the Police Academy in Perth, and while serving in the police force in Western Australia had felt prejudice and discrimination simply because she was female, she was new, and she had an accent. Her sense of humour, determination and skills earned her respect, and after three years she applied for a transfer to Victoria to progress into detective work. Training to become a detective was her driving ambition. When her older brother Brendan arrived in Melbourne on transfer from a successful London career, they were able to establish accommodation together and create a comfortable, stable base.

Linda was recognised as a talented potential detective and had been given a chance to prove herself when given a temporary transfer to the Ballarat Police Station to participate in a murder inquiry involving three deceased persons. Involving the full participation of police personnel from different divisions, a surprising but successful result had been achieved in that case.

Since the successful stint in Ballarat, Linda had been involved in a variety of criminal cases. These ranged from domestic violence to death through 'hit and run', accidental drowning and the biggest and ugliest of all, a widespread paedophilia ring. The hunting down of child sex offenders is not only difficult but controversial. Linda was part of a dedicated police team of experts and the case was for her very intense. The activities of grown men against prepubescent children she found abhorrent. For much of the time police see the activities as another form of pornography, and they try to focus on the offence not the offender. It is not one of the glamourous crimes to follow or chase, but is certainly one of high damage and emotion. Many offenders are in need of serious psychiatric treatment. It's ugly.

Luckily for Linda she had her mature brother Brendan at home with whom she had the happy ability to talk freely to relieve pressure. Brendan was a senior executive in an international trading company that exerted pressure on its own employees to achieve results, so he understood occupational stress. Having grown up in South Africa as children they had plenty of experiences and nostalgia to chat over.

Linda's personal life was progressing in a warm but not demanding or career-distracting way with her partner Jeremy, with whom she had a loving and appreciative relationship that included plenty of humour and support. The relationship with Jeremy was different, but in some ways familiar. He was a senior company executive who had never gone down the boring path of asking why on earth a woman would want to be a police officer; no doubt he liked the police association, but he never flaunted it. Commercial training and skill had moulded him into an excellent listener, and he was fascinated to learn about apartheid and South African history. She told him about the brutality of apartheid, home help, and things like game parks and the wide range of animals that could be seen in her old home country.

The best part of their happy and loving relationship was when they got together in the evening over a drink in their favourite pub and relaxed as they each related a funny or strange event of the day or week. They could feel the tension seeping quietly from their systems as they spoke, but no confidential details or 'pack drills' were disclosed.

The culmination of these evenings was usually about destination and food, and finished up with "Let's go home and make love." That was usually to Jeremy's place, as he had an apartment in Footscray, not far from where Linda and Brendan lived.

They were enthusiastic and ardent lovers. Linda would smile at Jeremy as she led him into the bedroom and impatiently started to remove his clothing. She made short work of cuff links and tie removal, belts and shoes and socks. They had seen one another without clothes often enough, but each time the excitement rose, the mood accelerated and their shared enjoyment was exhilarating. Erotic ideas sometimes crashed, in particular if there had been much discussion during the evening about exotic animals and their habits! The final wonderful intrusion to the interior was for the comparatively new lovers one full of joy. They lay together often for hours enjoying their own pleasure and solitude. What release and relaxed empathy.

4

Incident No 1

It was 7.30 am and the Woodend Police Station was activated into urgent attention by a telephone call, the integrity of which they had no reason to question. A man walking his Labrador dog in Quarry Road, Woodend, somewhat breathlessly reported a dead body floating in the small dam by the entrance to the Shire Council Tip. A well-known spot.

Sirens blaring and lights flashing, the patrol car rushed the three kilometres to the site in under five minutes. The man who had rung in was by the dam with his dog on the leash and almost guarding the area, although there were no houses nearby and not a soul in sight.

It was quickly evident that the person was indeed dead, face up with what looked like a sharp wound to the head. There was some blood on the clothing of the deceased. With a curt instruction to the man with the dog to, "Touch nothing and please wait," the police officer moved off to called up his Sergeant, and in an emotional tone reported the scene. He was instructed to take it easy and calm down, secure the site, touch nothing, and get details from the witness. He confirmed he had done most of that.

The Sergeant said, "Help is on its way. Do you by any chance recognise the victim?"

It was a negative to that, so the Sergeant swung into full police protocol for such an event and sent a message off to his District

Superintendent to alert him of possible consequences and publicity. Macedon Ranges was part of Victoria Western Division 5 that encompassed a range of police stations.

Quickly the officer made his way back to the scene. It was still deserted of any public by the time he arrived. He was well aware that the Critical Incident Response Team would have been informed and no doubt the Criminal Investigation Unit would be allocating personnel to the job. This to include detectives and the forensic pathology team.

At the station, Sergeant 'Jack' Jackson knew that all hell would break loose very soon in his otherwise quiet and well-run station. The Coroner's Court had to be notified and a Coroner's Court liaison officer would be appointed. A forensic pathologist was needed to establish the time and cause of death and to examine the scene in detail as soon as possible. Was it helpful that a constable from Woodend now thought he recognised the dead man?

It was the responsibility of the Coroner and the local police to order a post mortem and to set in motion the process of identifying the deceased and communicating with next of kin. The body would initially be moved to a local undertaker with an approved mortuary, then be transferred to the Melbourne City Hospital mortuary for further examination.

An initial examination seemed to indicate death had resulted from a single bullet to the forehead, probably from a hand gun at close range. In addition, the man's thumb and two middle fingers had been roughly severed. Identification was a priority and the Woodend constable was now sure he recognised the body as one of the well-known local Moretti twins. From first impressions it seemed likely that the man had been dead for several hours.

His clothing was smart and stylish. A light-blue collared shirt, dark-blue sweater and black leather jacket. Slim-fitting fawn chinos and high-quality leather ankle boots completed his expensive-looking outfit.

Later, when the pathologist arrived, examination revealed there was nothing in his pockets, not even a wallet, to aid identification. The remoteness of the old quarry site at 7.30am meant it was no surprise that there were no public around or potential witnesses to aid identification. Similarly, there were no tyre tracks or any debris obvious on the bitumen access road. An intensive search of the immediate area was ordered although it seemed possible the victim had been killed elsewhere and just dumped here.

The preliminary post-mortem described the victim as having brown eyes, narrow clean-shaven face, well-groomed black hair, and apart from the missing digits and a bullet hole in the forehead, no other apparent signs of violence.

Urgent messages were sent for photos of the Moretti twins and to enquire if there was anyone closely available who could positively identify either Luca or Giovanni, prior to informing members of the family. The possibility of the cadaver being a member of the Moretti family set alarm bells ringing in the minds of Woodend police personnel and prompted Sergeant Jackson to urgently contact his Inspector to alert him to the many consequences he could envisage. Alessandro Moretti and the entire family had a high profile of community respect and generosity that would result in media inquisition. He also warned his chief about the possible involvement of what he described as the 'loose cannon twins': It seemed at this early stage of the investigation that the victim was one of the boys, who were generally described at very least as bloody nuisances! Now 25 years of age, the twins had created a courier and freight carrying business of doubtful integrity, totally separate and independent of the rest of the family enterprises. The Inspector simply said "Thanks for the heads up" and brought forward his trip to Woodend.

5

Incident No 2

At 8.30am the same day, a distressed-sounding man telephoned the local Gisborne Police Station to say he was walking his dog around the swamp next to the Steam Engine Park, just off Station Road, Gisborne, in the Macedon Ranges, and had discovered what looked like a dead body. Calmly the duty constable took details and the officer in charge dispatched two officers in a patrol car, thinking it was probably something that had blown across from the display park next door. With flashing lights but no siren they arrived on site in under 15 minutes and hurried across to where they could see a warmly dressed walker and his retriever dog now on a leash. Not another soul was in sight.

What an incongruous situation. A beautiful sunny morning, no wind, the soft burring hum of vehicles driving along the nearby motorway, and 200 metres away the fenced off Steam Engine Club museum with its huge variety of old and antique machines in various stages of restoration. The fully clothed corpse lay face down in the scrub and long unkempt grass. Wisely, the dog walker had not touched the body, which appeared to have a bullet wound in the back of the head. The spreadeagled arms revealed severe damage had been done to the right hand, which was covered in dried blood.

The constables called back to the station with an element of alarm and urgency, asking for instructions and backup. The sergeant on duty was brief and clear, "Totally secure the site with ribbons, touch nothing, get full personal details from the witness, be careful where you walk, and request the witness to remain until back-up arrives

The Sergeant knew this had all the ingredients for a major incident and he also knew all the necessary steps that had to be followed. More than that, he was smart enough to telephone his boss to alert him of a developing scenario. The Superintendent had a roving responsibility over the entire Macedon Ranges police area and an office in the Gisborne complex. It was understood that he should always be kept in the loop, and the Sergeant wanted to speak with him for that reason. After his succinct outline of the circumstances, the Super's response was a little curt, "Are you pulling my bloody leg, Matthew? It's a bit early in the day for that!"

Respecting his Superintendent, who he knew well, the Sergeant responded earnestly, "No, Anthony, I am not, even though the detail has just come in. I thought as a courtesy you should be pre-warned." The Super then in milder tone explained that by coincidence, a remarkably similar event had been called in from Woodend Station about half an hour ago!

This news set off urgent communications in many directions and a call for the express assistance and involvement of the Critical Incident Response Team in Melbourne, who would be immediately assigned to the incidents. They would contact the Coroner's Court and forensic pathology unit and organise the handling and storage of the corpses—immediately a logistics headache as there were at least two sites to secure and examine.

The initial inspection of the body at Gisborne indicated that the young man had been killed elsewhere—opinion was at least eight to ten hours previously—and dumped in the scrub. It was thought the body should be easy to identify as apart from the obvious head wound, the only other damage appeared to be that two fingers and a thumb had been severed from the right hand. Despite amounts of dried blood on his right arm and his clothes, it was obvious that the deceased was young, well groomed, and expensively dressed. The usual police protocols swept into motion and urgent signals were sent in every direction to determine the identity of the victim and equally urgently to establish cause and time of death. The forensic pathology team was despatched from Melbourne as was the police dog unit. An intensive search was initiated over every centimetre of ground where the body had been found and the associated car parking areas.

It was agreed that the person had been killed elsewhere.

6

Co-ordination

By mid-morning senior police officers realised they had a major
catastrophe to deal with. Not just one murder but probably two,
involving the same family. How devastating would that be? Decisions
were made by the Critical Incident team to use the Gisborne Police
Station as the control base. A Chief Superintendent was appointed to
co-ordinate and control all activities and communications relating to
the events. He would be based at Gisborne and would pull together
the necessary team to work the case.

Positive identification of the body from Woodend was first to be
achieved as Sergeant Jackson took the initiative by calling the office
of the Carry-On Company and asking the senior clerk to accompany
him to look at the body. The man was very distressed to have to
agree it was Luca Moretti. Then Jackson went to the Moretti head
office in Woodend to seek one of the family to confirm a next of kin
identification.

It was by now mid-morning. Sergeant Jackson was informed that
Dominic was somewhere in Sydney, Bria was in Ballarat at the Bicycle
Centre, and Alessandro was probably still at home, as his usual habit
was to arrive at work about 10.30am after breakfasting at home with
his wife. Sergeant Jackson was on nodding terms with family members
and took it on himself to telephone the Moretti home in Tylden, where
the call was answered by the housekeeper. She confirmed that both

Mr and Mrs Moretti were at home but unavailable to speak. Sergeant Jackson identified himself and requested her quite forcibly to advise them that he would be there in fifteen minutes 'on an urgent matter'. He was there in ten!

Jackson drove his police vehicle to the front door and parked under the portico. He rang the very stylish door bell and the door was immediately opened by Corina—she had obviously been waiting to let him in. Alessandro was standing not far inside as brief greetings were exchanged.

Alessandro was dressed in an immaculate, loose-fitting, long-sleeved white linen shirt with motif on one pocket, neat chinos and brown leather moccasin-style shoes: his usual outfit for his semi-retired daily work routine. Corina was more fashionably stylish in her cream linen blouse, slightly tapered brown trousers and brightly coloured scarf. Her hair was severely pulled back from her striking face into a pony tail that was held in place with a brightly coloured ribbon matching her scarf. Neat, comfortable low-heeled shoes completed the look. What had been dark wavy hair of Alessandro was now speckled with white and grey, and Corina was a careful mid-blonde. Jack Jackson could see an obvious family likeness to Luca and Giovanni.

The couple both looked in fear of the necessity for a visit from Sergeant Jackson. He was politely invited to sit on a couch in the spacious reception area, where he noted a very smart leather jacket was draped ready for Alessandro to go off to work.

Sergeant Jackson got quickly to the point of informing them in the most sympathetic way he could manage that both Luca and Giovanni were dead, and had, in fact, been murdered. The delivering of bad news to next of kin was not uncommon for police, but there was no routine method and it was always stressful for all parties. Both parents' faces drained of colour and Corina fainted right away. Alessandro was hardly able to move, but called out in a harsh, cracking voice for Sally the house keeper who came rushing in and she then hysterically yelled for another staff member. With impressive control, Alessandro supervised the recovery of Corina. It took time for everyone to regain some composure, and Alessandro issued instructions for Sally to urgently contact Dominic and Bria and get them to telephone him. Still ghastly pale he did his best to console a weeping Corina.

Alessandro then set his whole attention on Sergeant Jackson, seeking all and every detail. He was still stunned and disbelieving, and became angry, even enraged, as he demanded full details of who had done it, where, and when. Amongst his anguished pleading he familiarly called the sergeant 'Jack', hoping for greater truth. As tactfully as he possibly could, Sergeant Jackson informed Alessandro that he would need to identify Luca and Giovanni at the mortuary as soon as possible. The sergeant expected and witnessed another horrible reaction of distress and rage, and waited sympathetically for some calm to be restored.

The pathologists had agreed to have the bodies temporarily stored together at a mortuary facility at Gisborne to minimise the family's ordeal, before moving them to Melbourne. With quite some composure and dignity, Alessandro carried out the identifications.

The cause of death was similar in both cases—a single bullet to the head—and both twins had had the two main fingers and thumb of one hand brutally severed: Luca the left hand and Giovanni the right. Alessandro was able to confirm that Luca was left-handed and Giovanni right. The only other difference was that Luca had been shot in the forehead and Giovanni in the back of the head. There was no other physical damage, however each had had a small circle and star tattooed on one buttock. Near enough the same position for both of them, and a tattoo not known to Alessandro. The mortician volunteered in a low tone that in certain circles, it meant that "the recipient was close to an arsehole". No need to emphasise that on this occasion.

With rising bitterness and a heavy heart, Alessandro, returned home where the whole family were gathering, including immediate relations and some intimate lifetime friends.

At both sites where the bodies had been found, full and exhaustive searches, including by the dog units, went back and forth over the scenes, photographing anything of potential interest. As the searches progressed it became very clear that both victims had been killed elsewhere and dumped, as each site was remarkably clean.

The Chief Superintendent appointed to run the case, Ronald (Ron) Brunton, was a long-serving, highly respected Victorian policeman. In his early career he had done stints in Geelong and Lakes Entrance areas, but in more recent years he had focused on Melbourne Central as a career path. He knew his way around. His first action was to convene a full meeting at the Gisborne Police Station for 5pm with a warning that it could be long and late and he expected minuscule details of everything so far known. Forensic Pathology was asked to contribute initial opinions on manner and times of death, as well as other details about body damage and results of tests on body swabs and finger nails.

Chief Superintendent Brunton arrived at 3pm and brought along with him Detective Sergeant Linda Alexander. He had requested Linda because of her rising reputation in the CIU and because she had done well in an investigation in Ballarat where she had gone deeply into the community. By happy coincidence a constable in Ballarat at the time called Beth Jenkins had now transferred to Gisborne as a two-stripe senior constable, and could help to build an efficient and compatible team. Ron Brunton was a smart team man.

7

Incident No 3

"There is but an inch of difference between a cushioned chamber and the padded cell." – GK Chesterton
"Children begin by loving their parents. After a time, they judge them. Rarely, if ever, do they forgive them." – Oscar Wilde

Some weeks prior, Carry-On had had a major problem to deal with. The twins' pride and joy, the Kenworth semi-trailer in all its glory, had gone missing. On this occasion neither Luca nor Giovanni had been driving. The job, clad in mystery, had been allocated to a newly appointed but experienced and fully licensed truck driver. The destination was South Australia—the outskirts of Adelaide—with the cargo undesignated. Overnight travel had been expected, but after 24 hours and no communication from the driver, alarm bells began to ring for the twins. Within the organisation they were the only ones who knew full details of the transaction. The driver probably had an inkling of the type of freight forwarding being carried out, but he was being adequately rewarded not to enquire.

Although a bit early to panic, Luca did a surreptitious check on the insurance policy on the full vehicle rig and felt assured they were covered. No need yet to contact the police to report a missing vehicle. The nature of their clandestine activities was secretly and closely guarded, not only from staff and law enforcement agencies but also from not-so-friendly rivals who bitterly defended their own turf. No on-vehicle stock insurance had been issued. In the early days of Carry-On, when the twins had really been a 'cash for carry' unregistered business doing illicit jobs for unsavoury types, they had on occasion crossed swords with motorcycle gangs who considered the upstarts were straying into their territory.

Meanwhile, unnoticed for some time on a remote back section of a derelict, overgrown farm, there was found a large trailer section of a semi-trailer—no cab, just a totally burnt-out trailer with no tyres remaining. The farm was at Chewton, just outside the town of Castlemaine, and it seemed strange that no one had seen or heard when the fire took place. It became evident on inspection that accelerants had been used as the fire and heat had distorted parts of the structure, but nothing else of significance remained. Some grass and weeds had been incinerated but the location was far enough from the road not to have been witnessed at the time. There was definitely no survivable stock from the truck.

There was no urgency felt by the local police to identify the burnt-out wreckage as there had been no notification of a theft. Days went by until a curious officer climbed over the fence to begin inquiries. The burnt chassis and twelve wheel rims were still in the empty paddock, well back from the Chewton primary school and a comfortable walk from the Red Hill Hotel. A bit late to be looking for track marks from the trailer or the delivery tractor or evidence from fingerprints or clothing! The police officer was smart enough to believe the trailer probably had a logo or code number somewhere that would identify the manufacturer. Logically he contacted Hayes Trailers of Woodend as they were well known in the Macedon Ranges.

The production manager was very helpful, "Oh yes, we are extremely proud of our products, and our trade mark, initials and code numbers indicating the date of manufacture are --"

The officer interrupted, "Too easy!" and relayed the details to him.

The answer from Hayes' manager was, "Yes, it's definitely one of

ours and was supplied to Carry-On freight forwarders of Gisborne."
He was even more helpful in adding that it was owned by L & G
Moretti with NAB having a financial stake. Date of build available.

The Castlemaine police realised they had been slow and casual
with their inquiry but contacted the Carry-On company with the
news and location of the trailer. Luca and Giovanni received the
information with growing dismay. Earlier they had received an
envelope containing a single unlined page bearing a message formed
with pasted-on letters that said simply: "When you do not pay on
time it still costs Ya."

A day after the call from Castlemaine they received another call
from the police, but this time from Bendigo. The office clerk had
directed the call on to Giovanni as the policeman had asked to speak
to the general manager. The officer identified himself and asked,
"Have you by any chance lost the tractor prime-mover from one of
your road rigs?"

Very carefully, Giovanni admitted that was possible. Easy to
establish it belonged to Carry-On because of the paint job, the
registration and Kenworth unit. The Sergeant said, "Well, you'd better
make arrangements to come and get it. Although it has been well
hidden it seems it may not be damaged. We are surprised it hasn't
been reported stolen. It is a very clean vehicle!" Police had found no
fingerprints and no surrounding evidence. Photos had been taken.

The officer went on to let Giovanni know that when he was ready
to collect it, he must liaise with the Sergeant first as he was to be
accompanied to the site, and there would be questions about the use
of the vehicle.

Giovanni and Luca urgently met in seclusion over a beer in a back
corner of Keatings Hotel in Woodend, knowing they had a full-scale
emergency on their hands. First things first: they needed to clarify the
parameters of the situation. Reports to police and insurance of missing
vehicle. What had happened to their driver? What could they report
as missing goods? What had been paid for, what were they obliged

to deliver and pay for, and to whom could they now turn for help and/or support? An urgent imperative was to destroy their mobile phones and all incriminating evidence. Huge and terrifying actions as they were well aware of the reputations of some of their 'fringe associates'. Sweating profusely, the pair were quickly onto a second beer and resisted the temptation to use even the hotel telephone to call Alessandro for assistance. They realised they were 'big boys' now. What about the driver? They both conceded that their checks may not have been that thorough, as they had been overkeen to employ a driver they could rely on to carry out instructions without questions. It now dawned on them he may have been a 'plant' and they reflected for a moment on the dubious references they had been given. Too late now.

Pressure was mounting on them. On the back of an envelope, they tried to add up their financial obligations relevant to the missing vehicle. Now with no prospect of any income from projects, they concluded that the stock alone totalled tens of thousands of dollars, a fairly high percentage of which they had already paid for, but far worse was that they had to pay in full for the stock that was on the vehicle and undelivered. That was illicit cigarettes from across state lines, plus the usual small amounts of well-hidden drugs locked in secret boxes.

Oh god! They were in big trouble! And they knew it. Very quickly their financial position had gone a full 360 degrees and their cash flow had evaporated. Worse still, they did not really know how to make direct contact with their nefarious associates and 'benefactors'. What negotiating tools could they use to work their way through or out of the mess? They were paralysed by fear and lack of ideas. "Let's have another beer," was all they could manage.

By now, a couple of locals in the pub had noticed the men's agitation and knew to keep away. Luca, the leader, finally suggested that they return to their office, sit down calmly and reassess their position. They walked briskly past their two administration staff into the sparse office, and made a quick list of things of value the company owned. It became even more obvious their position was untenable. There was now nothing of real value with the exception of $8,500 in their bank account at the NAB. They owed in excess of $150,000 for the delivery that could not be made, and more for the stock that had been on the truck and not paid for. Plus what was still owed on the Kenworth rig!

8

Police Work

Chief Superintendent Ron Brunton immediately set up his own style of incident room and knitted together his immediate team. Jack Jackson was given senior status because he was the local sergeant from Woodend, he knew the Moretti family and their foibles, and he had a working relationship with Alessandro. DS Linda Alexander, a well-respected career officer from Central, with a reputation for pursuing every possible lead. Constable Beth Jenkins, by coincidence now working at the Gisborne Station, was an immediate inclusion as she had previously worked well with DS Alexander at Ballarat.

Additions would be made as needed and the cooperation of regular officers at Gisborne was understood. Senior Sergeant Matthew Simpson of Gisborne was a close associate of Jack Jackson so interaction was assured. Two-striper Ian Ingram, also from Gisborne, was a welcome addition to the team and his wry Scottish sense of humour would be needed.

The first meeting was presided over by Brunton, who quickly got to the point. An ugly family tragedy with multiple ramifications in multiple directions. His first question after the introductions and welcome was, "What do we know, and what are the facts up to now?" He said he would give a summary and then would welcome theories, suggestions, ideas and random thoughts.

The Chief was succinct and listed the following:

—obviously a professional hit carried out away from where the bodies were discovered. The killer, or more likely killers, had gun expertise. Nothing about the brutal finger removals suggested surgical expertise. The manhandling of the victims suggested two or more in the 'hit' team and the use of at least one vehicle. Suicide was out of the question.

—probably an unpaid debt involved, and sending a message. To whom? Personal, private or business payback? Other family?

The Chief Superintendent posited that the killings were most likely connected with the Carry-On business and the products they transported. There was no known police information in that area but plenty of rumours. As an aside, he asked if the premises and in particular the office of Carry-On had been locked down. If not, he ordered that should be done—now! And a police guard put on it. What about the twins' home premises? Freeze their bedrooms at home.

More contributions followed, including the pathologist's report which said there was no obvious indicator of drug use by either of the victims. Still, drugs were always a possible connection. Any known internal family rivalries or tensions? What about the wider range of relatives?

To add fuel to the fire, the Super added the news about the missing Kenworth semi-trailer as now reported from Bendigo Police Station.

9

Family Summit

Almost simultaneously, Alessandro had called a family meeting at home in Tylden.

In attendance were Corina, Dominic and his wife Maureen, Bria, and Alessandro's closest and best friend almost from childhood, Daniel Russo, who also happened to be a highly qualified barrister who had guided the family through all of its early days. The only other non-family member in attendance was Roy Sinclair, who was the Moretti Group Operations and Administration Manager, long-time friend of Dominic and, in reality, the top executive.

This was the biggest crisis the family had ever faced, was how Alessandro greeted everyone. Almost as they met, the news arrived about the 'stolen or lost and damaged' Kenworth rig. The Bendigo police sent full details to the Gisborne incident room and that had filtered on to Daniel Russo.

Alessandro invited Daniel to lead the discussion. His first question to all was, "OK, exactly what do we know?"

Responses were hesitant and incomplete. It was clear that Luca and Giovanni had been murdered in a professionally orchestrated, precisely detailed killing, clearly intended to send a message.

Alessandro posed the obvious question, "What's this all about?"

Daniel suggested, "The boys must have really upset someone bigtime?"

Questions galore followed. They indicated a lack of knowledge about both the personal activities of Luca and Giovanni, even though the brothers still resided at home, and their commercial involvements in Carry-On. There was a huge disconnect among the family.

Was any part of the 'message' meant for other members of the Moretti family? Russo's opinion was, "Probably not, as no contact has been made. Is that right?" he asked as he looked around at everyone and received no response, indicating absolutely nil.

Alessandro now took over with the clear intent of closing ranks and protecting the reputation and integrity of the family.

Dominic said, "Maybe it's a good time to ask if any of us have the remotest idea of any activities that we are involved in that could have us connected to such an evil outcome"?

Roy Sinclair volunteered that on a few rare occasions, and now months ago, Carry-On had been used to do some work when a Moretti van had been out of action. All completely legitimate and paid for. Bria, slightly embarrassed, admitted she was in a relationship with her manager at the Ballarat Super Bike Store but there should be no repercussions as they were both single, but he did have a police record. Dominic revealed he knew about the relationship with Cliff Richardson and Alessandro also nodded that he knew, so no need to be embarrassed!

Daniel asked if the police had yet asked to inspect the boys' bedrooms? In a low voice, and with accompanying body language, Alessandro replied no, and then broached several sensitive subjects. Firstly, should the family be pursuing positive steps for retaliation or revenge? Did anyone have ideas or theories on who were the perpetrators? Nothing from anyone. Any suggestions that there may be more outstanding debts as yet to be called up? Alessandro was suspicious that it may be drug runners who were unpaid.

Secondly, should they let 'sleeping dogs' lie and simply let justice take its course, as the behaviour of the twins over many years had been embarrassing?

Finally, how co-operative with the police should they be? Totally, it was agreed, and that Daniel Russo should be volunteered as their representative. It was also agreed that Alessandro should visit Carry-On to appoint Roy Sinclair as interim manager.

It was agreed that their communications would be kept open and confidential, and they would await and welcome police contact.

10

Back to Basics

Back at the incident room in Gisborne, Chief Super Ron Brunton was in full flight. What, when, where, why, how? Motives, beneficiaries or losers? Revenge seekers? He wanted—in a big hurry—all telephone records and any other messages to or from Luca or Giovanni over the past month. From anywhere, on any telephone. A request was put in to their telephone providers, as their mobile phones were missing. All fax, email, text or written documents available to or from Carry-On and Luca and Giovanni were also requested.

What stock, from whom and for whom, was the missing semi-trailer carrying? Were there any records—invoices, delivery notes or receipts—in existence? What had happened to the driver? Who were the known associates, business partners, and customers—legal or otherwise—of the business and the owners?

These enquiries revealed little other than the fact that much of the business was informal and most details were unrecorded.

Some answers were obvious and easy from the beginning. The two victims had been killed in similar ways, and with the same mutilation of hands. They had not been killed where they were discovered. They were killed within a similar time frame so it was reasonable to assume probably at the same physical location. Totally unknown was the motive; though in both cases it was probably revenge for an unpaid debt and to give a message to others.

With this summary, Chief Brunton looked around and asked, "Any advance on these points?"

A lot of thought was given to the Chief's report before finally Jack Jackson offered, "A very dramatic way to make a point, so it's reasonable to assume whatever was outstanding was, in the eyes of the perpetrators, very significant, and unrecoverable."

That was agreed.

Random thoughts were bounced around. Was the sale of illegal products such as cigarettes and drugs involved? Was that how the semi-trailer got involved? How would the brothers be enticed to a suitable remote location to be threatened? Was it remote, and were they threatened? Phone records would be really important.

Was it a professional hit by a non-involved third party? Was it gang-related over turf? More remotely, were there any personal jealousies, family vendettas, history of previous financial rescues? Any known mental illnesses close to home?

Dozens of questions with few known answers! Jobs were allocated to Sergeant Matthew Simpson, and his Senior Constable Ian Ingram was given the urgent task of descending on the premises of Carry-On in the industrial estate in Gisborne. He was to freeze everything then delve into every corner of the business. He was to closely question the two staff members and also all neighbouring businesses, including the local café proprietor, and even the postie!

DS Linda Alexander was given the family connection to investigate, with assistance from Sergeant Jackson and also Constable Beth Jenkins when more appropriate. The very first telephone call Linda made was to Bria Moretti at the Ballarat Super Bike Store, with a request to meet there and to also include the manager, Cliff Richardson. That was arranged for the next day, and she took Beth in full police uniform with her. This was a fact-finding mission.

Bria had an attractive office looking down over the main retail area which held a spectacular array of modern and expensive bikes and accessories. Strategically placed displays added to an attractive store with appropriate background music. Linda and Beth were given a genuinely warm welcome by Bria with introductions. Cliff Richardson almost immediately joined them with equally warm greetings. Coffee and biscuits followed to help the informality of the catchup for Linda, Beth and Cliff.

Linda recalled Cliff from a police encounter in Ballarat a few years before. He was still a big man, now well-groomed and attired in smart casual dress, who had an engaging personality and all the confidence and charm of a nearly thirty-year-old successful businessman. Linda had done her homework on the relationship between Bria and Cliff and could understand how they would be attracted to one another.

The police officers expressed deep sympathy to Bria Moretti over the tragic loss of her brothers. They included Cliff in their condolences even though they were aware he had had almost no interaction with the twins. Pleasantries continued for a while and then Bria said, "Let's cut to the chase, please". It was helpful when she added, "You know, there was no love lost between the family and Luca and Giovanni. They were a nuisance and an embarrassment."

Linda by now felt brave enough to ask, "Do you think they were embarrassing enough to have to be removed"? That provoked an instant response of, "Wow! Wait a moment! I definitely did not mean any such likelihood!"

Linda hastily added, "No personal implication was intended, but I am aware that Cliff's known history and police connection has been raised in prior police discussions."

That sent a shockwave through the meeting, and although Cliff remained calm, Bria was outraged. Beth had to use her best reconciling skills to get the meeting back onto the track intended.

Linda's intent had been to ask Cliff for some help or guidance about motorbike gangs. In particular, did he have any information about the 'Bendigo Bandits' or perhaps, drawing a much longer bow, the 'Infidels'. He responded that the Bandits had a softer reputation, members including middle-aged executive types on their Harleys, while the Infidels were a serious gang of a hard and sometimes vicious mould, made up of ex-military types and dropouts who sometimes were involved in debt collection and protection activities. She also asked about any leads on how to infiltrate.

The meeting now back to a more even, harmonious atmosphere, Bria and Cliff wanted to help but were unclear how. The police officers, choosing their words with great care, asked if they thought it possible that anyone in the larger Moretti family or business could have commissioned such a terrible act? Bria and Cliff both gave the question the serious time and concentration it deserved and then separately and emphatically responded, "No".

More relaxed, the conversation proceeded into personal enquiries and updates particularly about Ballarat history, friends and associates. Naturally they progressed on to inquiring about Cliff's close friend Glen Robertson, who had been a fellow suspect in a double death and fire in Ballarat a few years ago. Cliff and Glen were still sharing accommodation in a house owned by Glen Robertson, who had quietly increased his real estate portfolio in and around Ballarat, and their friendship had survived the changes. Glen had encouraged and supported the return to education and acquisition of knowledge and degrees that helped Cliff to become the well-respected manager of the Moretti's new Super Bike Store.

Beth had researched some of this information and knew that Cliff had purchased a very nice Harley-Davidson Road King bike over a year ago, and he and Bria used it regularly for 'escape' time. Cliff had joined a motorcycle group but had not found it to be particularly enjoyable. He occasionally joined up with Glen Robertson for longer and more adventurous rides. It did appear that some of the 'big four' bikie gangs tried to infiltrate the milder groups for potential members, drugs, and for associations with tattoo shops.

Through their Ballarat Super Bike Shop, Bria and Cliff knew several of their customers who were active in the local Champions motorcycle club which, with its preponderance of over-forties, was often referred to as the 'Old Men's Club'. Their tongue in cheek motto: "Planning, growing old, disgracefully".

This background encouraged Beth to venture further into the murders of Luca and Giovanni. She carefully checked with Bria that she was not outwearing her welcome when delving into such a family tragedy. Bria assured her that solving of the murders was a high priority for the whole family (and which clearly included Cliff).

Linda put forward one of the theories—that there had been unpaid debts and intrusions into other people's turf re freight forwarding of illegal products interstate and even from overseas. Bria reacted with real surprise and said, "You no doubt know the boys were quite an embarrassment to the traditional family culture, and had been since they were kids. But I'd be amazed if they were up to those tricks!"

Beth said, "Extreme behaviour can create extreme reactions."

The most extreme of the local outlaw gangs, apart from some loose cannons among the other gangs, would seem to be both the Gypsy Jokers (the WA chapter of which was famous for the murder of Detective Don Hancock a couple of decades before), and the Veterans MC, with military veterans among its members.

Linda asked, "Are any members of such outlaw clubs known to you?"

As anticipated the answer was no. She then asked them, "Could you, would you, please put your ears to the ground for the remote possibility of any information that might help. We need to catch the killers!"

On that sombre note the meeting broke up with action expected by everyone.

11

Continuing Grind

Back at the station some immediate issues were raised.

What had happened to the missing driver of the undamaged semi tractor? Who was he? Had the twins left any formal wills or instructions about their finances? Were all company records and finances up to date, especially regarding their employees? Should immediate enquiries be made into school years at Salesian College, checking out close friends or known rivalries? Was there any history of bullying? A check to be carried out on their non-productive days during the so-called 'wasted year' at university.

Members of the investigating team were sent to Carry-On for onsite questioning. The two administration staff members were careful and hesitant with their answers. They clearly knew some of the company activities were dicey, if not straight out illegal. They hid responsibility as best they could by insisting little was delegated to them and there was a part-time accountant who handled most financial matters, including their wages. The accountant was a sixty-year-old widow called Renee Noble, who was a long-term Macedon resident who seemed to know just about everything and anything and who the twins relied on to resolve most problems. She was their 'Ms Fix It'.

Renee Noble was invited urgently to a meeting at Carry-On, where she told them that the missing driver's name was John Fraser;

he was on the payroll and he had been employed by Giovanni two months previously. His credentials had appeared genuine, and she produced his given address. The police follow-up indicated this was a false address and probably a false name as well.

Renee was known in the Macedon Ranges neighbourhood as a bit of a busybody, but with no known misdemeanours to her name. When asked about the financial position of Carry-On and whether either of the brothers had a will, she became very nervous. "Definitely no wills, as they did little or no financial planning, and no comment on the business position!" she answered. This was much too evasive for Sergeant Matthew Simpson and Constable Ian Ingram from Gisborne Station; they could see she knew more. Their subtle and not-too-subtle questioning finally elicited the answer that Renee was aware that tens of thousands of dollars was outstanding in debts, and the twins had been in a panic as to how they would pay it. However, she was unaware of details. Or was she?

To put more pressure on Renee, the two officers transported her to the Gisborne Police Station for a formal interview, where she was informed that everything was to be recorded for official purposes.

Sergeant Simpson and Constable Ingram conducted the interview and stressed the need for truth and co-operation. They told her they were aware that there were two parts of the business; legal and illegal. They wanted to clarify how much she was involved. Their first question related to the missing driver John Fraser.

Her response was, "I really didn't like him. He was a sleaze, and he was always 'distant' from us. He seemed to have a special relationship with Giovanni and although he was on the payroll, it seemed he was receiving special cash payments on the side." She hastily added that neither she nor other staff ever received cash, even though Luca and Giovanni always seemed to be carrying large amounts.

When asked for details of the stock that was transported on the semi-trailer, she was not very clear. When it was first commissioned one of the brothers usually drove it as they were very proud of it.

Renee could recall the first large load carried to and from Adelaide for a large supermarket chain, and the associated PR that Carry-On got from the deal.

However, she recalled that Luca had been quick to comment after all the invoices were processed, "Nice idea but a bloody loss—we can't afford that too often!"

Carry-On's big truck and the two vans had regular work which was processed through the company in a normal commercial manner. The glamor of driving the big Kenworth covered with attractive logo and paintwork had declined for the twins, and that had been the trigger to employ a specialist driver, Renee thought. The business's morphing into more unofficial 'cash jobs' to fewer routine destinations was developing. Renee offered the opinion that the driver John Fraser may have been 'offered' to Giovanni or Luca as someone 'who knew the ropes.' She repeated she had not liked him. She said the other two members of staff were basically honest but could on occasion look the other way for a small reward.

Back to the most important questions that Sergeant Simpson wanted answered, "What stock was involved in the last trip, and who was the buyer?" And then "And who was the seller? Where was it coming from and where was it going?"

Renee wanted her answer to be off the record, or clearly given only as an opinion. That was agreed. Her answer was, "Almost certainly coming from South Australia or even over the border from West Australia. It was most probably cigarettes, stolen electronics, maybe some drugs. Totally illegal." Renee emphasised that she had become very stressed by her growing concerns about what was going on!

With further prompting she added, "I think the two Mr Morettis have got themselves deep in trouble because in the last few weeks they have been searching desperately for cash resources. Maybe within the family?"

Both policemen reacted with, "What the hell does that mean?" and she quickly backtracked, withdrawing the implication by a full denial.

"Ms Noble," said Matthew, "our most important priority is to identify the buyer and the seller of the missing load." With heavy emphasis they asked her for further help. She offered that she had occasionally overheard snippets of telephone conversations, always a male, and with a European-type accent. It had appeared to her that there were sometimes raised voices, and threats.

Asked if any such person had visited Carry-On, she replied, "Not as far as I know."

As soon as the two policemen had reported on their interview to the Chief Superintendent, he instructed Linda and Beth to reconvene a meeting at Carry-On premises to include the two administration staff members and Renee Noble. That was arranged for morning tea the next day, with instructions, 'Softly, softly… what was the cargo?"

Everyone arrived on time and the office seemed deserted, quiet and inactive. The policewomen brought coffee, biscuits and juice and began softly and slowly. Linda completed all the pleasantries with the added message from her boss ringing in her ears, "Strike while the iron is hot!"

The two police officers appeared to be quite different but worked well together. Constable Beth Jenkins was neat in her immaculate police uniform—two-stripe status clear to see—with her blonde hair pulled back firmly into a ponytail and police cap correctly placed. She wore regulation dark stockings and well-polished black brogues. Detective Sergeant Linda Alexander was casually dressed in a neat, fitted beige skirt, a light orange long-sleeved blouse, casual jacket and stylish low-heeled cream fashion shoes. Her long blonde hair was also drawn sharply back into a ponytail, and adorned with a bright green ribbon.

They chatted with the staff about how and if the business could be continued, and the likelihood of an administrator being appointed. Linda wanted to explore any unusual happenings or behaviour in the last few weeks. They were clearly trying to establish empathy and whilst they were talking in generalities it was easy to seek opinions.

Linda asked, "Was morale good?" "Did staff feel as if they were part of a 'team'?" A resounding no to that!

Beth asked if they were aware that the semi-trailer had been found in two pieces in two different locations and that the trailer had been burnt out? Another resounding no.

Linda then asked the next question, "Any ideas about John Fraser, and any part he may have played?" All the staff members could offer was a dislike for the driver and that he had never fraternised with them. They really couldn't give a damn about him.

Bringing attention back to Luca and Giovanni, Linda suggested that they were probably part of a syndicate involved in moving illicit products. One of the clerks agreed that may have been possible, and the others nodded. They went on to agree with each other that the 'boys' were loud-mouthed braggarts who spoke at high volume to impress how big and bold they were. No discretion or respect for the other staff.

Linda took the opportunity to ask, from conversations they had heard, "What products do you think they were carrying for the unofficial customers?" A surprisingly direct answer came back: "Almost certainly tobacco, cigarettes, and whisky."

When Linda asked, "How do you know?" "Because we could smell it!" was the response. The staff offered no real suggestion of close associations with outlaw motorbike gang members.

Beth took over and more directly asked Renee for a comment about Luca and Giovanni apparently raising their voices on the phone and appearing to be stressed and pressured over unpaid debts. Renee was reticent to confirm that she had had knowledge of urgent steps being taken to find cash to settle outstanding debts.

One of the clerks confirmed that from snippets he had heard, there was a serious crisis. Putting together what he had overheard, he thought the problem was very big. When the truck went missing there was an urgent check on insurance, but much more serious was the payment due for the stock on the truck. It seemed the ultimate recipient had paid upfront for half of the consignment in cash, but most of that had already been spent by the twins. The load picked up in the semi-trailer was immediately due for payment to Carry-On, but of course had disappeared with the driver or been burnt.

Much of this was supposition but seemed to highlight the problem.

12

12 Burning Leaves

On the strength of preliminary evidence, the Chief Superintendent instructed Constable Ian Ingram to research illicit tobacco trading. The first surprise Ian received was how big the trade was and how seriously the government viewed it. The Taxation Administration Act 1953 and the Criminal code Act 1995, following on from the old Excise Act 1901, were used to prohibit the unlicensed production of tobacco plants and the manufacture of tobacco products. An excise licence was required and there were no licensed growers. Breaches were viewed as serious tax crimes and organised criminal groups were involved

The growing of tobacco plants in various parts of Australia was not difficult because of the country's size and varied microclimates. Hundreds of tonnes were grown and processed into cigarettes, cigars and loose tobacco (chop-chop). The criminals associated with illicit tobacco had lavish lifestyles and combined their activities into wider criminal enterprises. The huge loss of revenue involved encouraged government departments federal and state to disrupt, dismantle, and prosecute those involved. Harvest time was usually November and May, and unsuspecting owners of remote and/or little-used properties did not suspect that the land they leased out was used for illicit crops.

Illicit products require illicit users or retailers. 'Under-the-counter' sales were made and 'butt legging'—or interstate bootlegging

—was common. Chop-chop was usually packaged in small plastic bags with other dried and processed leaves, rolled and pressed into tubes and sold as cigarettes. Rudimentary manufacturing! The criminal syndicates were also usually involved in circumvention of taxes through sophisticated exports and imports of tobacco in its various forms and 'counterfeit' cigarettes from as far away as China. Sometimes it was as simple as buying the last of an over-run of a well-established legal brand and rebranding it with cheap printing and packaging. It was difficult to tell the counterfeit from the genuine in quality or presentation, and difficult for authorities to identify.

Illicit tobacco trading cost the government millions in lost taxes and in the negative community health implications. Huge national and international criminal syndicates—even into terrorist groups—motivated by easy money and greed and determined to maintain or even grow their power bases were behind the industry.

The tobacco summary presented by Senior Constable Ingram was very informative and gave the group a new perspective on the possible immense size and value of what Luca and Giovanni had stumbled into.

13

Incident Room Summary

An updated forensic pathology report confirmed there was no dispute about how the two men had been killed and that they had not been killed where they were found. It was not yet confirmed if they were killed by the same gun. Also not yet confirmed was whether the mud on their clothing was the same type. No information as to the likely murder location, or methods of transportation. There was only speculation about what may have been used to carry out the digit amputation, except it was clear that the job had been very rough, and possibly done by the same person. The perpetrator or perpetrators apparently knew that Luca was left-handed and Giovanni right-handed, to add emphasis to the apparent message.

In an effort to narrow down possibilities as to who the prime suspects could be, there was consensus that the following groupings were unlikely candidates to have initiated the murders: former fellow students at Salesian or university, workers associated with Carry-On's legal endeavours, or social friends. The costs of such meticulous planning as was evident and violent actions would be so high that the involvement of most local and casual small criminals was deemed unlikely.

So back to establishing a list of prime suspects, local or imported. Jack Jackson led the discussion in the absence of the Superintendent. His approach was less formal but equally inquisitive. In his quite friendly way, he stressed that he expected everyone to dig harder—be more curious, more assiduous, even more intrigued than they had been already. He did not want to hear anyone saying "I didn't like to seem aggressive."

"We have two cold-blooded killings right here in our neighbourhood, in a respected family, with understandable complications and repercussions. It is apparent the victims had accrued huge debts by our standards that triggered this unimaginable retaliation. Sorry about the big words," he added, tongue firmly in cheek, "but I'm trying to summarise the situation."

Every one nodded in agreement. In a moment or two Sergeant Jackson carried on in his easy style.

"It seems the illicit products were tobacco, alcohol and drugs. Unknown; could well be a syndicate of criminals, money lenders and gamblers, gang members, motorbike groups, or of as yet unknown heritage. To date no one has been identified. I'll take a breath and welcome input!"

There were a lot of concentrated and concerned faces looking at Sergeant Jackson.

The first hand up was from DS Linda Alexander. "Historically a high percent of aggressive personal murders are carried out or planned by members of the family. Are you excluding them from your 'potentials'?" she asked.

In his comfortable and laconic fashion with a smile on his face, the Sergeant replied, "I thought you might ask that very sensible question, Linda, and recalling some of my meetings over many years with Corina Moretti, when she was defending or excusing bad behaviour by Luca or Giovanni, singularly or jointly, I can imagine her protection, defence or aggression in defending her children could be extreme! No, I'm not excluding any family member at this point in time, and let's look and listen, but concentrate on the most likely which seems to be a professional hit for outstanding debts of some kind." That received general agreement.

Jackson was a career police officer who had worked hard to earn the respect in which he was held by the force, the community, family and friends alike. Now in his mid-forties, he was calm and resolute and knew how to bind together a team that wanted to succeed. He had early on recognised the talent, drive and intelligence that motivated Linda. In his own thoughtful way, he was determined to give her every opportunity to utilise her skills.

He asked for opinions on the most likely areas for concentration on the basis of, "Now! Now!" The four most urgent targets the team agreed on, and who would concentrate on them, were:

No 1. What was the cargo in the truck? Where is the driver, John Fraser?

The consensus of opinion was that Fraser was likely in South Australia. He had a police record, was aged about thirty, was perhaps a hardened crook, and was an efficient driver used to long hauls. Sergeant Jackson and Constable Ingham to pursue.

No 2. Who supplied the stock and to whom was it being delivered? Telephone tracing and message interception was paramount. Constable Beth Jenkins was to concentrate on this and recruit help from within Gisborne Station or wider if possible. Central Police to enquire undercover on tobacco, alcohol, and low-level drugs, e.g., marijuana. Someone must be hurting!

No 3. Where were the victims killed, and how were they lured there? What vehicles were used? A van or similar must have been used to pick up and/or deliver the bodies, and that must surely be in the Macedon Ranges area. If there was a driver or assistant involved —not the murderer—they must by now realise the magnitude of the offence. More telephone tracking, seek further opinion from forensics and pursue public observations of odd vehicle behaviour. DS Linda Alexander to concentrate on this.

No 4. Seriously big money seemed to be involved and the classic line of 'follow the money' was classic for a reason. Easily earned money usually meant wildly spent money. This would involve a request to

Police Headquarters to crank up their undercover assistance into casino attendance and gambling, and to keep an ear out for any information heard 'underground'.

Sergeant Jackson went on to emphasise with solemnity, "How do we get the murders into perspective? We are dealing with 'real heavies' who will stop at nothing to make their point, including the cynical and brutal removal of body parts, so be mindful that these are serious, vicious criminals, and be very careful." He stressed that the area of activity was narrow and the smallest lead could be critical. "Let's make sure we don't miss it," he added as he closed the meeting and added "good hunting!"

14

Forging Friendship

As the meeting concluded around 6pm, Linda took the rare spare moment to ask Beth if she would like to join her for a coffee or a glass of wine at the nearby Majestic Hotel. The offer was gladly accepted. Quickly and easily over a glass of shiraz they got up to date. On ordering a second drink they decided to have a pub meal and chat on as they enjoyed one another's company.

Linda related how male-dominated the detective area of Police Command was, and said that as her rank had advanced some officers almost choked on addressing her as Sergeant, or having to give her due respect. She admitted that she dressed and groomed herself in a conservative manner so as not to invite sexist comments from either in or outside the force.

She added that her relationship with Jeremy, who Beth had met, was not perfect, as he could not or would not see her as other than a policewoman and as his best friend's sister. He was not really a passionate lover and she did not see him as a long-term partner, which was what she was beginning to want.

Beth responded, "Lindy, I have one of those, but to be truthful I'm not ready or wanting to settle down yet to family and kids. I want to further my career in the police force."

Linda went on to remind Beth that her upbringing in South Africa had been narrow and closely protected through a single-sex high school, and after that she had been seen as a 'prissy superior kid' attending university from home. No wild high jinks or random sex in her life! Indeed, she confided, she was very inexperienced when the family moved to Australia.

That led the conversation onto, with more relaxation, expounding on 'men's attitudes' and how most men only had one thing on their minds. They laughed and giggled over reminiscences as they relaxed together as trusted friends. Linda expanded on her experience as a lowly constable in Perth indulging in sexual groping and penetration in the impossibly restricted space of a police car with her then lover, who was a married senior constable of Indian heritage.

That got a gasp or two from Beth who added to the 'true confessions' with her tale, "It's a long time ago and our group then thought we were so sophisticated and thus prepared to 'have a go' at most endeavours. This night was planned to be wild and the house where the party was being held was very dimly lit, so we almost had to feel our way in and then creep from room to room. As I slid into one room, I could hear noise from a corner accompanied by ugly grunting and feminine gasping. I had a pretty good idea what was happening. In the half-light I saw a girl I recognised bent forward over the back of a lounge chair with her dress held up around her chest, and a young guy with his trousers down around his feet, banging away with energetic freedom from the back! He was thrusting away and she was very much enjoying it. I kept watching, fascinated, as I hadn't previously contemplated such a position!"

Beth looked closely at Linda to watch for a reaction. Linda had now had years in police work and suggested that on another occasion she would offer better early experience!

Promotional opportunities within the police were covered in a more serious discussion just before they agreed it was time to go home. Linda dropped in her favourite aphorism, the Yiddish proverb, 'The girl who can't dance says the band can't play.' Adding that had applied to her and had been helpful!

On a professional note, Beth added that her intuition strongly told her that one or both of the clerks at Carry-On must know of some dicey van owners or drivers who could suggest a rogue or two. Apply pressure tomorrow! Off they went, both to sleep well, as they had enjoyed renewing the friendship and the confidentiality that had developed between them.

15

Progress

Next morning over coffee the Superintendent had quite a bounce to his step as he announced, "A breakthrough!" An apparent spokesperson for the Rebels motorbike gang had claimed overnight that they had carried out the killings on behalf of a Hong Kong millionaire. Great excitement for an hour or two until Police Central from within their own resources and underground contacts, came back with a denial. It was absolute BS and not worth tracking down.

Linda and Beth sought approval to vigorously pursue their intuition about Carry-On's clerical staff, and separately to seek more information from motorbike members, on the basis the gangs did not welcome pressure. Two actions followed promptly. Beth telephoned Cliff Richardson and asked for his help in directing her to any member of the 'old men's' Champions Club, or any other motorbike club, who could refer her to someone who at least could confirm no involvement of a motorbike club. Of particular interest were Beggars of Bendigo who had a reputation for helping the underprivileged and were more sympathetic to eliminating mindless violence.

Linda arranged a meeting at Carry-On in two hours' time to indicate the urgency and add pressure. She and Beth worked well together; they had become like a well-oiled machine.

After their arrival, Linda indicated the meeting was being recorded and then set the atmosphere with a quote from Schopenhauer, "It is only cold-blooded animals whose bite is poisonous," and then they got into full attack mode. Only the two clerks were at the meeting, so close proximity was possible. One of them asked why Renee Noble was not included and was informed, "We don't think she has any useful information, while we think you do!" The clerks both seemed to shrink back into their seats.

Linda looked forcefully right into their faces and said, "Today we want to find out who is a regular visitor to these premises driving a panel van, who comes and goes at odd times doing odd jobs for one or both of the boys. The driver may even have a key to the gate."

That genuinely did not seem to ring a bell with the staff. Beth tried to stimulate an answer by asking what vehicle had been driven by the unlikeable driver John Fraser. They thought probably a Toyota Corolla. That then sparked a memory about a similarly unlikeable and uncouth 'friend' of Giovanni's who did call in occasionally for no apparent reason, always driving a large black Range Rover SUV. Their best description was, "Tall and a big build, usually dressed in black, fashionable stubble—an arrogant prick! We think he lives somewhere near Hanging Rock."

"He's a show-off," said one, "and we both thought he was always trying to belittle us."

Not much more was forthcoming except that this man was always alone and was either coming or going to 'have coffee with some associate' as he informed everyone in a loud voice. The police officers hurried back to the station to get searches underway.

The response that had filtered back through pressure being applied to the motorbike gangs was very interesting. In its mildest form, with many colourful adjectives deleted, it was along the lines of, "Back off pigs, we are not involved in your little problem; get off our backs. Perhaps you should look closer to home at the local Mafia— maybe there's an affiliation with a family member."

The pressure was mounting in every area and direction. The three local newspapers were adding to the public awareness and concentration that the police were asking for to help identify unusual activities. Quite coincidentally, a young university student, Gordon, (who had graduated from his old farm bike to a newish road motorbike), was using it not only to get to the local railway station, but also to try it out around his local roads. These roads were anywhere from Woodend to Lancefield and even Romsey. The motorbike was fun and the roads were not busy, and being local he observed changes. Gordon had mentioned to his parents that many months ago a big farm shed had been erected on a property close to the Hanging Rock Reserve Park and Tennis Club. He often went for a burn early in the morning or at twilight as that suited his study regime. His parents respected his common sense and riding skills and did not worry.

Over breakfast one morning Gordon said, "You know I mentioned that huge big shed going up near Hanging Rock about a year ago? Well, that bloke now drives a big Range Rover Sport and I often see him parked by the tennis club! He drives very fast!"

Gordon's father had seen an article about the double murder in the Kyneton Advertiser newspaper and decided to ring the Woodend police station. They referred his call to Gisborne, where he was transferred to Sergeant Jack Jackson. The caller being a local resident of many years, and his son Gordon having been coached by Sgt Jackson at the local Hawks AFL club, Jackson felt there was no doubt about the veracity of the information. He looked into the office occupied by his Superintendent, saw it was clear and walked in to explain the phone call, its significance and his plan to go and look.

"Sir, I think we may be onto a break! Firstly, DS Alexander and Constable Jenkins have sprung information about a shady visitor to Carry-On and we have just received information about a perhaps equally shady local from around the back of Woodend, who may be one and the same person."

He went on to summarise the details and Chief Super Ron Brunton urged him, "Go for it, Jack, with all the usual care not to frighten the 'natives'—and you'd better take Linda with you."

Sergeant Jackson replied, "I was just going to suggest that!" accompanied with a smile.

16

The Big Shed

The two police officers arrived in an unmarked car to meet Gordon and his father to seek additional information. The father admitted he knew absolutely nothing about the shed's owner, not even a whisper of rumour or comment from members of local clubs. Gordon could offer no useful information to identify what the man looked like, but did add that he was usually alone, as if waiting for someone. Vary rarely, he had seen a second person in the car—he thought it was usually a man because of the size of the figure. Gordon thought he probably had been seeing him off and on for six months.

Linda said, "I have to ask, you don't think they were lovers having it off?"

Gordon laughed and said, "There was no rocking or rolling!"

Sergeant Jackson suggested they all go for a 'drive past' as anonymously as possible and asked for more information from Gordon as they drove. There was nothing remarkable about the property. Well preserved brick and tile house set back from the road with a double garage and a shed close by, typically used for hay, tractor, and farm equipment. Further back along the extended driveway was the remarked upon new 'Big Shed.' It looked like it was straight from a magazine, with a peaked gable roofline and double doors, all in a dark muted grey tone. By very rough dimensions it looked about 16 by 12 metres minimum, and very smart. Electricity was clearly connected.

The property appeared at the moment uninhabited.

They drove by at normal speed while Jack noted the address to follow up, just off South Rock Road, did a U-turn and went back a little more slowly. Further along the road he stopped and called into the nearest farm to enquire if anyone had met or knew the neighbour. No help there, so they dropped Gordon and his father home, asking them to keep the enquiry quiet.

Back to the station and urgent enquiries to establish the owner and full details of the property, purchases and recent additions. Immediate surreptitious surveillance was sought on the property. A plan was formulated to keep observation on the property 24/7 and to make a raid and arrest if appropriate. Urgency and excitement percolated through the taskforce.

The incident room looked alive and energetic and maps appeared of local roads and suburbs - in particular, the area surrounding Hanging Rock. The road from Woodend to Lancefield through Newham and all of the small farm byroads were highlighted. Jack visited the General Store and Post Office in Newham. This store, on the corner of three local roads, was undoubtedly the centre of the local community, and it was less than five minutes from the premises under surveillance. The store was almost next door to an acclaimed winery and less than five minutes from the famous Hanging Rock Racecourse. A busy corner spot used by locals to meet over coffee and purchase household goods and alcohol.

Sergeant Jackson asked the proprietor of the General Store to respect the confidentiality of his questions about the 'owner' of the address under enquiry. "This is a very low-key request for information about the resident at 'Lane X', as we assume he shops here and collects his mail?" he asked. Proprietor Mr Naylor answered in a most helpful manner, "Yes, but we hardly know him as he is an infrequent customer."

He was a little surprised when the Sergeant then asked, "Can you tell us his name?" Helpfully again he responded, "I think that would be Kenneth Wiltshire, as registered mail does come for him and I believe he has been trying to enrol his daughter at Braemar College up the hill. He drives a big black Range Rover Sport."

More information than Jack could have wished for and he answered, "Many thanks indeed!" Then he added, almost as a joke "Anything else you can tell me?" Mr Naylor with a smile volunteered, "Well, he is a Brit of some description."

In a hurry to get back to the office, Jack took his leave and headed back to the police station so they could urgently get underway with the new information. What a feast that had provided!

Enquiries told them that Ken Wiltshire was his real name, he was only slightly known to the police as a 'fringe crook', originally from Yorkshire, who had become an Australian citizen twenty-plus years ago. He was around forty years old and separated or divorced from his wife, the mother of their fourteen-year-old daughter. He was known to frequent the casino, horse racing (both gallops and trots) and mix with some 'sharp' associates. No history of violence, but could he be involved in money laundering?

The property at Hanging Rock was registered in the name of Kenneth Wiltshire with no mortgage details. The purchase had been settled a year previously. His description as tall with black hair and facial stubble corresponded with the description from the staff at Carry-On. The phone data results were slowly coming in and showed that Wiltshire had telephoned Luca or Giovanni at Carry-On but only very rarely. There was now immense pressure to try to connect other telephones to any phone used by Wiltshire. The mobiles used by Luca and Giovanni were concluded to have been destroyed.

As soon as Ken Wiltshire stepped onto his Hanging Rock property, police in the Homicide Squad were alerted and they swung into gear. A 6am raid was planned and, as would be expected under the guidance of Ron Brunton, it all was carried out with efficiency, with a low-key perfect result.

The main protagonists were Sergeant Jackson and Detective

Alexander, supported by three uniformed constables. It went well as Wiltshire was in his bed in his pyjamas, and unaccompanied, as they swooped. He was read his rights, arrested and eventually taken to the holding facility at Gisborne Police Station. The 'seize and freeze' rule was applied with particular emphasis on telecommunications equipment, and on his one mobile phone in particular, to trace his regular contacts, and on the Range Rover for possible blood or other evidence. The Range Rover was immediately taken off to Forensic for minute inspection. Wiltshire willingly gave up the car keys with a surprisingly relaxed expression on his face. Beth muttered behind her hand to Linda that he looked like a pirate with his thin moustache and pointed beard starting to form through his stubble. By the time he was dressed in his usual dark clothes he looked even more like a caricature of a criminal.

When Sergeant Jackson politely asked for the keys to the garage shed and also the big new farm shed, Wiltshire's response was less relaxed.

"The garage shed is unlocked and the farm shed is not mine so I do not have keys or access!"

Jackson was no mood to be fooled around with and he angrily retorted, "Now listen up, Mr Wiltshire, cut out the rubbish; we know the property is in your name and with or without the keys, you are going to witness us in one way or another entering that bloody shed!"

Everyone present was in awe watching their Senior Sergeant in full action as he added, "And take that smug look off your face. This is a double murder case and we don't have the time to be tolerant."

Wiltshire quickly became more amenable then explained how he saw his position, "I think I can find keys for the shed, and maybe the keys for Luca's Toyota are in it." There were some surprised looks amongst the police standing by as he went on, "The shed is not mine —in fact I'm not a bit worried, as I'm really just referred to as 'Mr Middle Man'.

Linda couldn't resist throwing in, "That lame excuse won't

absolve you from any responsibility, so you had better increase your co-operation while you have the chance!"

Wiltshire rummaged around in a cupboard and finally exclaimed, "Ah, here they are," and led them off to the big shed, where he easily opened the well-oiled doors and switched on the lights. Sergeant Jackson and DS Alexander and the team all mentally exclaimed, "Oh my god, it's an Aladdin's cave".

Stacked in orderly fashion were hundreds, even thousands, of packets of cigarettes and tobacco, and in separate areas, alcohol of all types and labels. Woodend Police were aware that large amounts of marijuana were being grown in the area (fixed wing heat-detecting aircraft had detected it previously) and had wondered about distribution methods. Here was some of the dried stock!

Well down the back of the shed was the Toyota panel van that belonged to Carry-On.

In his usual understated manner Jack quipped, "Well, more than we had bargained for!" He immediately phoned Superintendent Brunton to update him and request backup, and to suggest forensic pathology experts should be sent over, as it may be the scene of the crime - or at least the hiding place of an involved vehicle. He was locking down everything until help arrived.

Brunton asked that congratulations be handed on to all involved and said he was looking forward to meeting and interviewing Kenneth Wiltshire. All the wheels of the formidable police force rolled into action.

At Gisborne Police Station, in the specially allocated criminal investigation area towards the rear of the building, the interview rooms with appropriate one-way windows were available. Wiltshire was checked in and prepared for interview.

Superintendent Brunton was in the interview for an opening statement, giving Wiltshire a succinct summary of the evidence police had obtained which obviously implicated him. Brunton underlined the seriousness of the charges Wiltshire faced—including double murder, and elaborated the consequences for Wiltshire if he was found guilty. For clarity, he formally introduced Senior Sergeant Jackson and Detective Sergeant Linda Alexander as the investigating officers and urged Wiltshire to be honest and co-operative for his own good.

As he stood to leave the interview room he said, "You say you are just the middle man, so your best first step is to tell us who 'Mr Big' is!"

Stony silence, not even a blink of the eye, from Wiltshire. Chief Super Brunton left the room.

Linda took up the conversation by outlining how the arrest looked to her; Wiltshire had been identified as a regular visitor to Carry-On premises for confidential meetings with either or both of the murdered men, i.e., Luca and Giovanni Moretti. The company held no record of any formal business transactions with him. Police investigations had confirmed who he was and his financial status. Company telephone records indicated recent calls from him that could now be further confirmed from his mobile phone, which was being further analysed.

Linda added, "From witness statements we've received we know you have used Hanging Rock Park for meetings, and we now believe we can trace your arrangements with the two Moretti men to meet at Hanging Rock to discuss settling a large overdue debt for goods supplied. We know of your use of the south-east shelter in the park for some of your confidential discussions and your regular horse racing and money-laundering activities. It is clearly advisable for you to dismiss any idea of misleading us."

Sgt Jackson followed up with his analysis of the probable scenario.

"We believe you got your instructions to arrange a meeting with the Morettis, as your boss 'Mr Big', was sending his representative to settle the matter. No violence at this stage was suggested. You called in to Carry-On but the Morettis were not there, so you telephoned Luca and made an urgent appointment to meet at the entrance to Hanging Rock."

He went on: "It was not all that convenient for Luca as he had arranged to meet someone at 4pm at the Macedon Railway Hotel and later at 6pm at Keatings Hotel in Woodend. We know he cancelled the Macedon appointment but he advised the Keating Hotel friends he would be a bit late, as he was meeting with Giovanni and two interstate commercial associates at Hanging Rock at 4pm. We believe the twins then travelled together to Hanging Rock, but they did not leave there alive."

Jackson said much more harshly, "Mr Wiltshire, you and your interstate 'friend' killed them!"

Wiltshire leapt to his feet yelling, "Jesus Christ, no bloody way, I didn't kill anyone! I'm not the hit man!"

"Then perhaps now is the best time to tell us exactly how it all happened and who is your Mr Big," suggested Linda in her mildest possible voice.

Still looking defiant, although also somewhat fearful, Wiltshire was reluctant to begin talking until Linda added, "We are well aware of your domestic situation and your undoubted ambition to do the best for your daughter by getting her into Braemar College. But if you want maximum help from us to minimise your very grim position, we suggest again your best move is co-operation."

It was almost as if a light bulb had gone off in his head. Yes, Wiltshire admitted, he was the owner of the property, it had been bought with financial help through a legal firm, and the new shed had been paid for in a similar fashion on the basis it was for the exclusive use of a nominated person. His method of contact was through a convoluted series of text messages and telephone calls always initiated from 'their' end. He had been rewarded with an upgraded status for past services rendered over many years in dishonest activities. He admitted that he had taken a sneak look inside the shed on more than one occasion even though he had been warned against doing that. Yes, he was aware of what was inside and of the nocturnal delivery activities. He felt he was well paid for his use and he still considered himself to be only a middle man.

Sergeant Jackson burst in to the calm description, "Wiltshire, you must be bloody wet behind the ears if you think you can justify your involvement in a double murder in such an innocent and remote fashion! You have carried out instructions from your boss, set up the meeting of all those involved. You clearly have been a participant in the meeting on your premises, which location in our opinion was where the double murder took place."

Kenneth Wiltshire knew he was in deep trouble and his demeanour changed. Sergeant Jackson repeated, "What we want from you is full details of your 'Mr Big'."

Now almost crying and with hysterical jerking body language, Wiltshire pleaded, "I definitely cannot go there, you have seen what they can do! I fear for my life, and they know about my daughter and other family. No! No! I can't and won't go there!"

An earlier recommendation by the police officers that he contact his solicitor—which he had turned down—was now repeated and this time was accepted. The call was listened to but it was only to a local solicitor who had acted for him in the property transactions. Wiltshire insisted, however, that the solicitor make contact with "You know who", for support and guidance. The solicitor clearly caught on and asked to speak to the officer in charge. He indicated he would be coming to the station immediately and to hold any questioning until he was present. He was based in Kyneton, thirty minutes away.

After the arrival of the solicitor, Jack and Linda resumed their enquiries, for a while in a more conciliatory fashion as they pursued information about the fourth person who had been at the meeting.

In essence their questioning was, "Was he the hit man, who was he, and where had he gone?" Wiltshire looked for a nod of approval from the solicitor before responding. In vague terms all he conceded was that one other person had been at the meeting, he had come from Adelaide, he was in charge of the meeting, and he had instructed Wiltshire to invite the brothers to the meeting to discuss settlement of an outstanding debt.

Wiltshire further confirmed he had initially met the twins at the gate to Hanging Rock, and then adjourned with them to the big shed on his property. The atmosphere had been amicable up to arriving at the farm.

Linda then asked, "Well, who is he? What's his name? How do you make contact with him?"

Wiltshire began to answer and was cautioned by the solicitor to be very careful. Undeterred, he said, "The only name I know is Ben. I have only previously spoken to him twice by telephone; he or any of his associates have never left me a contact number, and all contacts are initiated by them." If he ever asked them about making contact himself, the answer was always, "No worries! We will always contact you when necessary and our mobiles are throw-away 'burners' so useless for you to try."

Linda jumped in with a surprise question, "We understand you knew and instructed the Carry-On driver, John Fraser, on what he was to do?" Wiltshire emphatically denied anything to do with Fraser.

Linda went back to her next question: "You have identified the probable murderer as 'Ben' (unknown), so how and when did he meet up with you, Luca and Giovanni at Hanging Rock Park?"

Somewhat more relaxed, Wiltshire began, "I had arranged to meet----" when his solicitor interrupted and stopped him, saying warningly, "Perhaps he contacted you and arranged the time and place, which was agreed to be Hanging Rock?"

"Yes, yes, that's how it was," replied Wiltshire.

Jackson now joined in, "You no doubt remember roughly the time of day and what vehicle he was driving?"

Wiltshire agreed. "It was about 4.25pm, and he apologised for being late as he had got lost. The vehicle was a silver Kia van of some type, almost certainly a rental as he blamed the sat nav. It was quite large."

The police thanked him and set in motion an exploration with rental companies for any details on the hire of a similar vehicle around the dates.

Linda added, "You apparently all moved into the big shed that contained the contraband products? How did that discussion progress? And are we assuming 'Ben' controlled the proceedings?"

Wiltshire anxiously, hurriedly, confirmed that was how it was and added, "I was merely a bystander."

Jack and Linda exchanged sceptical glances before they homed in on how things had proceeded. Wiltshire was keen to preserve his position as an uninvolved witness but they were not going to allow that. The detectives wanted confirmation that Ben had outlined and forcefully confirmed the size of the well-overdue debt. Wiltshire confirmed he had heard a figure in excess of $350,000. Luca and Giovanni apparently had nodded acceptance of that amount. Ben had asked in a nasty and aggressive manner, "How the bloody hell do you plan to repay us?" Giovanni apparently had whimpered that Dad might help. Wiltshire went on to state that Ben had then said, with a snort of extreme derision, "You could be so lucky, spoilt 'Boyo'—we have already asked and were told to 'go fly a kite'!"

That was a surprise for the investigating team, and indicated the Moretti family knew much more than they had admitted.

It was clear that Wiltshire was in awe of, and even terrified of, the power and menace of 'Ben'. Linda could see Ken Wiltshire as he really was; a small-time opportunist 'would be if he could be' crook without putting in the necessary dirty work. She could feel her contempt for him rising as she said, "Well, let's get on with it, what happened next?"

Wiltshire fiddled around, muttered incomprehensibly, and his eyes rolled as he looked to the solicitor for guidance, which was not forthcoming.

He stumbled on, "Ben became very angry and demanded answers and made suggestions about payment. He first threatened physical violence, then grabbed Giovanni by the throat, marched him across the floor and forced him down on one of the chairs in the shed." It seemed he had chosen Giovanni to pick on first.

Wiltshire continued, now sweating profusely.

"Giovanni was terrified and had more ideas about how they would pay it. Ben suggested getting money from other family sources, trust funds, hidden products, gold, or sale of works of art or even family heirlooms. Luca had been standing watching his brother being pushed around and exploded, 'Leave him alone you bloody bully, it's got to be fucking obvious even to someone as thick as you, we don't have the wherewithal to pay you'!"

Wiltshire said that was as close as he could remember to what was said. The reaction from Ben had been immediate—he pulled from his jacket a hand gun that he waved under the noses of Luca and Giovanni. Wiltshire paled just in the retelling. He added that it had flashed through his mind that the gun looked like a police Smith and Wesson pistol that had recently been featured on TV as a new semi-automatic weapon. Ben's wild waving around of the gun certainly got attention from all there.

Wiltshire seemed to want to stop at this point and his voice dried up. Linda volunteered to get water or coffee.

After a short break, Sergeant Jackson commanded Wiltshire, "Get on with it, what next?"

The solicitor whispered some instructions and cautions into Wiltshire's ear and nodded for him to proceed. In a very low voice, with extreme caution, he recommenced, "Ben was threatening and shouting, getting more and more agitated, and he threatened Luca that he would shoot Giovanni first to get some action. Luca was personally strong and seemed unmoved by the threat, but Giovanni was crying. Ben suddenly shot Giovanni and quickly moved on and shot Luca. They both fell to the floor, shot in the head!"

Wiltshire mumbled on about what he could recall, "Now, with just the two of us alive, with two clearly very dead bodies, Ben acted like a real psycho! His instruction to me was, 'Now you will help me dispose of the bodies.'"

Fragmented descriptions followed. Wiltshire admitted he was completely terrified by the bizarre circumstances. Ben appeared to be in a trance and had a smirk on his face. He started barking out instructions to move his van around to the doorway of the shed, open the back door of the van and bring in the big sheets of black plastic that presumably he had anticipated the need for. The single-minded actions rattled Wiltshire even more and when he was given detailed instructions on how to roll the two dead men into the plastic like a body bag, he had realised just what sort of cold-blooded killer he was dealing with.

He did as he was told and paid careful attention to everything Ben said, particularly to the clear warning about not leaking details to any authorities. A concerted effort to clean up blood on the dirt floor was the final act, and with little more ado Ben climbed into his rental van, said he had to 'deliver a message', and left!

Wiltshire admitted he had been in a complete funk and dithered around in shock for hours, trying to make sense of things. Linda interrupted his train of thought, "And at what point did the butchering of their hands take place?"

She was also showing a level of shock and distress at what had taken place.

Wiltshire denied anything like that had been done in his presence. Shaky and almost incoherent, he was as adamant as his voice and body would allow, "No cutting of hands happened at my place, there was no other blood or mess in the shed," he insisted. He was shaken just talking about it.

Sergeant Jackson called a halt to the interview, and his thank you to everyone was followed by the exit of the solicitor and Wiltshire being locked up in a holding cell while further enquiries were pursued.

On the basis of that interview it was assumed that the mysterious Ben, the 'Hit Man', had severed the fingers before dumping the bodies. Had anyone seen the silver Kia delivery van? Anywhere? Descriptions were broadcast widely, as were detailed descriptions of Ben with the police focusing on the airport and car rental agencies. Wiltshire, under pressure, had thought that he might have seen a

Europcar sticker on the van, but was not sure. That turned out to be wrong. Searches of airline records showed no trace of anyone fitting the description of 'Ben'.

A much more likely person flew out of Tullamarine mid-morning for Sydney, after returning a silver Kia van to Budget Car and Truck Rentals booked under the name of William Blake. The same name as the passenger used on Qantas. Police enquires suggested it was a false name. So much for the theory that the action was all based in Adelaide. Searches continued in every direction and forensics descended on the property at Hanging Rock. A hope that they might even find the gun or used shells did not come to fruition.

17

Back to Moretti's

The next incident room assembly of all involved police staff was chaired by Chief Superintendent Brunton. He employed his usual 'friendly but never friends' efficient manner as a boss and reported the current status and summary of events, and thanked everyone for the real progress achieved.

"Now the next important steps to be taken are as follows, and suggestions or additions would be welcomed."

The first point he made was that they now had at least one established person to concentrate on. That was the apparent professional hit man, the mysterious Ben. It seemed he was a murderer for hire, a psycho killer, used to using hand guns and not immune to using other forms of physical violence. The chief's voice hardened as he went on, "I will take responsibility to track down this evil bastard through the use of every resource available to the Australian police forces and even wider if appropriate! This type of behaviour must not be allowed!"

A little more calmly he added, "Immediately and with accelerated energy we want to find where and when the assailant stopped his van to hack off the fingers of the two men and dispose of them— and whatever weapon was used for that—and what happened to the weapon used to shoot them. The location has to be within a circumference of Hanging Rock, Woodend, and Gisborne. That would seem to be probable as our mystery man then headed to Tullamarine Airport."

Either mentally or mumbled very quietly to themselves, everyone noted, 'very good point, Sir!'

Chief Brunton added with more emphasis, "We are ordering in another six police personnel to help us search, and drain if necessary, sites where such weapons could have been disposed of." A slight hesitation then, "Any points or input up to now, please"?

After a moment Linda Alexander raised her hand and said, "Wiltshire, who we now have in custody, has given us a description of 'Ben'. Surely, he must be able to lead us through solicitors to his employer, or to him?" Brunton was delighted by the question, "Thanks Detective, for a good common-sense question because I will be going on to the allocation of new tasks and that is one to be on your list." All with a smile of appreciation.

The Chief informed them that forensics had gone to pick up the van from Budget Cars to go over it with a fine-tooth comb. It seemed that an amount of black plastic sheeting had been purchased from Mitre 10 in Woodend by a look-a-like for Ben. He acknowledged that some form of police protection was under consideration for Wiltshire and his daughter. Another interview was scheduled for Wiltshire to be conducted by highly skilled police psychiatrists to try to glean further relevant information. The Coroner was being informed of progress every step of the way.

Brunton then made the point that as he was not at the station on the case every day, the team should refer every piece of information through Senior Sergeant Jackson, who was working in close liaison with Senior Sergeant Simpson of the Gisborne precinct.

"OK, here are the next steps to be taken. Linda, as you enquired, your immediate steps are to take Constable Jenkins with you to interview Alessandro Moretti and find out everything about his telephone discussion with whoever about paying off Luca and Giovanni's debt. This may be emotional as the relationship between father and sons is not known, so take it gently. And go and see the solicitor who Wiltshire called—and don't take any stonewalling from him!"

The Chief Superintendant turned to DS Jackson. "Jack, take Senior Constable Ingram to visit Dominic Moretti, and concentrate on his connections with his father and perhaps longer family connections back to the old days when discretion was not always front of mind. Progress on to Bria because she might know a lot more than is obvious."

Finally, the Chief stated, "We need to use the media to crank up pressure and exposure and to maximise input from the public. We have plenty of expertise within the police but local participation often turns up surprises. Any suggestions welcome."

There was silence as everyone digested the information and the meeting concluded with a feeling that positive action was underway. Just as he was exiting the office, the Chief Super turned back and added, "Don't forget we are still looking for a Smith and Wesson and a mystery man called Ben who uses the name of William Blake. Keep asking everyone and anyone if they know of such a person!"

Linda and Beth made an appointment at the Moretti head office in Woodend to meet with Alessandro Moretti. They were interested to see if he would be accompanied by a legal adviser but he was by himself after one of his staff came in and took orders for, and then delivered, coffee. Alessandro was friendly and warm in his welcome to them. Once the pleasantries were over, Linda gave an up-to-date summary of the current status of the murder inquiry. His face hardened and his attitude became clearly meaningful.

He said in a blunt fashion, "So at this stage you have no prime suspect identified for the horrendous, violent murder of my two sons!"

Linda, who knew she looked every inch the Senior Detective Sergeant, replied, "That could be a non-flattering summary, but we are well on the way to establishing the perpetrators." She added, "The word 'perpetrators' is chosen carefully as we know more than one offender is involved."

Alessandro's face flushed in anger as he raised his voice and shouted at the officers, "I'm telling you right now I'm going to use every last piece of my energies and resources to catch those bastards and carry out 'just' revenge for treating members of my family worse than animals!" More threatening words followed. Linda and Beth looked at one another for reassurance before attempting to lower the level of extreme rage.

Beth looked impressed as Linda suggested, "We completely sympathise with your anger, Mr Moretti; we have never before been confronted with such barbarism to civilised members of the public." Alessandro in silence absorbed the full meaning of that statement and it seemed to help defuse his belligerence. More like his usual self, he then said sadly, "You know, they were no angels, and they were a bloody handful as kids, but surely they did not deserve this?"

Trying to continue the now civil conversation, Linda softly asked, "Would you have any names or suggestions about associates they may have had who would have such violent tendencies?" Alessandro's reply was sorrowful. "No. You know, I hardly knew the boys, and even less so in the last few years, as they really ran their own destinies."

Both Linda and Beth thought what he said was indeed really sad. But they had to progress into the subjects they had come to pursue. Qualifying their next questions with apologies in advance, they moved on; the first question was whether the Moretti household overall owned any guns; especially a Smith and Wesson hand gun? Definitely no to the hand gun, but Alessandro did have a double-barrelled shotgun. As far as he knew, though, the boys had none. Not quite the answer to the real question of whether others had guns, but it would do for now. Much more likely to create a reaction was the major reason for the visit, and it was presented by Linda in the most careful manner she could muster.

"We believe you had a telephone call from an unknown caller

suggesting you could pay in full the outstanding debt that Luca and Giovanni owed, and apparently you declined or were unable to honour?"

Linda and Beth waited for the explosion. It didn't happen. Alessandro looked at them with new and different respect. He had been secretly admiring them for their professionalism as well as their appearance, and the question added a new appreciation of the police inquiry. In by far the calmest manner since their arrival he replied, "That's a very good question," and then added with an apologetic smile and a laugh, "You are obviously both much more than just pretty faces!"

Alessandro, then with his best manners back in place, revealed that he and his associates were in the process of tracing the telephone call. They had the matter in hand and did not need help from the police. It was a matter that the family would handle to carry out retribution as they saw fit! In short, he was telling them to 'butt out'.

Beth could not let that pass and her body language as she moved forward, emphasising her uniform, demanded attention, "Sir, with the greatest respect, and recognising your family's pain, we cannot stand by and let you take matters into your own hands. How about we try to do this together, combining our energies and expertise to achieve the proper civilised result?"

The co-operative and concise way Beth made the point, together with her quietly authoritative air, sat Mr Moretti back in his chair and even surprised Linda. She had to restrain herself from clapping! The two policewomen could almost see Alessandro mentally shaking himself before, in a strained but accepting manner, he asked, "What do you need from me?"

The women started with the list they had prepared. It included an authority to search telephone records of all personal and private phones of Alessandro, Corina and the Moretti head office. Alessandro protested about Corina's phone, and they agreed to be discreet about enquiries of family members, and even to exchange confidential information as it developed. He gave them the name of the person who had telephoned with a request that the Moretti family satisfy the outstanding debt, and admitted there had been a follow-up tracing on who had made the call. He elaborated that it was from a company of lawyers based in Adelaide. The firm was big and appeared to be a conglomerate of contract lawyers who carried out individual consultations.

The lawyer who had made the call to him was a Max Rowe, who was a mid-level comparatively newly qualified solicitor. Alessandro then helpfully added that his enquiries had revealed that a senior partner had requested the phone call to be made, and he in turn had advised 'No comment'.

Alessandro was willing to hand over any other relevant details he had, as he acknowledged that police no doubt had more strength and power to follow through with legitimate actions designed to disclose more details. He agreed to fully co-operate with all police enquiries, and to issue instructions for his staff and family to be helpful.

Linda respectfully asked him to cool his anger and aggravation, particularly in public, to minimise the obvious public reaction to the murders. He reluctantly agreed it was appropriate. Linda and Beth again expressed their sympathies, and assured Alessandro all possible steps would be taken. As they departed, they mentioned that Senior Sergeant Jackson and Constable Ingham had made an appointment with son Dominic to follow up various points.

Only hours later Jackson and Ingham were in the company foyer to meet Dominic. The police activities were obvious to everyone, as was sympathy for the family. Dominic greeted them warmly and led them into his own office and offered tea or coffee which they accepted. Dominic was dressed 'smart casual' as would be expected of the chief executive, and also with his being less flamboyant than Alessandro.

There was less idle chit chat as they were known to one another. An update of the previous information exchanged with Alessandro was acknowledged by Dominic as he had been briefed by his father.

Jack got straight to the first point, "Dominic, you know someone purporting to be attached to the Rebels motorbike gang has phoned in and claimed responsibility." Dominic agreed he was aware of such a claim.

Jack went on: "We have attempted to track the call but it obviously was from was a throw-away phone. I know it's a long time ago that you had any involvement, but could you enquire among the 'bikies' if anything is known about who the caller might be and why?"

There was no reply forthcoming so Jack went on, "We know how angry and vengeful Alessandro is feeling, and how out of step the boys were, but we believe they were also in trouble with gambling debts and money laundering. Any comments or help in these directions?"

Dominic then replied in a thoughtful manner, "Bikies! I really don't know where to start. Maybe Bria? Those bloody twins were out of control and had no sense of loyalty to anyone or anything. It was a diabolical outrage! But the bastards must be caught and punished."

Constable Ingram, full of obvious empathy, agreed with his comments but expressed caution on the family about taking revenge action. He added, "Do you think your dad has invited help from some of his older associates?" Dominic thought that unlikely, as he believed those days—as were his own with motorbikes—were well in the past. Focusing on more recent times, the officers asked if Dominic knew anything about the Carry-On business and its involvement in the illegal tobacco trade. Dominic gave the question serious thought before he replied, "You know, I don't know a damn thing about it. How in God's name did they get involved!"

He was clearly very angry and frustrated about Luca and Giovanni and said, "For the life of me, I can't imagine the world of illicit tobacco, who smokes it and how it is distributed! It's beyond me how the boys were involved!"

Sergeant Jackson, clearly with sympathy, volunteered, "Well Dominic, they weren't personally involved in that shady side of small and sneaky distribution, they were simply into the illegal growing, theft, and distribution of bulk quantities of tobacco, alcohol and drugs—all activities that attach serious penalties, and huge profits! They were involved purely for the lazy, easy way they could make big money. You should remember that when planning any retribution on your own!"

Dominic looked silently at both policemen and acknowledged the point with a grimace. Constable Ingram was keen to make the point that they were seeking leads that might provide information on the methods of communication that had to exist. They said that it was probable that instructions had come down from Adelaide using a firm of lawyers as a conduit. Had he heard of this? A reaction of real surprise was all they got. The meeting went on amicably with Jack asking after Dominic's family of Maureen, Alice and Andrew, and concluded with confirmation from everyone of full exchange of all matters to do with catching the culprits. A request was left for Dominic to let them know when and where the funeral would take place.

18

Adelaide

What a lovely city Adelaide is, especially for the older well-established families with forebears going back more than a century. Their world is centred around Rundle Street. This is more accurately 'Rundle Street East' as opposed to Rundle Mall. Depending on how you view your status. The real centre of the universe, however, is perceived to be the Adelaide Club, an exclusive gentlemen's club in North Terrace, with a history going back to its founding in 1863. Building commenced in 1864 when 120 members were admitted without election. The largest group were pastoralists, followed by businessmen and lawyers, and government officials were also prominent. The majority of members were Anglicans, a few Presbyterians, and one or two Roman Catholics or Jews. The Club adopted the Grass Tree as its crest.

Membership was 288 by 1920, and the membership reflected the economy. Pastoralists were joined by manufacturers, warehousemen, newspaper proprietors, and later more 'businessmen'. There is no real rival club, thus reflecting the unity of the power elite in South Australia. The Club was unashamedly modelled on similar elite clubs in London. Today the Club has over 900 members, many of whom are fifth or even sixth-generation of their families being members. An exclusive club for the influential elite. Historically and architecturally the building remains a significant structure in South Australian history.

The term 'The Adelaide Establishment' came from the group of wealthy landowners and industrialists who have been influential in South Australia's history. The power of the Adelaide Establishment has declined over decades but continues its exclusivity, closed membership and culture even today. A long-serving member of the Club is Mr Gwynn Hassett, a senior partner in the large and respected legal firm of PGG and Associates. Gwynn was well used to entering the two large green doors into the traditional foyer of dark timber and chandelier lighting, with smartly dressed men in suits greeting incoming members by name with a warm smile. A home away from home where plans and actions are hatched.

A motto never mentioned is, "The first rule of the Adelaide Club is that you do not talk about the Adelaide Club!" Within the security of the four walls there is a quiet dignity, a gentrified atmosphere, where professors, doctors, lawyers, successful entrepreneurs, the old and established, discuss in confidentiality matters of choice. A serene climate where hands are much too clean to be sullied by ill deeds! There is no 'dirty money'.

Gwynn Hassett had a close friend within the membership, going back many years to family, school and university days. The term 'Old Boys' was a sinecure that applied to them. Gwynn made a point of sitting down in comparative seclusion with pastoralist George Fisher. In a low, confidential voice and manner, he whispered, "We may have a developing problem connected to the interstate smoking disease."

The mild, modulated response, "How serious could that be? I presume the drawbridge can be lowered to douse the flames?" Gwynn nodded sagely and took that as an action instruction. That immediately meant 'gofer' Max Rowe from his legal firm would be sacrificed.

19

Wiltshire

Kenneth Wiltshire was back in the interview room. He was accompanied by his lawyer, and was warned that apart from the murder charges there was a range of additional offences for which he was liable to be charged. He appeared depressed and physically tired, as if he had just now realised the seriousness of his position. DS Linda Alexander told him there were two matters that needed answers. Unequivocally, they wanted Wiltshire to confirm that his telephone call when arrested was to his 'contact' within the scam. Wiltshire replied, "Not quite correct. The solicitor who came to assist me had only done the conveyancing on 'my' property but had to contact an associate in the legal firm in Adelaide."

Trying hard to be helpful he added, "My opinion is that the whole illegal operation is masterminded from Adelaide."

In her friendliest manner Linda asked, "What about your close associate and friend Ben, aka William Blake!"

The response was swift. "Not my friend, not my associate, he actually terrifies me, and my opinion is he is a contract assassin! I hope to God I never set eyes on him again!"

Moving on, Sergeant Jackson tried to explore the illegal tobacco trade and how, where and who were the customers for the stolen goods. Wiltshire was more relaxed about the methods of distribution and pickup arrangements. He handled no money and those collecting goods had only to provide a delivery/pickup document. He could remember some details. Shady retail groups, bikies, and gambling junket tour operators were regular collectors. On rare occasions a client from interstate picked up a large order.

The police officers closely questioned Wiltshire about his personal activities and whether, with his style of dress and apparent affluence, he was a regular player on pokies or at the Casino. He freely admitted he was a regular on the pokies at the Regent Tavern in Gisborne and at Crown Casino in Melbourne. It was a 'form of relaxation' from his life of stress, he stated. When closely questioned about money laundering it became evident he was nothing more than a player for his own fun.

Reviews and summaries were constant within the investigating team and allocation of jobs and partners changed in line with skills and priorities. Team members seemed happy and often refreshed by changed emphasis. Chief Superintendent Brunton had a happy knack of maintaining 'esprit de corps' through what was often a hard grind of continual digging and perseverance. For a change, he paired together Senior Sergeant Jackson and Detective Sergeant Alexander to stay at the Gisborne Police Station to pore through and revisit every shred of evidence that had been accrued, and sent Senior Constables Ian Ingram and Beth Jenkins to make highly visible visits to the Regent Tavern, and an even more noticeable presence at the Casino. For the constables it was a rare opportunity to do some meaningful research in an environment where their uniform and presence were mostly greeted with respect. They were proud to be doing the part of their job which gave them pleasure. They wore their uniforms with pride.

There were no surprises beyond what was already known about what went on at Gisborne and who the main players were. The Casino provided the two officers with a range of results that certainly widened their personal knowledge. They had some appreciation of 'junket tour operators' but not necessarily how they operated and how they were one of the many ways laundering of money could take place. The 'junket' is an arrangement between a casino and a tour operator to facilitate gambling by one individual or a group of players to a casino. In return the casino or casinos pay the tour operator a commission based on the collective gambling activity of the players on the junket. It is a haven for organised crime.

Another method they learned was what is termed 'cuckoo smurfing', were money is deposited into an account at the casino using the name of a third person or identity—a stolen identity, or disguise, or even genuine identities—with or without approval.

The major value of the public display of police activity was to rattle cages: sending messages or attempting to encourage useful information to come to them, primarily from or about 'mavericks' involved or fringe players in the grotesque double murder. The constables expressed genuine thanks to the many contributors to their increase in knowledge of how these parts of society worked, and returned to Gisborne stimulated by their enquiries.

Jack and Linda were still slaving away over screeds of evidence, so the suggestion of adjourning to the Majestic Hotel for a drink or two was agreed with acclamation. Once the second drink was in front of them or gone, Jack excused himself to go home, Ian went off to call his partner to get a leave pass for an hour, and Beth rang her husband to suggest he join her and Linda for a pub supper. All very routine and domestic and reminded Linda of when she had recently been home to Perth to visit her parents, and how important they were to her. She recalled the dramatic life and background her parents had lived in South Africa and what the family had sacrificed to move to Australia ten years previously to escape the inequities of apartheid. Their recent few days together had reinforced her love for them and underscored the total family agreement on the decision to become Australians, which they now were. Her few days break in the West had given Linda a rest from the intensity of the detective work which she so enjoyed, and a better appreciation of family togetherness. She understood how couples needed empathy to succeed.

When Beth's husband arrived, he had with him a friend from work who had clearly been informed about 'the detective'. After everyone unwound, had a laugh and ate a simple meal together, and as evening farewells began, the new man to the group lingered awhile to talk to Linda, and now addressed her as 'Lindy' before suggesting he would like to get to know her better, and could they exchange telephone numbers? Very politely, and she hoped graciously, she declined, indicating she had a steady long-term partner, and she was a career police officer with no time to complicate her life. She apologised for the bluntness as she added she had enjoyed his company. As she walked off, she was aware of her own slight swagger and had to recognise the truth of her ambitions.

Parts of the investigation quite suddenly ramped up—yet another dog-walking citizen and a grisly find. A lady walking in New Gisborne had her dog pick up and present her with a small suspicious-looking thing that looked like bony mangled meat, and because of the publicity about the murders she immediately took it to the Police Station where it was quickly identified as a finger. The reactions were intense and fast in every direction, not least in the immediate recommencing of a detailed search of the area where the dog owner thought the object had come from. The whole area around the Steam Engine Club premises was closed off and police personnel equipped in gumboots and wet suits began to trawl the land and the lake, hoping for more evidence—possibly even the hand gun. It seemed clear that 'Ben' had made that area a last destination to dispose of bodies and associated articles before flying out.

This discovery intensified the search in New South Wales for a person with the reputation of 'killer for hire'. Authorities held the opinion that unless the protagonist had fled the country, associates who knew him and resented the pressure being exerted would give him up. After a day or two, a name was leaked through the unofficial channels that suggested a possibility was Benjamin Bates—an elusive, rarely available or used, but known and feared, 'pyscho'. The profile seemed to fit the person police were looking for and extreme pressure was brought to bear on police informants for a tipoff as to where to look. It took time and police were all instructed to use extreme caution as Bates was clearly violent.

The communication trail was now of singular importance. Wiltshire handed over the phone number of the solicitor who had done the conveyancing work on his property at Hanging Rock. With approval from Chief Superintendent Brunton, Linda visited the solicitor in Kyneton. Without much ado he volunteered the name and telephone number of his contact in Adelaide from whom he received 'instructions'. He had nothing else to offer about the relationship. Although he was a partner, he qualified his involvement by stating, "Ours is a traditional old country practice respecting confidentiality and acting within the law."

Linda concluded that his activities were routine. After reporting back to Chief Brunton, it was agreed that she should book an airfare to Adelaide and interview Max Rowe at his legal firm, PGG in Rundle Street. The Chief Super arranged the appointment using his full rank to ensure priority. The flight details allowed Linda almost a full day to dig as deeply as possible. She arrived at the Rundle Street office promptly at 10am and was greeted by the receptionist as was expected. Linda noted the number of lawyers listed as partners, but they did not include a Maxwell Rowe.

Rowe came into the reception and introduced himself and invited her to follow him into a very stylish interview area. Coffee was offered and the normal pleasantries were exchanged until Linda asked if he knew why she was there? He was evasive but admitted he had received a call from Kyneton. Linda, taking on an aggressive manner, asked, "And what were you told? Were you informed that a special Criminal Investigation Unit is investigating a violent double murder?"

Rowe was surprised and even more taken aback when Linda added, "We have our best people trying to solve this horrendous crime and we are well aware that the influential family of the victims has vowed to catch all those involved to carry out their own retribution. Naturally we are flat out to have the rule of law prevail!"

She let that sink in, took a sip of coffee, and proceeded in a quiet and professional manner, "Your co-operation is sought as we are well aware of your role as a communicator, and I'm here to listen."

Rowe was clearly ill at ease and quickly responded, "Yes, yes, you are assured of that; how can I help?"

To underline the severity of the situation Linda added, "This is such an ugly high-profile crime, I need to make the point that everyone involved will one way or the other be punished by one or other of the parties searching." There was an implied threat that was intended to hit home. Linda went on, "So, cutting to the chase: right now I need full reasons and details of why you contacted Mr Alessandro Moretti, and your associated solicitor in Kyneton. Dates and times are recorded, so don't muck around or try to be clever!"

Rowe looked shattered for a moment but quickly recovered and trotted out the standard response, "That type of information has client confidentiality and therefore 'no comment'.

Linda these days was an assured senior detective used to employing her authority as needed. She stood up and said, "This is a serious double murder investigation with the full power of Victorian Police concentrated onto it, so I will give you one minute to reconsider your answer, or I will be going to your senior partner. You are no doubt well aware that using a 'murderer for hire' is a criminal offence."

Mr Rowe fidgeted around, now notably pale and uncomfortable. In a slightly shaky voice he responded, "No comment".

Linda purposefully gathered her documents into her briefcase and directed Rowe to accompany her to whoever he reported to. They strode along the hallway to the reception area, where she ascertained the name of the firm's senior partner—a Mr Gwynn Hassett. Without hesitation she demanded to see him, but was told he was not in the office. "Please get him on the phone for me—or better still request his presence here immediately with an explanation that there is a murder charge involved and he would be well advised to talk to Mr Rowe for an update." Linda then indicated she would wait as long as necessary to meet Mr Hassett.

Hassett was eventually contacted, and indicated by telephone the best he could do would be to be in his office at 10am the following morning. Linda decided she would stay in Adelaide and let Rowe and Hassett stew overnight while she asked for support from Gisborne.

She had in mind Jack Jackson as she felt comfortable with him and she could convey to him how she had progressed and her thoughts on the case. On the phone to him she said, "Jack, to be honest I think Rowe is lying, and I'm going to go really hard on him." Her request for support was quickly agreed to and Senior Sergeant Jack Jackson arrived next morning on an early flight for the 10am meeting, in full police uniform.

As soon as he and Linda were seated in senior partner Gwynn Hassett's plush office, with Rowe present, Jack aggressively asked Mr Hassett if he was up to speed with all the circumstances and had he discussed the subject with Mr Rowe? There was no preliminary chit-chat. Jack also indicated he was recording the interview.

In a rather condescending, supercilious manner, Hassett agreed that he had spoken with 'Rowe', and went on, "In fact, I can't add much to what I believe he has explained to you."

Jack Jackson knew how to use his authority when riled and brought his seniority and presence to bear on the lawyers. He said, "I believe DS Alexander has informed Mr Rowe of the facts and the seriousness of these two murders, and that he has indicated a total lack of co-operation with our investigation when it is clear your firm holds a key to progress!"

The reply from Hassett, continuing in his superior manner, was that company lawyers handled their own clients.

Linda jumped into the conversation. "Mr Rowe clearly indicated to me yesterday that he reported directly to you, and took instructions, introductions to clients, and overall supervision from you—

particularly in the instance of the telephone messages and response to activities around the Victorian property." That brought a surprised silence, followed by Hassett making a denial and requesting a break with Max Rowe.

In obvious annoyance Jackson responded, "OK, but make it quick!"

When the lawyers returned the atmosphere was icy cold between them. In a more conciliatory tone Hassett indicated he was handling the matter and said it was necessary to outline some circumstances that would no doubt be "treated with confidentiality" to aid the formal police inquiry. Hassett advised that what Mr Rowe had told DS Alexander the previous day had been inaccurate in many ways, although there was some truth in what he had said. Within the firm of PGG Lawyers, Rowe did in fact report to him on routine company relationships but each lawyer 'ran their own' clients. Yes, he liaised with Mr Rowe on many routine matters but he, Hassett, did not dictate with whom or for whom Rowe acted. There were no internal records of any communication, by any methods, of instructions that related to the 'problem' being referred to.

Linda in her own mind said, 'Surprise, surprise.'

Gwynn Hassett went on, "There have been a few issues with Mr Rowe over the years that may have contributed to some activities beyond those regarded as professional behaviour." In a slightly conspiratorial tone he added, "He has had serious financial problems, no doubt contributed to by his excess alcohol consumption and gambling, plus family health worries, with his mother having advanced dementia. To his credit he has been active in groups pressuring for assisted living and 'right to die' laws. He has been under outside pressures."

Max Rowe sat through this entire pantomime totally without expression or sound.

In what Hassett thought was a conclusion to the discussion he went on, "I suggest, Sergeant Jackson and DS Alexander, you pursue the matter further with Mr Rowe and leave PGG Lawyers out of the picture." He then rose to his feet to exit the meeting, but not before Sergeant Jackson had added, "With due respect, sir, we will be contacting your company with an official report of this meeting and indicating what further action to expect."

Jack and Linda gathered up their paperwork, and with Max Rowe in obvious shock, informed him he was required at the Adelaide Central Police Station at 2pm for an additional interview.

They took their leave and hurried to a local café where they prepared their tactics for the meeting before they were to fly back to Victoria. What had been clearly established was that Rowe was a scapegoat to be sacrificed. The real question was how much blood would be let!

In the meeting with Rowe at Adelaide Central Police Station, they formally charged him with being an accessory to a homicide, giving misleading evidence, and being part of a contract to hire a felon to carry out a murder. All offences, they assured him, that could result in prison. Rowe was clearly shattered and broke down in tears. His only coherent spluttering was that he was being "screwed". He wobbled on about Hassett being "Mr Clean Hands", and how it was obvious that he, Rowe, was being "cut adrift".

The meeting was short. He was allowed police bail and was cautioned not to leave Adelaide, but that he would be required for further interviewing, probably in Gisborne, to view evidence and help with further enquiries.

Jack and Linda were then able to catch a later flight back to Gisborne and Linda chatted to Jack as an associate and friend on the trip. She related some of things she had learnt from attending the Police Training Academy in Perth, and talked about the emphasis they had put on 'keeping on – keeping on'! The stress had been on hard, thorough and dogged persistence. Feeling relaxed after two full and busy days in Adelaide, she opened up to Jack on her experience and learning on crime solving.

"Gather up absolutely everything about everyone, even the tiniest morsel. Check out the victim, the suspects, the relatives, friends and lovers. Where they live, have travelled, legally or illegally. Build an up-to-date picture of habits, acquaintances, workmates, even enemies, and convictions. Like a big happy 'American dream' story," she said. Jack nodded occasionally in agreement as the plane droned on, and Linda finished with a flourish, "You turn it all upside down, shake it vigorously, and wait to see what pops out!"

They sat in silence until Linda quietly added, "Sergeant, I know you have all this stuff off by heart, and even though I came top in my exams, I'm still adding actual experiences to my education. I love this job!"

Jack waited a bit then said, "Lindy, you're doing great. Let's nail the bastards!"

Back in the incident room next morning, as everyone was brought up to date, several points were agreed. The crude chopping off of fingers was believed to be simply a basic message about the consequence of not paying bills. Max Rowe in Adelaide was a prime suspect who would be cracked, but would that lead to 'Mr Big'? Ken Wiltshire was to be kept in custody to use with Rowe. The arrest of Ben Bates, the hit man, was urgent. A new meeting with Bria was to be arranged, and plans to monitor everything about the Moretti brothers' funeral were put in place.

Linda and Beth were delegated to revisit Bria at Ballarat, and Bria chose to include Cliff Richardson in the meeting.

Bria gave them a sombre but friendly welcome and the greeting from Cliff—clearly there as an executive and as part of the extended family—was genuinely warm. Coffee was made available as updates and information was exchanged.

Bria asked, "Has a culprit been established? Has progress been made in catching them?"

Linda admitted that the current position was that almost certainly a professional hit man had been employed to send a message that unpaid debts would not be tolerated. She added, "We have a trail of instructions given, and persons involved, one in custody, and an identified criminal we are seeking. The situation is bigger because there is an unidentified 'Mr Big' interstate involved in wider crime who we are trying to catch. We really are making progress, and we're asking for your help."

Bria and Cliff wanted more detail and gave positive offers of help, if at all possible. Linda declined to reveal any further progress, and went on to ask about funeral details. She added that they understood the bodies had to be released by the Coroner, and was it going to be a 'family only' ceremony? Police would co-operate in any way necessary to protect privacy as they knew the press was constantly badgering the family. Beth also suggested that a major reason for their visit was to ask for help from Alessandro and Corina, who no doubt were very distressed. The police wished to be seen as sensitive to the family's emotions, so Linda asked if there were any things owned by Luca or Giovanni or Carry-On that rightfully belonged to them? Linda took her time to listen to their responses before moving on to the other subject for the visit: they needed to know if anything was amiss in the fitness industry.

She outlined that the large and growing 'personal exercise' trend had grown out of all proportion and expectation. Well-promoted brand names had added colour to an otherwise industrial product and huge commercial opportunities existed. The fitness emphasis added diet, training regimes, music, and 'clubbing' routines into the genre. Linda then asked, "Is there a dark side to the health and fitness industry—in particular, has it had been infiltrated by crime to help distribute their products?" She admitted it was a 'heavy' subject but it was known that crime was alive in leisure products. Crime networks were as efficient as big business, and Linda admitted there was a real possibility that the twins had brushed into that territory. Not necessarily overlapping but an enquiry of interest. Both Bria and Cliff firmly asserted not to their knowledge or experience.

To help establish a comfortable rapport, Beth—as a fitness

disciple—asked if they could be given a quick conducted tour of the store. Linda added that as a fellow 'exercise freak', she also would appreciate a tour. Bria and Cliff were flattered by the request so a relaxed and interesting walk-around followed. The police officers were impressed by the range of body building equipment, and Linda quipped, "There is more here in one store than I thought existed in the world!"

Each section of the store only added to the wonderment both women expressed. When they got to the bicycle area the two were further taken aback by the huge space and the range and variety of bikes on show, and the myriad spare parts and additions available. In the assembly area, the number of mechanics at work seemed more akin to a car manufacturing plant. The size and scope of products was mindblowing and when they moved into the clothing area even more so, as the store became a fashion shop in its own right. Linda and Beth could not refrain from words of admiration. It was a small empire!

They adjourned back to Bria's office in now what had become a comfortable relationship, even more so as Linda made the comment, "You two must be very proud of the business; you are 'frontrunning' for the whole industry."

Bria replied, "It's a battle to stay innovative and a leader but we work hard at it, and Cliff in particular is always first here and last to leave."

Beth led the conversation back to enquiring about pressure groups or strong-arm tactics from any identified opposition. Bria looked seriously at both policewomen and said, "Truly, you both know Cliff and his integrity, and mine by reputation; no way known we are in any way mixed up with the shady side of commerce! It would be silly to say we have never been approached to accept stock of doubtful origin, or even products for free under duress, but probably because of Dad's established record of being 'squeaky clean' and the family reputation of not being bullied, we have been in a position of strength. It probably helps that we are financially strong."

All said with genuine pride. Linda expressed thanks but just wanted to enquire further about any fringe associations with tattoo parlours, gyms, health and fitness clubs, even boxing. "No, none of those," said Bria, "and although we have plenty of space, and we (and the bank!) own this building, we've resisted offers from sub-tenants. We are sponsors to bicycle riding clubs through this business and through a couple of smaller shops we are associated with."

Cliff added, "There are two major overseas suppliers of famous brand bikes and they supply some money and products to be used to support local events." Linda said she recognised that commercial support like this would be sought after. Cliff also added with emphasis that there were unscrupulous operators in every endeavour, but they were not and hopefully would never be in that area. Perhaps Cliff and Bria were overly sensitive because of current events.

It had been a pleasant and informative meeting and grateful thanks were expressed by everyone. Cliff added in parting that they had no relationship with any 'bikie' gangs or personnel! On the way home Linda said to Beth, "Lovely couple but a bit of a waste of time, and like Alessandro, they seem as clean as a whistle! I don't believe there's any mafia or bikie gang connection."

20

Back to Gisborne

Back at Gisborne Police Station, information received from the Australian Federal Police indicated they thought they had identified (and knew the location of) the much-wanted William (Benjamin) Blake, aka 'hit man Ben'. They had the feeling his whereabouts had been deliberately leaked, but as a known vicious criminal, they planned an overnight raid to the premises he was apparently living in. Although Ken Wiltshire had given the police a reasonable description, no one had seen him so there was no urgency to rush to Sydney overnight.

Next morning the position was greatly clarified by a call to Chief Superintendent Ron Brunton to advise the raid had been carried out at 5am to discover that William Blake was on the premises but was in fact dead when they broke in. The death was deemed to have occurred within the past twenty-four hours. The Chief Super made a decision, with approval from his NSW counterpart, that his Detective Sergeant Alexander would fly to Sydney to be involved in the investigation, to contribute details from the recent events in Victoria, and to see if there was any information available that could add in solving the double murder that Gisborne was trying to finalise.

It was all agreed and at very short notice Linda was on her way. She was greeted on arrival with the information that Blake (aka Ben Bates) had been killed with a single shot to the head from a hand gun at close range and his right hand had been disfigured by the amputation of his index finger, i.e. his 'trigger' finger. All very tidy. It had been a clearly orchestrated event that had caused no noise for neighbours. The local police had no doubt this was a direct message to all associates that leaking would not be tolerated; the code of silence must be respected. In a rare moment of humour, the local officer volunteered to Linda that the situation was getting "bigger than Ben-Hur!"

Resulting from the more formal exchange of information about the deceased William Blake, his background and reputation evolved. He was in fact a contract killer known to both police and the criminal fraternity. He was ex-SAS a long time ago, a military force which was known as a breeding ground for the slightly unbalanced. He was a loner, available at short notice, non-selective about jobs, and the fee for the double killing was probably in the vicinity of $50k.

Almost certainly the 'contract' was arranged via a cryptic message from a senior criminal leader in Adelaide to a similar remote leader in Sydney. Also possible was a new cypher system that was almost impossible to crack. The criminal 'lords of the manor' kept their turf and identities well protected. There was no way known they were going to allow the contract on the Moretti twins to be successfully investigated, so the best method of protection was total elimination of the end perpetrator. Back in Victoria on bail, Ken Wiltshire would no doubt be pleased to know of the removal of 'Ben'.

Linda spent time with the investigating crew in Sydney and was impressed by their camaraderie and willingness to exchange tactics and methodology. They wished her well in nailing the culprits in the Moretti murders and suggested it looked like they had bumbled into serious criminal territory. Linda flew back to Melbourne on an evening flight and was pleased to be in bed at a reasonably early hour in the local Gisborne Motel.

Next morning, walking in the bright sunshine the 20 minutes or so to the Gisborne Police Station and enjoying the beautiful tree-lined streets that fringed the prosperous town, Linda found it was a good time to reflect on the current state of progress, and to plot out next moves. She arrived at the Richardson Road precinct at 7.30am full of enthusiasm and ideas. Straight into the incident room with all its photos, diagrams, and notes all over the walls, and the first thing she did was put a line through the illustration of what was meant to look like William Blake. She then downsized the photos of Bria Moretti and Cliff Richardson.

In her mind the next person to concentrate on was the 'gofer', Max Rowe. She was going to suggest he be brought to Gisborne to be confronted by the full extent of current police knowledge, and perhaps even the evidence from Ken Wiltshire? As the police team gradually assembled and updates were given individually and then collectively, there developed a feeling of optimism as elements were eliminated and the focus was narrowed. Linda, fully supported by Jack Jackson and so automatically with approval by Chief Super Ron Brunton, made the recommendation to pull in Max Rowe to Gisborne Station. Full pressure to be exerted on him to find out more and to dig deeper into the role of his law firm's senior partner Gwynn Hassett, particularly when Rowe was away from his office. That was unanimously agreed and planning commenced immediately. The discussion was to be held in the interview room in Gisborne with one-way viewing window obvious and all the trappings of a serious crime interview. Wiltshire was to be brought into a holding cell to be confrontational as necessary.

A list of points to be covered was worked up, and Sergeant Jackson and DS Alexander were formally allocated to be the prime interviewers. Others including Chief Brunton to be available to add clout if needed. Enthusiasm was growing so the date was set for the compulsory meeting.

Max Rowe was not particularly compliant but the trip was non-negotiable. Air tickets were booked and he was picked up at Tullamarine by uniformed police and taken to Gisborne in a standard police car. He was, without any flourish, taken straight through the back private entrance to the interview room. Sergeant Jackson and Sergeant Matthew Simpson, both in uniform, began the interview without any offer of tea or coffee but in the very minimalistic room water was available. The recording equipment was obvious.

Jack had met Rowe in Adelaide, and started, "We intend to cut through all the rubbish, and as previously indicated we expect the truth. You have already been informed of your possible guilt by association." Rowe acknowledged with a nod.

"More than that, we do not accept that you worked alone on all or any of the communications you undertook relative to the murders we are investigating," said Jack. Both sergeants could see an almost imperceptible relaxation in Rowe's posture. Jackson proceeded, with Sergeant Simpson remaining silent. "It is undisputed that you made the telephone call to Mr Moretti, you were associated with Mr Kenneth Wiltshire and the property development, and it was Wiltshire who called you for help when we apprehended him at a crime scene."

As an aside, he added, "We have Wiltshire here today, so he can confirm you actually communicated with him by telephone with instructions on how to behave." Jackson went on to repeat much of what Hassett had said in Adelaide, in particular that Rowe was on his own, and that Hassett had stated that he, Hassett, was uninvolved. That brought a disgusted grunt from Rowe.

Matthew Simpson spoke for the first time, "That's what we want to pursue with you in great detail before you go anywhere!"

Jackson continued, "We are curious where all the money came from to enact the steps you authorised and we believe another man, Jake Wolkowyski, acting as the Project Manager for the Hanging Rock property, took instructions from you."

Rowe interjected, "Not quite true, although I know the name. I do believe he had direct dealings with Mr Hassett, and that may be worth your follow up." Spoken almost with pleasure as a distraction.

They took a break and Matthew was replaced by DS Alexander. With renewed energy the interrogation then focused on the relationship and responsibility between Hassett and Max Rowe. Linda suggested this was the major part of the meeting. She led by repeating much of what had been covered both in Adelaide and now, and she gave Rowe a chance to deny any of the accusations and encouraged him to repeat his indignation about being cut adrift. He didn't hesitate and confirmed he was aware that the conversation was being recorded. For the first time Rowe said, "It is now obvious I am being made the 'fall guy'. I am definitely being cut adrift and being screwed by the big boys. They are pretty bloody smart, you know."

Of course, that needed elaboration and coffee was now brought in. Encouraged by the small shift in atmosphere, Rowe tried to explain. He was barely middle tier in PGG Lawyers and was given 'pickings' by others when suitable. He was, however, mainly a 'gofer' to Gwynn Hassett who labelled himself as "an inch wide and a mile deep" in his area of expertise.

Rowe was not a willing participant because Hassett was regularly offensive. Hassett was disliked by all because, unlike other senior partners, he was aloof and arrogant. He was very proud of his 'Old School' and pastoralist family background.

With a mixture of sympathy and leadership, the police team encouraged further details on the man they were now sure was their main suspect for a major part in a major crime! In a funny sort of backhanded way, Rowe now launched into a defence of himself and what he had done by explaining that it was because he had been admiring and even envious of the position and power of Gwynn Hassett. The words now flowed from Rowe. How great it must be to be third-generation pastoralists, to have status among your peers, to be in a position of influence in a large and respected law firm, and to be wealthy enough to be able to introduce innovative farming practices—at high costs—even if they did not succeed.

He stressed that the ownership of the Hassett family's farming properties were well buried in family trusts and miscellaneous shelf companies to protect them from any threat. Rowe said admiringly,

"And well that may be necessary, as without a doubt the farms are huge loss makers that only the banks can keep alive whilst waiting for water, weather and farm product prices to rise".

He went on to attack 'The Establishment', particularly the Adelaide Club and its exclusive old boys' system that created a narrow commercial clique in South Australia. As he got that long spiel off his chest he returned to giving them more positive pieces of information. He told them that Hassett was a long-serving member of the Farmers Association, a pillar of the Presbyterian Church, a visibly caring family man to wife and children, a fighter for water rights, a Rotarian and a contributor to local charities. Rowe could not help adding in the same breath, "But it is well known he has a mistress to whom he is very generous and they both hide behind the façade and friendships that exist within the secrecy of the club. It's also known that he has some personal financial stress." More snidely he suggested a friendly bank manager within the 'system'.

It was clear that Rowe was looking for sympathy and an understanding of the position in which he now found himself. As a solicitor he was well aware of the consequences of his participation and that his life as a lawyer in South Australia was probably over. In a pleading voice he asked what he could contribute to solving the crime.

Quite out of the blue Linda suggested a break might be good and as it was nearing lunch-time, she suggested a short stroll along to Macca's almost next door. Sergeant Jackson agreed as clearly it would ease the tension Rowe was feeling. The three-minute stroll by the beautiful park and a twenty-five-minute break was shown to be a good strategy as Rowe confessed how distraught he was that his personal affairs were in such a mess. Much along the line that Hassett had used him to 'throw him under the bus'. Rowe went on to add that he actually did not like being a solicitor and was distressed about what to do with his future.

Back in the interview room, the police officers homed in on what they would welcome as a formal contribution from Rowe. They wanted a sworn declaration from him that all the communications and actions he had carried out relative to the Moretti case had been under instructions from his senior partner, Gwynn Hassett. After serious thought, Rowe wished to clarify the matter of the Wiltshire property, and to specifically exclude any connection with hit man Ben (William Blake), who he said must have been arranged from 'on high'. All routine property transactions had been through the solicitor.

Sergeant Jackson asked very directly, "What has your knowledge or involvement been in the illicit tobacco trade, locally or imported. And drugs?"

Rowe asked, "What do you mean?

Jackson retorted, "Simple enough question. MDMA, cocaine, methamphetamines…"

Emphatically Rowe replied, "No knowledge, no usage, and no associations!"

They talked on but it was clear to the officers that they had exhausted their probing so they summarised for Max Rowe and then asked Chief Superintendent Brunton into the interview room, after first having given him a quick update in his office. In full uniform and displaying a serious demeanour as his position warranted, the Chief Super intoned, "You know you are in big trouble, so your help could be appreciated. This is an ugly crime we are investigating and has big ramifications because of how far the involvement spreads. The wider criminal network is at work. We need your feedback to crack the Adelaide link. We expect to hear from you with valuable information within the next seven days! We realise you deny any real involvement but we expect to receive a response from you—by email, telephone, or even snail-mail: even the smallest snippet could help us solve this heinous crime. And some serious advice; be careful!"

With those parting words CS Brunton bade him farewell, and arrangements were made to get him to Tullamarine airport for a flight back to South Australia.

In Gisborne the following morning, Brunton attended the regular 8.00am meeting where the up-to-date position was summarised. He started with congratulations on progress and gave his opinion that the key was definitely in Adelaide and the involvement of bigger criminals and wider networks. He wanted to express a current police position about wealthy criminal groups that overreached traditions and barriers of old—certainly interstate and even internationally.

CS Brunton went on to explain at length, in the context of the current crime, how the lifestyles and behaviours of the wealthy and professional criminals were often interlaced. He took time to note that there were university studies which indicated that organised crime in general—and more particularly the networks that sustained it—were now a special focus of the police. In particular, the special attention given to the way people collaborated with each other in some types of illegal activity.

He quoted Professor David Bright, a noted forensic psychologist, about how crime networks shared many of the attributes of big business in their drive for profits. CS Brunton stressed how the wealthy of all descriptions were reluctant to sacrifice the lifestyle they enjoyed and often went to great lengths to preserve what they had. Again quoting Professor Bright on criminal behaviour he said: "They have to balance efficiency of the operation against the need for security because they are operating in the dark. They need to make their money but at the same time they don't want to be detected and exposed." It was all a small lesson on modern policing relative to the Moretti case.

Now in full swing and with everyone paying rapt attention, he proceeded with more quotes from Professor Bright, "For criminals wanting to expand their networks, the risks of allowing someone into their organisations who could inform on them, or to provide material to rivals, gets greater. So, their networks tend to remain very small. Criminal networks are driven by the profit motive so they often sacrifice security for efficiency. They repeat the same method over and over again. Example: drugs".

Chief Superintendent Brunton had a clear motive for this little motivational speech to back up his congratulations. He wanted to emphasise how everyone was vulnerable to the 'squeeze' and that was about where this case was at. He again stressed that modern policing, to succeed, needed the sharing of information and co-operation between states and law enforcement agencies.

To finish his address before going off to another meeting, he said, "The outfit we are dealing with is ruthless, powerful, and has a lot to lose. Please don't get brave or stupid by going it alone with any investigations. Well done again!" And away he went.

At much the same time, Rowe was back at PGG Lawyers in Adelaide, having been summarily commanded by Hassett to be there at 9am. No pleasant chit-chat this morning! A simple demand to know what the police wanted to know. Rowe appeared hostile. They had worked for the same firm for a little over three years as associates, and Hassett suddenly thought the discussion might go better over a cup of coffee in his office. He surprised Rowe with the offer, made in an effort to reduce the animosity that his high-handed summons to Rowe had created. However, coffee poured, he reverted to his previous manner.

"Well now Max, what was it all about?" The answer took time and several prompts along the way but Rowe admitted that the police had not accepted that he acted of his own volition to orchestrate the actions that they were fully aware of. Hassett probed for more accurate detail as Rowe tried to recall the range of topics.

Finally, he stated, "They were wanting to know about any shell and shelf companies that PGG utilised and if you were involved. They asked about Oakland Farm Holdings which they thought you may own. They were curious about subsidiaries and trusts. They were particularly interested about records of telephone calls to and from my company mobile phone, and internal and external telephone calls, texts, and emails. They suggested the records could be subpoenaed." That really did rattle Hassett and he asked for a repeat of what Rowe said. Then with further recall, Rowe added, "They seemed really interested about the Adelaide Club and your friendship with George Fisher, and I told them I knew nothing about him as he was only a name to me." That name certainly got the attention of Hassett. He tried to divert attention by suggesting another coffee and asked if there was any news about the possible 'hit man'.

Rowe answered that easily, "No, they are certain they have traced him in Sydney to the syndicate that arranges those contracts and anyway he is dead!" Silence followed, and Rowe remembered that the police had quizzed him closely about the illegal trading and transport of tobacco and drugs. He added with some pleasure, "I told them I have absolutely no knowledge or association in that world." More bravely he said, "They did accept that I did not have the position to act completely on my own and they found it hard to believe that you, Mr Hassett, were not my controller!"

Hassett spluttered and grumbled, stood up and walked around clearly distracted. Rowe then explained he had agreed with DS Linda Alexander to keep her informed of any discussions that took place and any new material that might be relevant.

Hassett regained his composure and with clear anger he advised Rowe that his employment was herewith terminated and that he was to vacate and clear his office of all personal effects and not to take with him any company records or equipment. Effective immediately. All necessary termination paperwork would be sent to his address. He emphasised that Rowe should look carefully at the contracts of confidentiality he had entered into and be extra careful about anything he said. A threat?

Max Rowe left the premises and immediately telephoned Linda to inform her of the situation, and to ask her to pass it on as promised to Chief Superintendent Brunton. Linda repeated her warning to him to be careful, and wondered, "Do you think you would feel safer if we gave you some obvious security backup?"

The answer from Rowe, "Good God no, I don't have enough

valuable information for them to be concerned." Linda suggested that if he could put his mind to it and email to them even the smallest snippet it may be useful. He responded that he was angry enough right now to do that, and then proceeded to send a summary.

The heading was short and sharp: 'To whom it may concern. Re Mr Gwynn Hassett.'

The content followed: "The following are facts in my relationship to Senior Partner G. Hassett at PGG Lawyers. I had my own small group of clients but my major role was as an assistant and back-up to Mr Hassett from whom I took instructions. Relative to the Moretti murders and associated activities in Gisborne, Woodend, and Hanging Rock areas, my contacts and actions were all under referral from Mr Hassett. I had no authority to question or contest instructions. Actions on behalf of Mr Kenneth Wiltshire were all carried out with the full approval of Mr Hassett as were telephone calls to Carry-On and a member of the Moretti family. On a more historic basis it could be worthwhile to enquire about thousands of dollars that went missing from the Adelaide Club when Mr Hassett was Treasurer, that was then refunded by a close friend from within the club, without fuss.

"Mr Hassett has a history of infidelity, and has two semi-secret illegitimate children who he does not support or acknowledge. Regular payments are made into a trust fund for their welfare. Check on Hassett's long-time friend within the Club, pastoralist George Robert Fisher, for illegal activities. Check on Hassett's current personal financial position due to previous large financial losses through gambling at the Casino in Sydney.

Some of this information is provided because of bitterness over how I have been treated but may add to your ability to convict the guilty people of an ugly crime. There is no doubt that either Hassett on his own, or on behalf of an anonymous client, or less likely on behalf of PGG, is regularly raising invoices for large sums of money for consulting services that have not been provided, to a company that hardly exists. When paid, that money is flicked through to an interstate third party, i.e., money laundering. Media exposure would surely bring him out from behind his façade of self-righteousness."

Rowe sent it all to the Gisborne Police Station marked for the personal attention of Ronald Brunton and Linda Alexander.

At around the same time, Hassett spoke over the telephone to George Fisher requesting an urgent and confidential meeting to discuss a potential problem.

Sergeant Jackson accompanied by Senior Constable Ingram made a new appointment to meet with Alessandro Moretti and asked for Dominic to also attend. It was not intended to be confrontational, in fact quite the opposite. They met in a private corner in the foyer of the very smart head office in Woodend. The clock tower almost opposite the front door gave an added appearance of strength and stability to their building. A staff member delivered tea, coffee and scones to the four men as they exchanged information. The meeting was held on a friendly basis that made confidentiality easy. Jack told them that the contract killer had been identified and was now dead, probably to silence him, and he was associated with a criminal group based in Sydney. The police believed that the group had an association with a parallel group based in Adelaide, who were suspected of being the criminals who had lost and stolen the tobacco and drugs central to the killing of the Moretti twins.

Jack quietly asked for comments, then more specifically said, "Alessandro, I know you and your family—with all of its contacts plus those you can call in as needed—have been hot on the trail of known groups in New South Wales and I wondered what progress you have made?"

Alessandro looked at Dominic and replied, "It is a bit of a long story and we do still have contacts deep into what some call the 'Italian Mafia', but two things are very clear. There is no current connection between our group and the perpetrators of this horrible event. Luca and Giovanni were immature naive criminals. We have identified the Sydney syndicate that employed Ben Bates the hit man, and more than that we know the connection to the head of the Adelaide criminal syndicate, and that person is very deeply protected. We expect to identify the name or names of the next level down."

Jack Jackson admitted surprise and admiration, and expressed a need for great caution. He said, "We are probably both at the same doorway and I will give you a name in confidence, to be sure we are pursuing the same target." He whispered the names PGG and Hassett, and Alessandro nodded and added, "Not quite the top."

Dominic admitted he had been following leads through some of his past motorbike cronies but said they had been totally unknowing of any connections, but the bikies were curious and making their own unofficial enquiries.

Jackson and Ingram expressed genuine thanks and all agreed to keep each other informed. The short drive from Woodend back to Gisborne left the two police associates pondering on the meeting as they progressed along the Calder Highway, not far from the site of the murders.

Gwynn Hassett and George Fisher, meanwhile, huddled together in a corner of the large lounge at the Adelaide Club in North Terrace, having indicated to everyone they were not to be disturbed. Adhering to a tradition going back to 1890 or even earlier, and with both of them having long family connections, they were left strictly alone. Fisher was anxious as Hassett had requested the meeting based on the comment, "We have a problem."

Fisher simply asked, "So what is the problem?"

Hassett began by saying that his uncle, who was the Police Commissioner, had told him off the record that there was a lot of communication going on between the Victorian Police, the AFP and the South Australian Police Force. It apparently was to do with a double murder in the Melbourne area connected to illegal trading in tobacco and drugs.

With an air of great indifference, Fisher looked at Hassett and said, "So, how can that concern me?"

Gwynn Hassett whispered, "Well one of my lawyers has been interviewed and apparently has sung like a canary about handing on instructions. It's all been emphatically denied but the Victorian detectives are persistent. I am nervous about the possible wider implications."

Fisher responded in his usual disdainful manner, "I can't imagine what they could be; things better be tidy!" Hassett assured Fisher he was confident there was absolutely no evidence of connection in or outside of PGG to the crimes.

Back in the incident room in Gisborne there was complete agreement on the next move as Sergeant Jackson joked a little about the famous saying of 'don't prod the bear' and related the actions of Max Rowe to a new version—as Jack Jackson saw it. He said, "Rowe was like the mouse that if you squeezed it hard until it screamed, it would lead you right to where the cheese was stored. Rowe was hurt and humiliated, so he was spilling the beans."

Those beans necessitated a search warrant for the premises of PGG in Adelaide, the home of Gwynn Hassett, and the premises of Farmland Products Ltd which Rowe had remembered was one of the slightly mysterious companies that was under the wing or hidden by trusts or a subsidiary. It was located close to Seppeltsfield in the Barossa Valley and close to vineyards and equestrian activities. Rowe thought it was run or managed by some cronies of Hassett's. Because the search warrants needed to be served outside of Victoria, time had to be spent clarifying under which jurisdiction the warrant would be served. The rules relating to 'evidential material' and the handling, selection of material, such as telephones, records, computers, and storage of the seized material had to be considered. Media involvement needed to be considered. Preliminary discussions fringed into considerations about including the New South Wales Police, as the main suspect of the actual killing had in turn been killed in NSW. Close co-operation between Victoria and South Australia would be the first thing needed to avoid possible mess-ups, and to ensure caution around the power elites of the Adelaide Club when enacting search warrants that could in any way be offensive, as this could result in defamation suits.

Chief Superintendent Brunton used all his experience, contacts and skills to organise the necessary permits, paperwork and personnel to carry out the search warrants in conjunction with the various other police forces. He was meticulous, to ensure there would be no leaks of the intended action. More than that, Ron Brunton was an intelligent member of the senior ranks of the inner sanctum. He had cross relationships with senior personnel at the AFP. With the possible need for support from the Federal Police when intruding into South Australia and New South Wales jurisdictions, he rang an old associate now with the AFP and invited him to share a cup of coffee at the café next to the Victorian Parliament House in Melbourne and beside the AFP offices.

Jason McStevens was delighted to see Brunton as he had a question or two he wanted to ask himself. Brunton was determined to clear all possible pathways to maximise the chances of apprehending the associated 'cleanskins', as he called the arms-length, hard to nail solicitors and associates. Over their second coffee Jason McStevens agreed wholeheartedly and stressed a request to be kept in the loop. He explained that heavy drug trafficking, particularly in methamphetamines, by sophisticated drug trading syndicates, internationally and through Sydney in particular, was driving the AFP to distraction. The use of disguises within coffee and tea bags, paper masks and vegetables…! The drug scourge was unending.

They chatted on about mutual problems of law enforcement and then Jason asked, "I believe you have Detective Sergeant Linda Alexander in your current team?" Ron Brunton was surprised, "As a matter of fact that is correct; why do you ask?" In a lowered voice, Jason explained in a friendly manner that the Feds were always looking for suitable recruits and the name of DS Alexander had been nominated by sources from both Ballarat and Footscray police with comments about her dedication, intuitive ability and apparent policing ambitions. Brunton was quick to respond, "Listen Jason, the things said about her are all correct, and she is a delightful young woman, with great people skills, but I did not come here to help you 'pirate' one of our best, so leave her alone!"—all with a smile. They parted with good humour and an intention to co-operate.

The decision was made to proceed with the raids which the South Australian Police would carry out with the added involvement of Victorian Police crime squad members. It was decided that Sergeant Jackson, Detective Sergeant Alexander and Senior Constable Beth Jenkins would be seconded to Adelaide as observers and participants if necessary. Constable Jenkins was by far the most excited of the trio to be involved. Wonderful new experience to add to her CV, she thought!

After careful examination and many private discussions, Commonwealth search warrants were specifically applied for and granted with the usual seven-day validity. The rules about evidence being sought and reasonable grounds for suspicion being established, they now had a cut and dried legal document authorising police to enter premises, to search for and seize evidence specified in the warrant which related to offences set out in the warrant. Other related evidence could be added if 'reasonable'.

Targets would be files, phones, and computers located on persons, location, or vehicles. To be confiscated and removed. It was accepted that challenges could arise over scope and validity. Some seized documents could be subject to legal professional privilege that protected communications between lawyers and clients, but that would be sorted out later. To add emphasis to the applications it had been specified that there were serious offences plus drugs involved. All necessary official copies of documents to be presented with the search warrants were ready. Emphasis was added to ensure confidentiality as leaks had been known.

The plan evolved into three separate operations. They were all to gather 'evidential material' on proceeds of crime that would help solve the prime matter of the murder of the Moretti brothers.

Search warrant No 1 was for PGG offices; for records, internal and external, of communications by Max Rowe with property purchases and instructions to named persons in Victoria. Internal communications between Rowe and Hassett that could indicate instructions and connections to ownerships or managements.

Search warrant No 2 was to the home of Mr Gwynn Hassett, with particular emphasis on his private study for files, computers, mobile telephones (burners in particular as investigators had already pinpointed) and an encryption system that was known to be used.

Search warrant No 3 was to be carried out at Farmlands Products Pty Ltd on the fringe of the Barossa Valley. This property had for a long time been suspected by SA Police as more than it appeared. Informer Max Rowe had nominated this property as highly suspicious. The property was a few acres with a large traditional old shed, and in front of it on the roadside was a comparatively new smart showroom and office. Annual tax returns showed little or no profits and all permits to be a retail business were in order. Directors were listed as Gwynn Hassett, George Fisher and a trust company nominee from NSW.

Chief Superintendent Brunton nominated Beth Jenkins to accompany the group entering the PGG premises as he anticipated there would be loud verbal and legal opposition to the raid for little or no resulting evidence.

Sergeant Jackson was to accompany the raid to the luxury home of Hassett, with particular concentration on the private study where it was anticipated they would capture incriminating records of transactions over a range of products and geographical areas. A number of unregistered mobile phones were expected. Most important in the search would be equipment used for encrypting correspondence. Angry resistance from anyone who was at home was expected, but they were timing the raid so that hopefully Hassett was not at home when the warrant was presented. Timing would be critical.

Linda Alexander was assigned to the Farmlands Products visit; all records that should be on the premises would need serious sifting. From snippets and tips received, these should be substantial, and materials discovered in this search may need interpretation.

The timing of each raid needed to be closely choreographed to maximise the effect and minimise any barriers thrown in the way. It was expected that the presentation of the warrant at PGG would probably cause immense ructions and produce little or no valuable evidence, but would present a huge distraction for Hassett. As that uproar was in full swing, the raid on Hassett's private residence was to be immediately and forcibly enacted. The visit to Farmlands Products Pty Ltd was to follow more quietly with less fuss, but extensive forced entries were anticipated over the objections of reluctant personnel.

Detailed planning was put in place and rehearsals were conducted. Communications for all and every step were in place and faithfully recorded. It was ready to go!

21

Search Warrants

Warrant No 1: Adelaide. PGG Lawyers, Rundle Street. 10am. Confirmation senior partner Gwynn Hassett is on premises.

Armed with the search warrant, the team of three police officers, under the command of a Senior Sergeant and accompanied by Senior Constable Beth Jenkins entered the foyer and issued a warning to all to freeze activities while the warrant was served. Exclamations and rising voices greeted the orders as panic and disarray erupted. The senior officer asked for the most senior administration staff member and a partner, as instructions followed. Material in particular wanted for seizure included all records and files relating to ex-employee Max Rowe, Kenneth Wiltshire, phone and computer records of communications with Wilson and Wetherell, Solicitors, of Kyneton, the Moretti family and William Blake (aka Benjamin Bates).

All hell broke loose as protestations were raised at volume. The office manager screamed that the police had no jurisdiction in a lawyer's office and she was quickly followed by the financial director with much the same rhetoric. Eventually senior partner Gwynn Hassett joined the chorus. Attempts to settle the chaos took patience and time, which was exactly what the police wanted.

Hassett had enough presence of mind to comply with the freeze order and to invite the police to detail exactly what they were looking for. Senior Constable Jenkins added to his anger by suggesting he was wasting police time by procrastinating over a very serious matter. Hassett exploded, "With all due respect to you and what no doubt is your limited knowledge of the law and search warrants, I request that you butt out of this conversation!" The Senior Sergeant took it calmly and simply suggested Hassett would be best advised to watch his manners. He then elaborated on the information being sought. Connections to Rowe, Wiltshire, Kyneton lawyers, Moretti, and dead criminal Blake. In his customary superior manner, Hassett gave a pompous dissertation on search warrants and protection of lawyer confidentiality. Beth could not restrain herself; "Yes, we were taught that in year one at the Police Academy."

Hassett responded acidly, "So young and naïve. But you will find nothing here."

Very patiently, the Senior Sergeant went through the procedures they would carry out and suggested co-operation would be the best idea, and cautioned Hassett not to hide or destroy evidence. All that elicited was an ugly grunt. The arguing and legal point making went back and forth and each side sought additional input from superiors on technical points, all of which added to the time the police occupied the premises. Hassett kept reiterating that it was a complete 'beat up'; a waste of time as there was no work connection between himself and the departed Max Rowe. That did seem to be accurate. Constable Jenkins, who was present mainly as an observer, finally dropped into the conversation that she had been informed that Max Rowe now had supporting witnesses to back his evidence.

The police departed after several hours, as expected taking miscellaneous files, computer printouts, telephones and records including Rowe's employment details. The comment about Rowe that Beth had dropped into the conversation was deliberately designed to rattle Hassett and was based on new evidence volunteered by an ex-employee of PGG Lawyers. Max Rowe had been a middle-level lawyer there with a non-intrusive and friendly manner who most people had liked and respected. He had been seen as a decent guy and it had taken many weeks for the way he had been treated to filter through to staff and associates. The consensus of opinion was that Rowe had been badly treated and Hassett had done his usual "not responsible" trick.

One of the senior clerical staff had told her friend, a recently departed PGG staff member, how Max Rowe had been wrongfully dismissed. The ex-employee, already disenchanted by the firm's treatment of her own retirement, now came forward to volunteer information about lines of authority and responsibility. Morale in the firm was so bad that her friend then told the police she would confirm and verify the lines of command. This needed to be treated carefully. Beth was finding the process of unwinding the witness evidence enthralling.

Warrant No 2: Home of Gwynn and Mrs Hassett, Stanley Street, Erindale, Adelaide.

The warrant specified contents of the study including files, telephones (plural), computers, and special equipment used to carry out encrypting. The team included an IT specialist. Knowing that Hassett was otherwise involved at his office, the warrant was delivered without distractions or interruptions. Mrs Hassett tried to contact her husband but he was taking no calls!

In a very deliberate way, the team descended into the study, collecting everything and labelling it carefully. Any devices, disks, and information that could help decode data was packed into cartons. Mrs Hassett was distraught but the raid was quick and efficient and the police had departed in less than two hours. They did, however, expect huge ructions to develop once Hassett discovered what had gone on at home. The natural progression for Hassett was to use all possible contacts and 'friends' in all levels of government, and particularly referral to contacts in the AFP to assist him.

Warrant No 3: Farmlands Products Pty Ltd, Seppeltsfield, Barossa Valley, South Australia.

The premises were a clean and tidy office and showroom with a large traditional shed-warehouse attached. The team of three police officers serving the warrant were accompanied by Linda Alexander from the Victorian special crime squad. New information now in her possession included company tax returns and the names of Farmlands Products' company directors: Gwynn Hassett, G.S. Fisher, and Steffanie Stewart, a nominee from a Sydney trust.

The police marched up to the front door to find only one employee doing some cleaning in the immaculate showroom and a forklift driver sitting idly in the lunch room. The Senior Sergeant presented the warrant and asked the employee, "You the boss?" to be answered, "No, not really, we don't have one here."

Keen to get into action Beth asked, "How long have you been here?" followed by "what happened to the person before you?"

Seemingly not a bit perturbed by police descending on the place, the man responded, "Well, I have been here three months; I don't know about the last guy, but it seems no one stays long because there is bugger all to do!"

When asked what the actual business was, he proffered, "Mainly a storage facility; not much else as there is only a limited range of products for grapes and farming at the top end of the price range."

A brusque instruction from the Sergeant: "Stop all activities and let's get on with our search."

Computers, phones, files and records were seized and recorded. The manager went off to call his 'boss' who he said was a lawyer called Mr Hassett. Beth suggested facetiously that he was probably busy.

In the front office and new shed there were fertilisers, sprays, reticulation pipes and pumps, brochures, and brand information. All very neat and tidy. The big back shed was securely locked and the manager was reluctant to find the keys and even more reluctant to open the shed, as it was a 'no go' area for someone of his status in the company. That cut no ice with the officers, and he was made to unlock it without further delay. Wide, well-oiled, double strengthened doors, opening onto a well-lit, clean and tidy, 80% full warehouse, brought a surprise.

Not just numerous bales of hay, but tobacco and cigarettes of all brands and sizes. As well, in smaller packs but easily identifiable, were piles of 'ice'—methamphetamine—ready for distribution. The sheer size of the discovery made everyone whistle. The Senior Sergeant was straight onto his phone detailing the find and requesting not only additional instructions for backup and to secure the site, but whether the staff should be apprehended. Beth Jenkins quickly called Chief Superintendent Ron Brunton with the exciting information.

22

Chasing the Big Guys

The level of excitement and anticipation throughout the police climbed at high speed. The information and evidence gathered had to be sorted, cross-referenced and collated. Experts were pulled in from everywhere. At the same time vociferous protests from Hassett about the legality of actions taken under the search warrants mounted.

Slowly but surely the evidence mounted. The Victorian contingent was instructed to return home apart from Linda, who was to stay on an extra two days to re-interview Max Rowe and the clerks from PGG who had volunteered to give statements. Police facilities in Adelaide were provided to her, including recording equipment. There was speculation within the investigating group as to how much 'wriggle' Hassett would be able to muster!

The order went out to arrest Gwynn Hassett and to secure all evidence gathered. The South Australian Police carried out the arrest and immediate steps were initiated to have him extradited to Victoria to face murder charges. He was arraigned on multiple charges including arranging the murder of the Moretti brothers and trading and transporting illegal drugs over state borders. Further charges were expected to be added to the indictments as the investigation went on. Hassett was incarcerated by South Australian Police to await the extradition hearing, accompanied by protests at every imaginable level of legal skill. Back in Gisborne, the special taskforce arrested

Ken Wiltshire as an accomplice in the murder of the Moretti brothers.

The case of George Robert Fisher presented for the police quite a quandary. Linda felt his apprehension to be a huge challenge on both the legal aspects and from the law enforcement angle, not to mention criminal protection issues. There was little or no identifiable commercial connection between Fisher and Hassett, except informally through the Adelaide Club and historically as fellow pastoralists, and through their both being directors of Farm Products Pty Ltd. Hassett was clearly the managing director but both Fisher and Steffanie Stewart could perhaps argue their innocence as hands-off directors. Linda planned to rigorously pursue the subject. She knew it was going to be a big mountain to climb. But in her own mind she thought, "I'll be all over them like a rash!"

George Fisher was many things to many people. First and foremost, he was a member of a well-established and respected pioneer pastoral family owning or leasing huge tracts of property over many years and generations. Over time the original farming operation had been diversified and expanded using trust funds, subsidiaries, shell companies and investments both locally and overseas. It had grown into a world-class group of enterprises and ghost activities. Clearly with the help of in-depth, sophisticated legal advice, an absolute labyrinth of commercial frameworks and connections had been established. This allowed many assets to be disguised or hidden and activities to be 'planted' in places of choice.

In the community arena, Mr Fisher was a prominent conservative and an official lobbyist. It had become more difficult for large-scale traditional farming to be profitable but it was carried on for the prestige. Being a stalwart of the Adelaide Club attracted similar status. Like many of his cohorts Fisher, as a young man, had used drugs but never to the extent of addiction. Quite the opposite—he saw an opportunity and made inroads into the underworld. As a schoolboy he had been associated with Gwynn Hassett who had a similar, but not quite as prestigious, background. Their university days had led them into different disciplines in life. Fisher was adamant that he was little more than a casual acquaintance of Hassett's, going back a long way to school days!

The two days Linda remained in Adelaide proved advantageous. Her interviewing and questioning skills were highlighted. First with Max Rowe, with whom she quickly established a rapport. She cut through his resentment and the vengeful attitude he harboured by joking with him about a cousin of hers called Rowe who had always been teased about rowing a boat gently up a stream. It relaxed the atmosphere of the interview and Rowe—a naturally reticent man— opened up, and actually enjoyed talking with her. Secondly, it turned out he had much more usable, credible evidence of instructions coming from Hassett than had been envisaged. Many phone and computer records were recoverable and irrefutable. With encouragement from Linda, Rowe began to recall details of messages that had been sent or received, through him, from Hassett to third parties.

The accumulation of information kept growing. Rowe had been made the sacrificial lamb but he was turning out to be something of a wolf in sheep's clothing; not quite the loser flunky Hassett had expected him to be.

Linda's skills in extracting information were again highlighted in her next two interviews with ex-staff members of PGG Lawyers. Her ability to relax the interviewees, with humour or a genuine compliment, got things going. Her own experiences with the law and its intricacies that had been taught at the Police Academy, and some episodes from her own life highlighting how women were so often put down, soon drew the two women out. She was not above relating some personal experiences that made her look silly. With some embellishments, she recalled how naively she had fallen into a doomed relationship in Perth when she had been lonely. The resulting empathy contributed to further volunteered information.

When it was all patched together and cross-verified, the evidence was compelling. Gwynn Hassett had undoubtedly committed indictable offences. However, his stance was still, through his legal representations, "I want immediate exoneration on all charges, and damages will be pursued!"

Linda, as a full Detective Sergeant, was able to hold a preliminary interview with Hassett in Adelaide prior to his transfer to Gisborne and then Melbourne jail. A senior officer from the SA force sat in on the interview, which was fully recorded.

It was conducted in polite terms. Linda observed that Mr Hassett appeared somewhat dismayed, tired, less arrogant, and perhaps more compliant now. She began in a formal manner, "Mr Hassett, you are probably aware that the encrypted messages sent back and forth between your associates have been unravelled and will be part of police evidence. You are probably surprised how the encryption keys can be found or cracked but in a murder case of this consequence we have available worldwide expertise to call on. We are aware of the '256 police protocol' and can pull back and recover a server's data records. What may have been considered destroyed can in some conditions be reinstated. Laptops are reformatted and police experts can 'hack' most systems. It is surprising the information available on videos collected from family and commercial sources!"

Linda deliberately took a few deep breaths to observe how Hassett was reacting. He was clearly shaken. She resumed on a different tack as she moved into exploring the relationship with George Fisher.

"Mr Hassett, we currently consider you to be an equal partner in many nefarious activities with your friend and associate George Robert Fisher. We have in mind that you are both in the category of, or close to being, 'Mr Bigs' in the criminal syndicate you inhabit." That made Hassett blink and he voiced strong denials.

Linda added, "You are probably aware that Mr Fisher has denied any close relationship with you."

That drew an, "ugh ugh" grunt from Hassett.

Linda quietly moved on, seeking any further comments from Hassett that may contribute to finding Fisher guilty of 'anything'.

In a frustrated and demoralised voice, he uttered, "So they have deserted me!"

Linda restrained herself from asking who 'they' were, and encouraged him to go on, saying, "You know lawyers never go to jail. Real criminals don't touch dirty money, and your Mr Fisher has plans for every possible contingency. It was at his insistence that all correspondence was by anonymous text and burner phones, everything was in cash, and instructions given where to pick up keys and cars, and the envelopes hidden under seats. Very thorough. And, importantly, it is not even him who is a director of Farm Products Pty Ltd!"

Hassett asked, "Who was listed as a director, then?"

The reply was, "It is a Gavin Sein Fisher, who is a cousin of Fisher's."

23

Gisborne Police Station – Incident Room

As the investigation moved towards its conclusion, the incident room was a picture of ordered chaos. The desks were grouped and scattered, the walls were plastered with photos of the murdered twins, the parents, all the siblings, cousins, and other connections: Ken Wiltshire, the farm boy, the truck driver, Ben the hit man, the Kyneton lawyer and other shadowy figures, and an array of vehicles. As well, photos of Rowe, Hassett and Fisher, PGG premises and the Adelaide Club. Strewn around were piles of files, printouts, videos and formidable pieces of IT equipment. It looked like an unfathomable mess! But it was the opposite.

Chief Superintendent Ron Brunton convened the special and celebratory final meeting of the full taskforce. Everyone who should be there was there, plus representatives of the media. CS Brunton was quick to congratulate the team and to point out it was unfair for him to be given credit as the team leader when it should go to his sergeants; and he was keen to acknowledge the SA Police involvement, all combined into a formidable and efficient team. Most of all he wanted to stress a wonderful result: the arrest of an evil criminal and the curtailing of a major part of the illicit syndicate. He went on to say he would invite comments from the senior sergeants shortly but first wanted to make some observations about the case.

The Chief Super wanted to pay tribute to Alessandro and Corina

Moretti and the dignity they and their family had shown through the whole horrible affair. The morale of the family had never wavered. Even more, the family had investigated the possibility of compensation or settlement of debts accrued from activities of Luca and Giovanni. However, this was not appropriate as all products and information seized by the police had been confiscated.

CS Brunton revealed he had asked himself was the family satisfied? He said, "They are probably not, but they were determined to revert back to normal as soon as possible, although the tragedy of the terrible twins would remain in many lives for years.

He commented that the large criminal syndicate involved had been bruised and while not eliminated, had undoubtedly been set back and made to appreciate police expertise. It was the considered police opinion that a major syndicate member had been permanently identified and constrained from future activities. That was a great result. Finally, and most importantly, it was his great privilege as the senior officer to congratulate the whole taskforce for the unrelenting effort made and the outstanding result achieved.

He added, "You are without doubt the most harmonious and efficient group of officers it has been my pleasure to work with. It will be recognised!" This was greeted by loud and long applause by all assembled.

The sergeants followed on with minimal information, and then members of the press asked multiple (and often obtuse) questions which resulted in no new information being given out. The formal briefing finished.

Linda and Beth hugged each other, and hoped their personal and professional paths would continue to evolve together as they realised how comfortable they were with each other.

Within days, the Gisborne Police Station reverted to its normal, not so exciting, routine in the heart of the Macedon Ranges group, ensuring law and order across the large geographical area north-west of Melbourne.

www.ingramcontent.com/pod-product-compliance
Lightning Source LLC
Chambersburg PA
CBHW072057020426
42334CB00017B/1542